ALSO BY DAVID SHIELDS

War Is Beautiful: The New York Times *Pictorial Guide
to the Glamour of Armed Conflict*

*That Thing You Do With Your Mouth: The Sexual Autobiography
of Samantha Matthews, as told to David Shields*

Life Is Short—Art Is Shorter: In Praise of Brevity,
coeditor with Elizabeth Cooperman

I Think You're Totally Wrong: A Quarrel, coauthor with Caleb Powell

Salinger, coauthor with Shane Salerno

How Literature Saved My Life

*Fakes: An Anthology of Pseudo-Interviews, Faux-Lectures, Quasi-Letters,
"Found" Texts, and Other Fraudulent Artifacts,*
coeditor with Matthew Vollmer

Jeff, One Lonely Guy, coauthor with Jeff Ragsdale and Michael Logan

The Inevitable: Contemporary Writers Confront Death,
coeditor with Bradford Morrow

Reality Hunger: A Manifesto

The Thing About Life Is That One Day You'll Be Dead

Body Politic: The Great American Sports Machine

Enough About You: Notes Toward the New Autobiography

Baseball Is Just Baseball: The Understated Ichiro

Black Planet: Facing Race During an NBA Season

Remote: Reflections on Life in the Shadow of Celebrity

Handbook for Drowning: A Novel in Stories

Dead Languages: A Novel

Heroes: A Novel

OTHER
PEOPLE

OTHER
PEOPLE

TAKES & MISTAKES

David Shields

ALFRED A. KNOPF · NEW YORK · 2017

Grateful acknowledgment is made to the following for permission to reprint previously
published material: Alfred A. Knopf, a division of Penguin Random House LLC: Excerpt of
"Esthetique du Mal" from *The Collected Poems of Wallace Stevens* by Wallace Stevens, copyright
© 1954 by Wallace Stevens and copyright renewed 1982 by Holly Stevens. Reprinted by permission
of Alfred A. Knopf, a division of Penguin Random House LLC. All rights reserved. Dover
Publications: Excerpt from *The World as Will and Representation* by Arthur Schopenhauer,
translated by E. F. J. Payne. Reprinted by permission of Dover Publications. Guardian News
& Media Ltd: Excerpt from "Odd One In" by Chloe Veltman, originally published in *The Guardian*
(www.theguardian.com) on June 12, 2006. Copyright © 2016 by Guardian News & Media Ltd.
Reprinted by permission of Guardian News & Media Ltd. Houghton Mifflin Harcourt Publishing
Company: Excerpt from *American Pastoral* by Philip Roth, copyright © 1997 by Philip Roth.
Reprinted by permission of Houghton Mifflin Harcourt Publishing Company. All rights reserved.
The New York Times: Excerpt from *The New York Times*, March 18, 1984, copyright © 1984 by The
New York Times. All rights reserved. Reprinted by permission and protected by the Copyright Laws
of the United States. The printing, copying, redistribution, or retransmission of this Content without
express written permission is prohibited. W. W. Norton & Company, Inc.: Excerpt from "Around
Pastor Bonhoeffer" from *Passing Through: The Later Poems New and Selected* by Stanley Kunitz,
copyright © 1970 by Stanley Kunitz. Reprinted by permission of W. W. Norton & Company, Inc.

Library of Congress Cataloging-in-Publication Data
Names: Shields, David, 1956– author.
Title: Other people : takes & mistakes / David Shields.
Description: New York : Knopf, 2017.
Identifiers: LCCN 2016022400 | ISBN 9780385351997 (hardback) | ISBN 9780385352000 (ebook)
Subjects: LCSH: Other (Philosophy) | BISAC: BIOGRAPHY & AUTOBIOGRAPHY /
Personal Memoirs. | LITERARY COLLECTIONS / Essays. | LITERARY COLLECTIONS /
American / General.
Classification: LCC PS3569.H4834 A6 2017 | DDC 814/.54—dc23 LC record
available at https://lccn.loc.gov/2016022400

Jacket photographs made by Robert Capa © International Center of Photography /
Magnum Photos
Jacket design by Chip Kidd

Manufactured in the United States of America
Published February 23, 2017
Second Printing, March 2017

Some names and identifying details have been changed
to protect the privacy of individuals.

Thanks to Artist Trust for the Arts Innovator Award
and to Arne Christensen, Kristen Coates, Erik Fenner,
and Russell Harper for their research assistance.

For Ann Close

You fight your superficiality, your shallowness, so as to try to come at people without unreal expectations, without an overload of bias or hope or arrogance, as untanklike as you can be, sans cannon and machine guns and steel plating half a foot thick; you come at them unmenacingly on your own ten toes instead of tearing up the turf with your caterpillar treads, take them on with an open mind, as equals, man to man, as we used to say, and yet you never fail to get them wrong. You might as well have the *brain* of a tank. You get them wrong before you meet them, while you're anticipating meeting them; you get them wrong while you're with them; and then you go home to tell somebody else about the meeting and you get them all wrong again. Since the same generally goes for them with you, the whole thing is really a dazzling illusion empty of all perception, an astonishing farce of misperception. And yet what are we to do about this terribly significant business of *other people*, which gets bled of the significance we think it has and takes on instead a significance that is ludicrous, so ill-equipped are we all to envision one another's interior workings and invisible aims? Is everyone to go off and lock the door and sit secluded like the lonely writers do, in a soundproof cell, summoning people out of words and then proposing that these word people are closer to the real thing than the real people that we mangle with our ignorance every day? The fact remains that getting people right is not what living is all about anyway. It's getting them wrong that is living, getting them wrong and wrong and wrong and then, on careful reconsideration, getting them wrong again. That's how we know we're alive: we're wrong. Maybe the best thing would be to forget being right or wrong about people and just go along for the ride.

But if you can do that—well, lucky you.

—PHILIP ROTH

CONTENTS

I. MEN

Listening to men attempt to talk to each other is like trying to get The Magic Flute *on Armed Forces Radio.*

—(SECOND LIEUTENANT) CAROLINE BECKER

The origin of enslavement is the invention of writing.

—FOUCAULT

COMP LIT 101: ADVICE FROM MY DAD

Good to get your long and candid letter, Dave. I must say I'm some-what perplexed by your reaction to your creative writing class. I think you have the accent on the wrong syllable, figuratively speaking. You're in this class to learn from the teacher, and perhaps from your fellow students. I think if you keep this in mind you'll loosen up a bit and get a great deal out of the course. All of your classmates are in the same boat; they're all just as apprehensive about revealing themselves as you are, even though some may be able to camouflage it better than others. I think it's great you were accepted in the class, and you should think so, too. Relax, and learn from this "famous" writer (though I don't know his books and had never heard of him before). A certain amount of fear and anxiety at the approach of a new experience is natural and healthy. I don't know any placid types who are creative people; intensity is what drives them to the outrageous thoughts and ideas ordinary people never think of. But anxiety also has to be self-controlled if it's not to become the dominant force.

.   .   .

I find Kosinski a good writer, very good. Nobody I've read recently writes a better, simpler declarative sentence—no extraneous language, not one extra word or sentiment. With your stuff I'm sometimes so busy untangling the syntax I don't know what you want to say.

Not to be involved with mankind is not to have lived; join up.

The Roth book you gave me for my birthday (thank you) grew on me. At first I did a foolish thing: I placed my own prejudices ahead of the novel. I wanted him to leave, for good, his absorption with his father and mother and their self-deprecation. I wanted him also to leave the novel told in the first person. Why doesn't he write novels like everyone else? Writing them in the first person is the lazy way, the easier way. I soon realized how utterly naïve and unsophisticated such an attitude was and settled down to enjoy the book, even that very contrived exchange of letters between David and Debbie, and David and Arthur.

I'm hoping that you won't wait as long as I did to learn how to make dinner, clean house, make sensible purchases, etc., etc. Just because one is a "poet" doesn't mean one has to be a schlemiel. I feel very strongly about this and look forward to talking about it in depth sometime.

The Front? I didn't like it. The blacklistings were serious. I want serious subjects treated seriously.

I went with your great-uncle Hyman to hear Elie Wiesel give a talk at UCLA this week. A very moving experience, comparable only to the talk I heard by Chaim Potok several years ago. Wiesel had been in Auschwitz as a teenager and so, of course, he spoke about the Holocaust and the baffling faith of the Jewish people in humanity. He opened with a tale of two Russian peasants who were sitting around drinking and talking. Jacob says to his friend Yosal, "Are you my friend?" "Of course," Yosal assures him. They talk some more and again Jacob asks Yosal if he's his friend and again Yosal assures him. Then Jacob asks him once more, "Are you really my friend?" And Yosal says, "Of course I am. Why do you keep asking?" "Well," replies Jacob, "if you are my friend, how come you don't know that I am hurting?" Wiesel closed his talk by quoting from documents that he'd seen recently, diaries and journals written by concentration camp victims who were forced to conduct their fellow Jews into the gas ovens and then later were themselves incinerated. They left letters and notes and descriptions in bottles and boxes in crevices in the crematoria—some discovered only now. If ever there were people who had the right to tell all the world to go to hell, these were such people, but they wanted humanity to know what had happened there, and by sharing their experiences and describing them, they demonstrated their faith in the survival of the Jews and their faith that people would remember and not ever let such horrors happen again. It was a respectful, quiet, and appreciative audience, and there wasn't a dry eye in the house. Hyman went through two handkerchiefs himself.

Don't stop the world because you want to get off.

A play—even a one-act set in seventeenth-century England—needs some "wasted" moments to make it work. Your protagonist, Lilburne, is alone way too much. Plus, he's a pompous martyr; he couldn't have been that self-righteous in real life. I want to see him in private, enjoying himself with his family, being witty. So far he's so serious as to be inhuman. Work it out in *emotional* terms, not intellectual ones.

It's been a long time since I've seen you. You've done a lot of greening and growing in the fourteen months since you were last here. I think I've done some, too. My old habits have been carted off to the dump. You'll see, I think, when you visit in March, although I thought I detected at the end of our last conversation a very conscious pulling away on your part.

. . .

John William Corrington writes in the darkly humorous tradition of a Barth, Donleavy, or Heller. He is concerned with the troubled spirit of this country and writes about it with gusto.

Peace in the world or the world in pieces.

I found that toward the end of summer I needed some distance between you and me because I was becoming so conscious of your writing, presumably about me. When you told me that after dinner with Hyman and me, you went downstairs and recorded our sodden trip down memory lane, I was disturbed by it, and after that I felt you were making mental or actual notes any time anything of an "interesting" or curious nature was discussed between Hy and me. I don't mind that you use any of your observations about me in your writing, but I do mind being made so conscious of the fact that you're doing it. If other people get this feeling, you may find that they, too, require distance from you, and this doesn't make for close, open, honest relationships. I've known quite a few writers and have never had the feeling with them that they were interested in me or observing me just for what grist I could provide for their mill. This is an attitude and approach that I think you will, in time, learn to cultivate.

Some think O'Hara's stories consisted of an introduction, a little character development, and the rest was dialogue of a most ordinary nature. O'Hara was more than that, much more. He said the lonely mind of the artist is the only creative organ in the world. His advice: inherit money, have a job that will keep you busy, be born without a taste for liquor, marry a woman who will cooperate in your sexual peculiarities, join a church, don't live too long. Oh, he had his wild and uncontrollable moments. He thought of his work as a personal reassessment against the history of his time. An important writer of the '20s, '30s, and the '40s and clear until the time he died.

. . .

I know from your letters and even the things you say to me during our too-brief telephone conversations that a considerable annealing has taken place, and I know it'll be very much in evidence in what you write.

This blacklisted writer (played by Luther Adler, I think, maybe not), after coming out of jail for contempt of a congressional committee, gets some work in the gray market and then has a chance to do a script on his own. He can't believe his luck has changed. Then, when he goes over to his friend's place to celebrate, his friend says, "Well, it seems that somebody has been doing some poking around, and you know how it is, this ain't the end of the world, times will change, you'll see, one of these days we'll look back on all this and laugh, but in the meantime you're off the picture and we have to put some schnook, a nebbish who can't carry your typewriter ribbon, on the picture." Adler looks at him, looks through him, and on Adler's face is written all of man's grief from the beginning of time. His friend sees him to the door, arm languidly on his shoulder—feeble gesture of phony friendship, but it's there. And he asks Adler, "What will you do now?" Adler says three words, and no more eloquent words have ever been spoken on screen, stage, TV, or anywhere: "Survive. I'll survive." He closes the door and walks off into the night. The scene haunts me still and I bet I saw it on *Playhouse 90* twenty-five years ago, maybe longer. That's real writing.

Why not take the reader into your confidence rather than play a game of wits with him? Illumine the human condition—that's all. Set it down one little word after another. No tricks or gimmicks.

Did you know I must have tried half a dozen times to get down on paper those stories Hyman told you and me about being a panhandler in New York during the Depression? I never could get away from the plain reportage of it, even though I strove to put in "local color" and the "bums" as Hy depicted them. On my now-and-then tries, I couldn't get past the obligatory opening scenes—descriptions of the Lower East Side, etc. Rarely got much further. "Fiction is not fact," wrote Thomas Wolfe (the real Thomas Wolfe). "Fiction is fact, selected and charged with a purpose." Which is exactly what you did—blending Hy's memories with your imagination to put together an absorbing story. I can't begin to tell you how much it moved me, especially the very end, when Tannenbaum says Kaddish. Beyond my poor powers of description. (One minor criticism: Why do you need such a cutesy title? How many people nowadays even know what a dybbuk is? Why not just something simple like "A Boy Grows Up"?)

BLOODLINE TO STAR POWER

My father's birth certificate reads "Milton Shildcrout." His military record says "Milton P. Schildcrout." When he changed his name in 1946 to Shields, the petition listed both "Shildkrout" and "Shildkraut." His brother Abe used "Shildkrout"; his sister Fay's maiden name was "Schildkraut." Who cares? I do. I want to know whether I'm related to Joseph Schildkraut, who played Otto Frank in *The Diary of Anne Frank* and won an Academy Award in 1938 for his portrayal of Alfred Dreyfus in *The Life of Emile Zola.*

I grew up under the impression that it was simply true—the actor was my father's cousin—but later my father was more equivocal: "There is the possibility that we're related," he'd say, "but I wouldn't know how to establish it." Or: "Do I have definite proof that he was a cousin of ours? No." Or: "My brother Jack bore a strong resemblance to him; he really did." From a letter: "Are we really related, the two families? Can't say for certain. What's the mythology I've fashioned over the years and what's solid, indisputable fact? I don't know. . . . We could be related to the Rudolph/Joseph Schildkraut family; I honestly believe that."

In 1923, when my father was thirteen, his father, Samuel, took him to a Yiddish theater on the Lower East Side to see Rudolph Schildkraut substitute for the legendary Jacob Adler in the lead role of a play called *Der Vilder Mensch (The Wild Man)*. Rudolph was such a wild man: Throughout the play, he hurtled himself, gripping a rope, from one side of the theater to the other. After the play, which was a benefit performance for my grandfather's union—the International Ladies' Garment Workers—my grandfather convinced the guard that he was related to Rudolph Schildkraut, and he and my father went backstage.

In a tiny dressing room, Rudolph removed his makeup and stage costume, and he and Samuel talked. According to my father, Rudolph said he was born in Romania; later in his acting career, he went to Vienna and Berlin. He and his wife and son, Joseph, came to New York around 1910, went back to Berlin a few years later, and then returned to the United States permanently in 1920. (Joseph Schildkraut's 1959 memoir, *My Father and I,* confirms that these dates are correct, which proves only that my father probably consulted the book before telling me the story.) Samuel asked Rudolph whether he knew anything about his family's antecedents—how and when they came to Austria. Rudolph said he knew little or nothing. His life as an actor took him to many places, and his life and interest were the theater and its people. The two men spoke in Yiddish for about ten minutes; my father and grandfather left. What little my father couldn't understand, my grandfather explained to him later.

"For weeks," my father told me, "I regaled my friends and anybody who would listen that my father and I had visited the great star of the Austrian, German, and Yiddish theater in America—Rudolph Schildkraut. What's more, I said, he was probably our cousin. Nothing in the conversation between my father and Rudolph Schildkraut would lead me or anybody else to come to that conclusion for a certainty, but I wanted to impress friends and neighbors and quickly added Rudolph and Joseph Schildkraut to our family. I said, 'They're probably second cousins.' Some days I made them 'first cousins.' Rudolph Schildkraut, as you know, went on to Hollywood and had a brief but successful motion picture career. I told everybody he was a much better actor than his countryman Emil Jennings."

In 1955, my parents were living in Los Angeles, my mother was working for the ACLU, and my mother asked my father to ask Joseph

Schildkraut to participate in an ACLU-sponsored memorial to Albert Einstein, who had died earlier that year. "After all," my father wrote in reply to one of my innumerable requests for more information, "Einstein was a German Jew and Pepi [Schildkraut's nickname] had spent much of his professional life in Berlin and was a member of a group of prominent people who had fled Germany in the years after Hitler and lived in the Pacific Palisades–Santa Monica area"—Arnold Schoenberg, Fritz Lang, Peter Lorre, Max Reinhardt, et al.

My father tracked down Schildkraut's phone number and called him, telling him he was a Schildkraut, too, and inviting him to speak at the memorial tribute. "After much backing-and-filling and long, pregnant pauses (his, not mine) on the phone," my father said, Schildkraut told my father to bring him the script. When my father went to Schildkraut's house in Beverly Hills a few days later, Schildkraut came to the door, greeting Shields (né Schildkraut) stiffly. "He was very businesslike—cold, distant is more like it." For a moment or two they talked about their families. My father told him about the backstage visit in 1923. Joseph knew absolutely nothing of the Schildkraut family's ancestry. "Joseph Schildkraut, I would say," my father said, "and I think it's a fair statement, was somebody who didn't think about his Jewish background." Schildkraut talked to my father for about thirty minutes in the foyer of the big, rambling house. "Later, in telling the story, I often exaggerated—said he clicked his heels, Prussian-like. He really didn't." Schildkraut said that he had to show the script to Dore Schary for approval. (Schary was a writer who had become the head of production at RKO and then MGM. Anti-Communist fears lingered; the blacklist was still in effect.) Schildkraut told Shields to come back in a week.

When my father returned, Schildkraut again talked with him rapidly in the foyer of the house—"On neither visit did he have me come into the living room, nor did he introduce me to his wife, who was moving about in the next room"—and wound up saying that Schary had read the script and said it was all right. The script was taken almost entirely from Einstein's writings on civil liberties, academic freedom, and freedom of speech. The memorial was held at what was then the Hollywood Athletic Club and later became the University of Judaism. Also on the platform were the scientist and political activist Linus Pauling; A. L. Wirin, the chief counsel to the ACLU; John

Howard Lawson, a screenwriter and the unofficial spokesman for the Hollywood Ten; Anne Revere, who before being blacklisted won an Academy Award as best supporting actress for her performance as Elizabeth Taylor's mother in *National Velvet;* and a novelist who my father insisted was once very highly regarded and who in any case had a name worthy of the Marx Brothers—Lion Feuchtwanger.

The event was free. Every seat in the immense auditorium was filled. Hundreds of people sat in the aisles. Eason Monroe, the executive director of the ACLU and a man upon whom my mother had an immense, lifelong crush, asked the overflow audience to find seats or standing room in several small rooms upstairs. Monroe assured them that all the speakers would come upstairs to address them after speaking in the main auditorium. The program started a little late, about 8:30 p.m., but Schildkraut still hadn't shown up. Monroe asked Shields, "Milt, where's your cousin? It's getting late." My father assured Monroe he'd be there. My dad to me: "He was too big a ham to stay away on such an occasion." His name had appeared prominently in the ads as one of the main speakers.

Finally, Schildkraut showed. Monroe greeted him and asked him if, as the others had consented to do, he would also speak to the group upstairs. Schildkraut said that first he'd speak to the main auditorium audience; then he'd "see."

The other speakers—Pauling, Wirin, Lawson, Revere, and Feuchtwanger—spoke to the audience in the main auditorium, were "warmly received" (whatever that means), then went upstairs to speak once again to the overflow audience in a couple of anterooms. "The occasion lifted even the most uninspired speaker and material to emotional heights," according to my father. "But then came Pepi, the last speaker on the program.

"When he got to the podium, the audience was noisy and restless. After all, people were feeling the emotion of the memorial to this great man. Schildkraut took one look out there and employed the actor's classic stratagem: He whispered the first line or two, and a hush fell over the audience. Then, when he was sure he had their attention, he thundered the next lines. When he finished, he got a standing ovation. And this for a political naïf, or worse: a man who certainly didn't agree with everything he had just read, or anything else Einstein stood for. But he was the consummate actor and he read his lines—to perfection."

When Schildkraut finished, my father asked him about going upstairs. Schildkraut looked right through Shields and walked out the door. "Now he truly was like a Prussian soldier. That's the last time I saw him. In person, that is. Of course, I saw *The Diary of Anne Frank* on the screen half a dozen times. And if it's ever on television, I watch it again."

Twenty years later, my half-sister, Emily, was working as a maid at a resort in Oregon. "Don't know how it happened," my father explained, "but Pepi and his wife were guests at this posh place." Emily introduced herself, told him who she was, and Schildkraut gave her one of his "stylish Borsalino felt hats, which he wore in rakish over-one-eye European style—always the matinee idol—as a souvenir." She gave the hat to my father, who "had it in the closet for years, but it must have gotten thrown out when I moved after your mother's death."

I told this story to Emily, who wrote back, "Concerning the story about Joseph Schildkraut giving me a hat—that's a total mystery to me! I did work for a short time at a resort in Cannon Beach, Oregon. I have no memory of this intriguing visitor (or even seeing him) except in the movie *The Diary of Anne Frank*. Either I was that spaced out in those days and have blocked out this significant event, or once again our Pop has fabricated another yarn for you from his rich imagination. Sorry."

I relayed what Emily had said back to my father, who wanted to know, "Then where did the Borsalino hat come from? I distinctly remember Emily telling us that when she learned Joseph was a guest at the Oregon resort where she was working, she went over to him, told him her father's original name, they talked for a few minutes, and then Pepi gave her the hat. He wore hats like a Borsalino in his stage and screen roles back in the days when all male actors wore hats. And Borsalino, an expensive Italian-made hat, would be his style."

Shortly afterward, in a truly weird coincidence, an old friend of our family's called my father and asked him to pick up two boxes of odds and ends that my father had left with them many years before. "The lid flipped open on one of the boxes, and on top there was the hat Schildkraut gave to Emily at that Oregon coast resort back in the early seventies. Thought you'd be interested to learn about my (accidental) archaeological finding."

The hat solves nothing. Schildkraut died in 1964, which means that Emily, sweetly seeking my father's appreciation, must have invented the entire story, my father invented the story, I've got the details wrong, or being in a family is indistinguishable from playing telephone. And yet the photograph in *My Father and I* of Schildkraut kissing Susan Strasberg on the forehead in *The Diary of Anne Frank* mimics exactly the melodramatic bad acting in two photographs of my father kissing Emily when she was very little. In so many photographs of Pepi or my father or me is a certain quality of mugging hungrily, of pretty-boyness (me till I was twelve, my father deep into middle age—"Your dad is a really distinguished-looking man!"—Schildkraut until he was dead), of stilted posedness, of on-your-knees-before-the-camera obsequiousness, of needing to be liked by the lens, of peasant smilingness, of overreliance upon previous modes of appearing in pictures. . . .

Schildkraut also had what is to me a disturbing (because familiar) detachment toward his own feelings. "Maybe there was no such thing as love in real life," he wrote. "These all-consuming agonies and ecstasies of love existed only on the stage." I once wrote about stuttering that "it prevents you from ever entirely losing self-consciousness when expressing such traditional and truly important emotions as love, hate, joy, and deep pain. Always first aware not of the naked feeling itself but of the best way to phrase the feeling so as to avoid verbal repetition, you come to think of emotions as belonging to other people, being the world's happy property and not yours—not really yours except by way of disingenuous circumlocution."

The tightest warp and woof I can weave comes from the sound of the syntax. Joseph said of Rudolph, "He was passionately in love with the sound of words. They intoxicated him." Joseph says of his mother, "She had an acute business sense, a talent for making every kreuzer count." My father would say, "You can bet all the borscht in Brownsville on that." He wrote, "It's been at least a year since that coffee-klatch-cum-current-events-discussion-group held its final meeting, but many people at Woodlake Village still talk about the explosive events of that fateful day." I write, "The tightest warp and woof I can weave comes from the sound of the syntax." Do you hear the keynote—the incessant buzz and hum of alliteration? I pointed out to my father what I saw as the link between Schildkraut's alliteration-dependent writing style, my father's style, and my own (as well as my stutter), and he wrote back, "About Joseph Schildkraut's style: I believe the book he wrote in collaboration [*My Father and I,* "as told to Leo Lania"] is the only thing he's ever written. Solo, or with somebody's help. Don't know how much his collaborator did and what Pepi contributed. My style? Strictly journalese. Marked by—riddled with?—too much, far too much, alliteration. The O. Henry influence: As a young boy of seven or eight, I read his stories over and over. My brother Phil had won a complete set of O. Henry in a writing contest and there they were for me to devour—and (sadly) to incorporate, lock, stock, and barrel, into my own writing."

I told my father that I hoped to travel someday to Eastern Europe to trace the Schildkraut ancestry, and he responded, "That would be a dream trip—you and me investigating the Schildkraut strain in Austria, Germany, and the Ukraine. Whenever you're ready, I'll be ready. It would be a great adventure." I explained that what I was most interested in was my need to get him to tell the stories over and over and over again and his ceaseless capacity to extend and reinvent the material. He replied (and this is what I've come to recognize as my father's signature and see projected forward in myself and backward in Schildkraut: an unshakable self-consciousness), "Writing about it, you'll probably use and exploit how I arrogated to myself the 'cousins, yeah, they're probably second cousins' relationship. And how I told and retold—dined out a lot on it, as the saying goes—the story of my one actual involvement, in person, with Pepi: the Einstein memorial night, etc."

Well, so, as my father liked to say, what? What is this correlation-seeking but a ghoulish attempt to back-form a bloodline to star power? What proof is it, in any case, to find common traits in a putative relative's memoir? Is he or isn't he? Was he or wasn't he? I don't know, I can't know, and I'll never know. Why is it important for me to believe there's a link? Why do I care about being related to someone who—on the basis of my father's stories and *The Diary of Anne Frank*—appears to have been a singularly unpleasant human being and painfully ham-fisted actor? In such other films as *Marie Antoinette, Idiot's Delight, Orphans of the Storm, Cleopatra, The Road to Yesterday, The Garden of Allah, Flame of the Barbary Coast, The Man in the Iron Mask, Northwest Outpost, Mr. Moto Takes a Vacation, Souls at Sea, The Crusades, The King of Kings,* and *The Shop Around the Corner,* he was equally self-regarding, studied, stiff, grave, dignified, and yet also prone, regardless of role, to a truly astonishing amount of bowing and scraping. Toward the end of his life, my father newly informed me that he believed—although he couldn't be absolutely certain—that we were related to Robert Shields (né Schildkraut), of the former San Francisco mime duo Shields & Yarnell, and I couldn't help it: I thought, *Well, then, maybe I'm also related to Brooke Shields;* toward the end of *Endless Love,* when she was crying in that dark New York hotel room, trying to say goodbye to David, and her hair was braided and rolled up in a bun, she did, it seemed to me, especially in the mouth and chin area, look at least a little the way I sometimes looked as a teenager. . . .

MR. BIG

My sister, Paula, and I were just kids in 1965—ten and nine, respectively—when an article about our half-brother, Joseph, my father's son from his first marriage and named (I long thought) for Joseph Schildkraut, appeared on Saturday on the front page of the *San Francisco Chronicle*. Joseph has always been the hippest person I've known. Walt Disney's death, he once informed me, was the greatest day in American cinema. His three favorite movies are *The Terminator, Thief,* and *2001:* all attitude. He once did a U-turn in a kelly-green Triumph (with me in it) across an eight-lane highway. He's always seemed very male (as a child he went in for the sheriff's costumes and Lone Ranger outfits that never had much appeal for me), endearingly vague, elegant, handsome, and cheerful, if a bit self-satisfied.

Now he owns a film-editing company, but in 1965 he was a senior at Berkeley and, according to the article on the front page of the *Chronicle,* "part of a vast and busy University of California drug-peddling operation." The article was headlined "Big UC Campus Drug Case—Hunt for 'Mr. Big.'" Joseph wasn't Mr. Big—"allegedly a Berkeley campus source of large quantities of narcotics and so-called mind-expanding drugs such as LSD and DMT"—but it was clear he was on speaking terms with Mr. Big: "Officers went to Shields's apartment at 1709 Channing Way and found therein, they said, 720 ampules of DMT with an estimated market value of $1,500." The usual retro pleasures are present when reading an old newspaper article:

> A meeting had been arranged for yesterday at which Detro and Jimenez were to buy $10,000 worth of LSD from Mr. Big. But Mr. Big failed to appear and had, in fact, vanished.
>
> Jimenez and Detro recalled that during one of their early meetings in the San Pablo Avenue bar, Mr. Big had demanded that they put up part of the money in advance. They refused.
>
> "Well, like, man, I don't know you guys," Mr. Big replied, "and you could be narcos (police)."
>
> "You know, the State got 50 new undercover men."
>
> Jimenez answered, "I never heard of a bust (arrest) at UC."

Joseph had to reassure my father that he was completely innocent—he had no idea what his roommates were doing with so many glass ampules; he thought it was part of a lab experiment—and my sister and I had to worry all weekend about what taunts would greet us at school on Monday. The funny thing was that no one, not friends or fellow students or teachers or the principal, seemed to have seen the article, or if they did see it, they didn't connect it to us, or perhaps they simply had the grace not to wonder aloud (it's a common enough name, I suppose, and we've never looked that much alike, Joseph and I). So what I did after several days of silence—and I've never known whether my sister did the same; we weren't prone to compare notes about this kind of an event—was to bring the article to school and wave it in people's faces and in that way glean at least a little glamour from the guilt by association.

FATHER'S DAY

My father came up from Los Angeles to visit for the weekend, and my Father's Day present, six days late, was box seats to a Mariners game. I was new to Seattle and this was the first time I'd been inside the Kingdome, which, with its navy blues and fern greens, looked to me like an aquarium for tropical fish. The Kingdome reminded my father of dinner theater and he wanted to know where was Joseph Schildkraut. My father was turning seventy-nine the next month; when he turned eighty, he wanted to quit his part-time job and drive a Winnebago cross-country, then fly to Wimbledon to eat strawberries and cream.

The sixth-place Mariners were playing the last-place Tigers on Barbecue Apron Night. Watching batting practice, we folded and unfolded our plastic Mariners barbecue aprons, which smelled disconcertingly like formaldehyde, and we ran through all the baseball anecdotes he'd told me all my life, only this time—because I pressed him—he told each story without embellishment. He'd always said that he played semi-pro baseball, and I had had images of him sliding across glass-strewn sandlots to earn food money; it was only guys from another neighborhood occasionally paying him ten bucks to play on their pickup team and throw his dinky curve. He used to say he was team captain for an Army all-star baseball team that toured overseas, and as a kid I convinced myself that he spent 1943 in Okinawa, hitting fungoes to Ted Williams and Joe DiMaggio. He was only traveling secretary, the most prominent player on the team was someone named Pat Mullins, and it was fast-pitch softball stateside.

In his fifties, my father looked uncannily like Dodgers manager Leo Durocher. Once, when we were living in Los Angeles, the garbageman supposedly shook my father's hand and said, "Sorry to hear about your marriage, Mr. Durocher." The actress Laraine Day had recently divorced Durocher; the garbageman was being sympathetic in a male mode—so went the story. And for some reason I always thought my father stood atop the trash in the back of the truck, hefted garbage cans with one hand, and cursed The Fishbowl Which Is Hollywood, whereas in actuality my father immediately told my mother about impersonating "Leo the Lip," she cautioned him against stringing along the innocent garbage collector, and my father chased down the truck to explain and make amends.

Before the game, there was a Peace Run around the field—some sort of marathon for a cause that I didn't quite catch because the PA system sounded like it was being filtered through a car wash—then the umpires strolled onto the Astroturf, but they weren't booed even a little, which disappointed my father. In 1930 he was the star student at a Florida umpire school run by Bill McGowan, who said my father could become another Dolly Stark—namely, a big-league Jewish umpire—but after a few years of umping in the minors my father begged off, citing his poor night vision. His favorite Bill McGowan story concerned the time McGowan, a former amateur boxer, grew weary of Babe Ruth's grousing and, during the intermission of a doubleheader, challenged the Babe to a fight. The Babe backed down. The hero of my father's stories was always someone else. It was never him.

The Mariners scored three in the first. Keith Moreland looked painfully uncomfortable at third for the Tigers. Ken Griffey Jr. made a nice catch in the fifth. We were Dodgers fans, though, so the game was largely devoid of any real drama for either of us—as my father said, like watching a movie when you don't care what happens to the characters. He grew up playing stickball in Brownsville; every few innings, he and his friends would run over to a pool hall to check the score of the Dodgers game as it came in over the ticker tape and was posted on a blackboard outside. Zack Wheat. Dazzy Vance. Wilbert Robinson. He moved to Los Angeles in 1946; nine years later, while my mother was nursing my infant sister and suffering blackout spells during a late-summer heat wave, he flew back to New York, ostensibly to attend his father's eighty-fifth birthday party but, more particularly, to attend the 1955 World Series and, even more particularly, watch the Dodgers finally beat the Yankees and, more particularly still, watch Jackie Robinson steal home under Yogi Berra's tag. I have my father's pictures of press row at Yankee Stadium. Look at the snap-brim hats.

In our family mythology, this flight of my father's was always painted in the darkest of colors, and yet when I was a child I would look first thing each morning at the box scores and cry ickily into my cereal if the Dodgers had lost. I remember defacing my Ron Perranoski baseball card when he failed to hold a huge lead going into the ninth, pushing over my grandfather's television set when it broadcast Dodgers right fielder Ron Fairly's transformation of what should have been an easy catch into a home run over Dodger Stadium's low right-field wall, engaging in a weird mock-Ophelia thing at the beach after the fiasco of the 1966 Series against the Orioles. What was this obsession we had with the Dodgers? "For me, it comes out this way," my father wrote me the week after this Father's Day visit. "I wanted the Dodgers to compensate for some of the unrealized goals in my career. What do they call that in Freudian terms—transfer, is that right? If I wasn't winning my battle to succeed in newspapering, union organizing, or whatever I turned to in my wholly unplanned, anarchic life, then my surrogates—the nine boys in blue—could win against the Giants, Cardinals, et al. Farfetched? Maybe so. But I think it has some validity. In my case. Not in yours."

No. Not in mine. Never in mine.

Although the Kingdome had, even by ballpark standards, notoriously bad food, we decided to stand in line at the concession, anyway, not because we were so hungry but because we needed something to do while a "wave" was going around the stadium. (The vilified wave was apparently invented or at least popularized in 1981 at a University of Washington football game.) Both my father and I got a hot dog and a beer, and we shared a bag of peanuts—which came to an amazing amount of money, for a meal my father said had the nutritional quotient of a rosin bag. To his astonishment, I topped off this indigestible dinner with a chocolate malt, which looked almost purple and tasted as bitter as coffee. We returned to our seats. The wave was still rising and falling, or maybe it was a new wave.

He was the sports editor and photographer for a suburban San Francisco weekly, for which he covered the Little League, Pony League, Colt League, men's fast-pitch softball, and women's softball. Three days before he came up to visit, he'd been trying to take a photograph of a Little Leaguer stealing third base, and the catcher's throw had hit my father in the ankle, breaking three blood vessels. Proud of his bruised ankle, he kept showing it to me while enacting the scene, saying with a sportswriter's mix of hyperbole and mixed metaphor, "It blew up like an egg."

He always used to send me the column he wrote for his tennis club newsletter. This is by far my favorite lead: "A hundred members and guests attended the annual Tennis Club meeting and, to coin a forgettable phrase, a helluva time was had by all and sundry. (Especially Sundry, who seemed to be having the night of his life.)" This Borscht Belt humor could—when I was in certain moods—completely convulse me.

Just as my father and I didn't stand up during the national anthem, in order to express some sort of vague rebellion, now during the seventh-inning stretch we didn't stretch, either, although I couldn't help but watch the full-matrix scoreboard, which was flashing images of fans stretching. Seemingly all fifteen thousand fans in the Kingdome were watching the scoreboard, waiting to find out whether they were beautiful enough to be broadcast, since without exception the images were Pacific Northwest idyllic: sleeping babies wearing Mariners caps, energetic grandparents, couples kissing. The moment people were shown, they pointed at the screen, then they pointed at themselves pointing at themselves on the screen, then everyone pointed at them pointing at themselves pointing at themselves on the screen. I continued looking at the scoreboard, wanting my chance to point at myself pointing at myself on the screen, and then I looked over at my father, who hadn't been watching the screen at all. He always kept score, and he was tidying up his scorecard. He was no longer looking to be lifted onto an empyrean matrix; he just wanted to eat strawberries and cream at Wimbledon, the following summer, on his eightieth birthday (he purchased a group package but, a timid traveler, canceled at the last minute). "Presley, Martinez, and Vizquel coming up for the Mariners," he said, and we went to the bottom of the seventh.

EULOGY FOR MY FATHER

On an Army transport ship taking my father and five thousand other soldiers from Seattle to Okinawa in May 1945, my father played in a poker game that continued for three days and nights; players left only to use the bathroom or get food or sleep. They'd all read about the bloody Marine invasion of Okinawa a month before, so there was, according to my father, a fatalistic feeling about the game of "Tomorrow we die" and "Hell, it's only money."

On the third day, my father was ahead a thousand dollars. They were playing 7-Card Stud. The first two cards he drew were kings. He immediately bet the two-dollar game limit, trying to drive out as many of the other players as he could—a poker strategy his father had taught him.

By the fifth card, there were only two people left—my dad and a young private from Georgia, "Rebel."

When my father bet two dollars, Rebel said, "Ah raise you, Sarge. It's two dollars and two better."

My father, seeing that Rebel had a possible straight, threw in two dollars to see him. Another poker lesson learned by my father from his father: Never let anybody bluff you, especially when you and the other player are the last two in the game. "You've got to keep them honest," he told him, "even if you have to put in your last dime to see them. Remember that."

On the sixth card, my father began with a two-dollar bet, and Rebel again raised him two dollars. My dad now had four kings and, looking at the cards Rebel was showing, he couldn't imagine what he might have that would beat four kings. My father saw Rebel's raise.

When the seventh card was dealt down and dirty, my father said, "It's up to the raiser. Up to you, Rebel."

"It'll cost you four dollars to see me, Sarge," he said, which got a laugh from some of his buddies.

My father saw Rebel again and asked him what he had.

"I got me a little old straight," he said, and started to rake in the seventy-five-dollar pot.

"Not good enough, Rebel," my father said, showing his four kings.

Rebel slammed his cards down on the table and said, "Y'all play like a gahdamned Jew!"—stretching out the word "Jew," according to my father, as if it had several syllables, making it sound like "Joo-oo-oo."

The chow whistle sounded, the game broke up, and my father asked Rebel, "Why did you use that expression, 'play like a goddamned Jew'?"

Rebel said that his father told him that all Jews were sharp poker players. My dad said that some of his friends back in Brooklyn were poor players, almost as bad as Rebel and his friends. Then my father told Rebel he was Jewish. Rebel didn't believe him; my father had blue eyes, blond hair, and a deep tan. My dad said that he'd provide proof if he'd just step into the latrine.

The comedian Danny Kaye and my father were classmates at P.S. 149. In the mid-1950s, shortly before I was born, Kaye gave a Hollywood Bowl one-man performance, which my father and mother and half a dozen of their friends attended. At intermission, Kaye walked to the front of the stage and asked how many in the audience were from Brooklyn. Quite a few hands went up. He asked how many had gone to P.S. 149. About ten people raised their hands. Then he asked if anyone remembered the P.S. 149 fight song. My dad's was the only hand still up. Kaye said, "Great, let's do it," and gave the band the beat. My mother tugged at my father's coat, saying, "Milt, you're embarrassing me. Please sit down." My parents' friends urged my mother to relax. Danny Kaye and my father sang their alma mater's fight song:

> 149 is the school for me
> Drives away all adversity
> Steady and true
> We'll be to you
> Loyal to 149.
> RAH RAH
> Raise on high
> The red and white
> Cheer it
> With all your might
> Loyal all to 149

The crowd went crazy.

In the early 1930s, my father worked as a minor-league umpire on the East Coast, teaming up occasionally with Emmett Ashford, who was something of a showman and who thirty years later became the first black umpire in the major leagues. Some people thought all of my father's behind-the-plate antics amounted to little more than "white Ashford." In the mid-sixties, we'd go to Giants games not when Koufax was the competition or bats were being given away, but when Ashford was calling balls and strikes. All game long, my father would keep his binoculars on Ashford and say to me, "Emmett's calling a low strike," or "Emmett was out of position on that one," or "If that guy gives Emmett any more guff, Emmett's going to give him the old heave-ho." Then I'd look up and Emmett would be giving the guy the old heave-ho.

It wasn't the major leagues that played at Golden Gate Park. It wasn't even the minor leagues. It was something called the industrial league. The Machinists would play the Accountants; Pacific Gas and Electric would play Western Airlines. Still, they played with a hardball, they played for blood, their wives cheered like enraged school-girls, and my father was the umpire. He'd leave on Sunday morning, carrying his spikes and metal mask, with his chest protector under-neath his blue uniform and a little whisk broom, with which to dust off home plate, sticking out of his pocket. I'll never forget the first time I saw him umpire.

It wasn't a stadium at all but an immense field without fences. There was a diamond, though, and dugouts and a half-circle of stands. I stood behind the screen, watching Denny's Restaurant play Safeway Market. Neither team meant a thing to me, and after a few innings I looked around for my father, who I figured must be working the next game. Then I realized the big man in blue, squatting behind the catcher with every pitch, was my dad. In certain sections of the country, in certain leagues and stadiums, the spectators are expected to focus all of their economic and sexual frustrations upon the lonely figure of the umpire, but in San Francisco, in Golden Gate Park, on at least one Sunday in the summer of 1966, they didn't do that.

Denny's and Safeway weren't playing up to par; my father soon emerged as the main attraction. When a batter took a called third strike, my father would parody the victim's indignation. When a bat-ter drew a walk, my father would run halfway to first base with him to speed things along. He was the only umpire working the game, so on balls hit to the outfield he'd run down the foul line to make sure the ball had been caught, and on balls hit to the infield he'd run to first base to be in position to decide. He signaled safe by spreading his arms and flapping them, as if readying for flight. He signaled out by jerking his thumb, and the entire right side of his body, down. Between innings he juggled three baseballs.

He worked all day, four long games, ten in the morning until six at night, and at the last out of the last game the fans applauded. It was only light, polite, scattered applause, and maybe they were clapping for the winning team, but to me it was a thunderous ovation and they were thanking the umpire. I stood up behind the screen and joined them.

Two of the things I love the most in the world—language and sports—my father taught me to love. I'm no longer much of an athlete at all. I have a bad back, tendonitis in my shoulder, a trick knee; I wear orthotics in my shoes to balance the unevenness of my legs; and I have a little pinch in my neck that's been bothering me lately, whereas through his nearly ninety-nine years my father's major ailment appeared to be tennis elbow. He got upset when it rained because that meant he could only work out in the gym rather than speed walk around the track and then work out in the gym. Deep into his mid-nineties, he speed walked, swam, played golf and, occasionally, tennis. He was the most vigorous person I've ever known. From his newspaper column about a raft trip our family took down the Salmon River: "I was up at 6 the next morning and volunteered to gather the kindling and other firewood. The other members of my family snuggled in their sleeping bags and made it just in time for the 7:30 breakfast."

On my tenth birthday, when my father was fifty-six, he pitched so hard to me and my friends that we were afraid to hit against him. "Get in the batter's box," he growled at us. One of my fondest memories is from about twenty-five years ago—the two of us sitting on his couch in the dark, listening to the radio broadcast of a Giants-Dodgers game; when Mike Marshall hit a three-run home run in the tenth inning to win it for the Dodgers, he and I looked at each other and both of us were, a little weirdly, crying. (Not in my case. Never in mine.) From the time I was six years old, the first thing he and I did every morning was read the sports page.

Games held us together, but also words. I always loved his love of puns, bad puns, and worse puns; admired his ability to tell a joke and a story. He flew to Providence to attend my college graduation, and the day before the ceremony we took a tour of John Brown House at the Rhode Island Historical Society. On and on the docent droned, giving us the official version of American history. My father and I tried not to laugh, but as we went from room to room, we were in an ecstasy of impudent giggles. SUBVERT THE DOMINANT PARADIGM—so goes the bumper sticker, which is now complete cliché. In so many ways, though, he showed me how to do exactly that: to not accept accepted wisdom, to insist on my own angle, to view language as a playground and a playground as bliss. He showed me how to love being in my own body, how to love the words that emerged haltingly from my mouth and (over time) less haltingly from my typewriter, how to try to love being in my own skin and not some other skin.

THE GROUNDLING

As a student at Brown in the mid-1970s, I admired my writing teachers, John Hawkes and R. V. Cassill, but both of them were more than thirty years older than I, so I admired them as father figures, from a distance. I wanted, instead, a teacher who was the older brother I never really had (I didn't grow up with Joseph and only now, in late middle age, am I getting to know him a little), a cool tutor, a hero to hang out with. Friends at Yale kept telling me about a creative writing teacher named David Milch. He had written speeches for Watergate felon Maurice Stans and songs for the Allman Brothers; he was an alcoholic; he was a compulsive gambler; he had written and discarded three novels of a projected four-book series that R. W. B. Lewis and Robert Penn Warren thought possessed genius; he had been or still was a heroin addict and had served time in a Mexican jail for possession; he was kicked out of Yale Law School for shooting out the lights on a cop car. Who knew how much of it was true? Who cared? I enrolled in Yale's summer session. I wanted him to show me not only how to write but how to live.

Milch looked like he'd never been released from *Rebel Without a Cause:* He wore black tennis shoes, blue jeans, a pack of Marlboros rolled into the sleeve of his white T-shirt, and a permanent smirk. The only person I've ever known who could convey genuine menace in a classroom, he paced back and forth, chain-smoked, lectured nonstop without notes, rarely allowed anyone to say anything, insisted that we call him "Mr. Milch," addressed us—with pseudo-politeness—as "Mr." or "Miss," and asked questions that somehow were impossible to answer without sounding either feeble-minded or overscrupulous.

When John Cheever visited class, Milch asked me whether I thought Farragut, the protagonist of Cheever's new novel, *Falconer,* was "pussy-whipped."

"Define 'pussy-whipped,'" I said. (I hadn't the faintest idea.)

Joan Didion gave a talk, and afterward Milch made me perform the duty that he'd been assigned—selling copies of *A Book of Common Prayer* in the foyer of the auditorium—while he and his sexy fiancée drove away on a motorcycle, reeking of dissipation and glamour.

One student in the class, the son of a famous *New Yorker* writer, had hilariously bad literary instincts. "Whenever you're about to say something," Milch told him in front of everyone, "say the opposite of whatever you're thinking, because whatever you think is always wrong."

No one else's opinion of me and my work had ever seemed so momentous, thrilling, potentially disabling. Although Milch warned us to "never, ever read a review," when we read Sherwood Anderson's story "I Want to Know Why," I looked up what Cleanth Brooks and Warren had said about the story in *Understanding Fiction,* since Milch had studied with both of them and now assisted them in the preparation of revised editions of some of their textbooks. The "correct" interpretation of "I Want to Know Why" was that it defined loss of innocence as an acceptance of the fact that human beings are not wholly good or wholly evil but a mixture of these qualities. I then rephrased this interpretation so Milch wouldn't recognize the crib, and got praised.

At my first conference with Milch he said, "You're a writer."

I said, "Well, sure, that's why I'm taking the class."

He said, "No: you're a writer."

To celebrate, I bought and ate twelve chocolate-chip cookies at a Greek deli on Elm Street.

However, I liked nowhere near as much as Milch did the tortuous circumnavigations of the books he taught: Conrad's *Nostromo,* Faulkner's *Light in August.* One time I pointed out an exceedingly minor inconsistency in *Light in August* about Joe Christmas, and Milch glumly agreed. When I swooned over Henry James's "The Beast in the Jungle," Milch quoted Mark Twain's remark about liking the one James novel he had read but that he wouldn't read another one if you gave him a farm. Milch, who as a child had been sexually abused by a camp counselor, was a hyper-masculine writer, like Conrad or Faulkner; I, à la James, wasn't.

Both Milch and I liked to write in the new underground wing of the Cross Campus Library, but I needed the complete isolation of an enclosed cubicle, whereas Milch would work on his stories and plays and screenplays at a table in the center of the room, drinking coffee, overhearing whispered gossip—surrounded by human activity. I allegorized and romanticized this difference: To me, writing was a revenge upon life, upon my life, whereas to Milch writing seemed to be part of life. He was the first intellectual I'd ever met who not only seemed to like life but who reveled in it—who, in Conrad's famous phrase, "to the destructive element submit[ted]." He was—or wanted to appear to be, or succeeded in appearing to be, or succeeded in appearing to me to be—that purest contradiction: a macho pedant, a Jewish cowboy. He frequently made sure to take me with him to meet his bookie.

Although Milch seemed to have picked up a faint southern accent from his association with Brooks and Warren and his mock-fastidious manners evoked for me lapsed southern gentility, he actually grew up in Buffalo, the son of a surgeon. I grew up in San Francisco, the son of journalist-activists. In Milch's class, I wrote elliptical but overwrought stories about this childhood: first kiss, first death, first peace march in Golden Gate Park, etc.—heavy on the water imagery. Milch called these stories "tropisms," which when I looked it up in the dictionary turned out to mean an "involuntary orientation by an organism or one of its parts that involves turning or curving and is a positive or negative response to a source of stimulation." The source of stimulation was my nonfictional family in its perfect righteousness; my response tended toward the negative.

One afternoon, in his nearly empty office in a baroque building, Milch said that I suffered from the "malaise of your [and, of course, his] race": an excessive preoccupation with narrowly moral rather than universally human concerns. As a result, he informed me, I had an insufficiently developed eye. Judaism is a faith rather than a race, I reminded him, but I'd recently started wearing glasses and I knew what he meant: I needed to stop judging the world and just see it. *Annie Hall* was the big movie that summer; Milch hated it. He excoriated all my favorite Jewish writers. They were like the boy in "I Want to Know Why"; they hadn't yet learned that human nature was something to accept rather than to protest. The only admirable Jewish American writers were Norman Mailer, who "at least has balls," and Nathanael West, who called Jewish women "bagels." When Milch played softball, he shouted anti-Semitic obscenities from the outfield. All contemporary Jewish American writing amounted, for Milch, to the climactic scene in *Making It,* when Norman Podhoretz has to congratulate himself for being able to enjoy a drink on Paradise Island. *Drink, drink,* Milch was trying to tell me, *drink it all in.* Instead, I endlessly repeated back to him his criticisms of me, altering the wording slightly each time so that the criticism didn't sound quite so thoroughgoing and devastating. (Much of Milch's allure is based on his persona as the first and only Jewish amoralist. This dichotomy between moralizing Jews and manly men shows up in nearly every TV show he's been associated with: *Hill Street Blues, NYPD Blue, Deadwood.*)

"You're classic passive-aggressive," he finally said.

I fiddled with this observation until he threw me out of his office.

Against Milch's advice and without benefit of his recommendation, which he refused to send since he said I needed to get out in the world and live, I went to the Iowa Famous Writers School. Milch had gone there a dozen years before, so I looked up his master's thesis, a work in progress entitled "The Groundlings," and pored over every line of the two chapters he'd written. The two phrases Milch had used most often in class were "strategy of indirection," which meant it should take the reader forever to figure out what was happening, since life was difficult, and "content tests form," which meant that since life was difficult, it should take the reader forever to figure out what was happening. It took me forever to figure out what was happening in "The Groundlings," but it had an undeniable narcotic pull, probably because there was so much Milch in it: a protagonist named

Torch, ruthless intelligence bordering on the sadistic, extreme emotional candor, incessant obscenity as a mantra of seriousness. Milch also had what he accused me of having: perfect pitch for how people talked and next to no interest in how the world looked.

The first chapter took place almost entirely in the men's room of an airport in upstate New York. The second chapter was replete, for some reason, with references to Catholic liturgy. Mark and Torch, brothers, spoke to each other in a curious mix of neo-Elizabethan diction ("Speak, knave") and street talk ("Fuck you right in the mouth, Torch"). It contained two crucial passages for me—for me, personally. Torch tried to talk Mark out of blaming himself for his father's death (Milch's father committed suicide):

> You've got this compulsion to have some moral relation to every move that's made in this vale of tears. I mean you made a move. That's all you can do. Okay, so now you'll go back to blaspheming, so everyone will call you a mind-fucker and a shit-bird, and if they don't, then you'll call them phonies, because they won't execute divine judgment. That's really a small-change operation, Mark. That's really a shitty game to play. And I mean it's so cheap. It lets you out of every situation, out of letting your moral position be defined by your response to things, by the way you act. You know, by your rules, you say if I am of two minds on a problem, I am not perfect, and if I am not perfect I am evil, and so you've got your position established without ever having to get involved with the problem itself.

Universally human rather than narrowly moral. And at the end of the first chapter, Mark said, "I picked up this guy. And I fucked his mind! He had just, see, killed his father. By indirection. So I catalyzed it. I got him to see the connection." This was precisely what Milch did for all his students, especially me: catalyzed connections that we knew were there but didn't (but did) want to see, so we could never stop talking about him.

A few years later, my girlfriend from Iowa, a poet named Rita, and I checked into the Hotel Lincoln in Chicago. Rita's father was a movie producer, so we didn't have a TV in our apartment in Iowa City. We were on spring vacation, though. One night a show called *Hill Street Blues* came on. It wasn't just that *Hill Street* seemed better written than most things on television; it also seemed instantly familiar, though I'd never watched it before. Bobby Hill bought Renko a prostitute for his birthday, and the prostitute wasn't supposed to tell, but she did. The scene was more effective than it had any right to be, and I told Rita the show reminded me of Milch—its mixture of academic and street idioms, its (I couldn't help it) "strategy of indirection," its very male existential gloom. The credits rolled at the end of the show, listing Milch as story editor, whatever that was. I bounced up and down on the springy bed.

"Take it easy," Rita said. "It's only TV."

I moved with Rita to New York that summer and scoured *Hill Street Blues* every week for the most minuscule revelation about Milch's psychology. The show was full of what were to me recognizable elements from Milch's life—gambling, loan sharks, heroin, Belker's relationship with his mother. One night that fall, Rita and I sat on the floor of our Lilliputian apartment; Milch had been nominated for an Emmy Award, so we watched the ceremony on our nineteen-inch black-and-white box. He won for an episode he'd written called "Trial by Fury," about Furillo's Cuomo-like conscience. Accepting the award, Milch stood at the podium as if he were back in class, quoting Stanley Kunitz, "You are all my brothers in the world." Kunitz was one of Rita's favorite poets; she knew the reference was to his poem about the Holocaust, "Around Pastor Bonhoeffer," which contained the question "*if you permit/this evil, what is the good/of the good of your life?*" We looked up "Around Pastor Bonhoeffer." The final section was called "The Extermination Camp":

> Through the half-open door of the hut
> the camp doctor saw him kneeling,
> with his hands quietly folded.
> "I was most deeply moved by the way
> this lovable man prayed,
> so devout and so certain
> that God heard his prayer."
> Round-faced, bespectacled, mild,
> candid with costly grace,
> he walked toward the gallows
> and did not falter.

Oh but he knew the Hangman!
Only a few steps more
and he would enter the arcanum
where the Master
would take him by the shoulder,
as He does at each encounter,
and turn him round
to face his brothers in the world.

For anyone ready to catalyze the connections, false modesty turned rapidly into whiplash judgment.

My first novel was published in the winter of 1984. I sent *Heroes* to Milch, who a year later left a message on my answering machine that he'd liked the book—"a nice novel about a kid growing up," according to Milch, whereas in actuality it's about a diffident Iowa sportswriter obsessed with a brilliant and uncouth college basketball player (me and Milch?).

A couple of years later I went to Yaddo to work on a new book—which wasn't nice, but it was a novel about a kid growing up (a self, stuttering). One afternoon, Milch drove into the parking lot with his wife and daughter. He got out of the car and told me to give them the tour. With the money he'd made from *Hill Street,* he'd bought a horse and had come to Saratoga Springs to watch it race. Since I hadn't seen him for ten years, I was surprised, and secretly delighted, that he recognized me immediately. He said that when he'd been here years ago he'd found it "a good place to dry out" but hadn't written a thing, and the only thing he'd looked forward to every day was reading the paper, because "at least it was a little hit of the real world." We walked through the ridiculously medieval main mansion. I pointed out that the founder of Yaddo had made his fortune in the railroad business and wound up being killed in a train wreck. "That," I said, "is known as poetic . . . something or other." Milch laughed. This was funny—to be smart enough to know when to pretend you don't know something. He gave me a phone number to call so we could get together; I called a few times and left messages and he never called back.

The book I had worked on at Yaddo was published in 1989. I sent him a copy, and shortly afterward his assistant called, asking whether

Dead Languages had been optioned yet, and I thought, *Yes, yes, sweet revenge; Milch likes the book so much he feels compelled to make it into a movie.*

He wasn't interested in making it into a movie and never had been. He was the executive producer of a television show called *Capital News* and wanted to know whether I wanted to make four hundred thousand dollars a year writing teleplays. He sent me a videotape of the pilot, to which I knew I was supposed to respond by coming up with new scenarios, but the show was dismal—*Capital News* was like *Hill Street Blues* on Thorazine—and I couldn't come up with anything. I pretended I didn't understand exactly what it was he was looking for from me and mailed him a lengthy, not to say interminable, critique of the pilot. When he never replied, I called him and was put on hold for the longest time. While waiting, I planned my speech about how I hoped he took my response in the spirit in which it was intended: as *constructive* criticism; how the show had a lot of good moments and plenty of potential and there was nothing about it that couldn't be fixed if—

He put me on speaker, explained that my critique was moot since the pilot was already in the can, dispatched me in thirty seconds, and started talking on another line before I'd even hung up.

What did I seek so earnestly from this mentor/tormentor, this charming bully, and why did he so steadfastly refuse to give it? Why did he always tease me by positioning himself close enough to view but just out of my grasp? Antagonizing me, he was also showing me in person what he wanted me to do on the page. "Strategy of indirection": Life is difficult. *Describe the difficulty.*

EVERYTHING I KNOW
I'VE LEARNED FROM MY BAD BACK

I'm not thrilled to acknowledge that I date the origin of my back problems to the period, twenty-two years ago, when I repeatedly threw my daughter, Natalie, then an infant, up in the air and carried her around in a Snugli. It's a dubious etiology, since another cause would surely have come along soon enough; my back, one physical therapist has explained to me, was an accident waiting to happen. It makes perverse sense, though, that in my own mind Natalie and my back are intertwined, because dealing with a bad back has been, for me, an invaluable education in the physical, the mortal, the ineradicable wound.

I wish I had gotten to indulge in the luxury of being lionized as Atlas by Natalie when she was little, but I didn't. I was still quite good at unscrewing bottle caps and pinning her arms when I was tickling or wrestling her, but if she was sitting atop someone's shoulders on a walk in the woods or getting tossed around in the pool, they were someone else's shoulders or it was someone else in the pool. I couldn't Hula-Hoop with Natalie and I can't dance with my wife, Laurie. Now, at parties, I look first for a chair, since I can't stand for more than a few minutes. When we take trips, Laurie has to carry the heavy luggage; at home, she moves the furniture. Atlas I ain't.

You might suspect—I might suspect—Laurie definitely suspects— that maybe I just have a pathetically low pain threshold. And yet my back doctor assures me that with my back, some people play golf and tennis while others have been on disability for fifteen years. I fall about in the middle: I've never missed a day of work because of my back, but I certainly complain about it a lot; it's weirdly toward the forefront of my consciousness. I'm not so much a hypochondriac as a misery miser, fascinated by dysfunction. Several years ago, I heard an elderly woman interviewed on the "Apocalypse" episode of *This American Life* say she welcomed entering the kingdom of heaven because she would finally be granted relief from her incessant physical pain. While I was listening to this, I was driving, my back was killing me every time I turned the steering wheel, and sad to say, at the moment she said this, I must admit: I could relate.

My father never even tweaked his back, never had a single physical ailment until the last few years of his life, and yet he was never prone to expressing gratitude for his near century of good health ("I've had to see more doctors from ninety-four to ninety-seven than I did from zero to ninety-four"). Over the last decade I've gone to innumerable physical therapists and doctors. One doctor said I should have back surgery immediately; he had an opening later in the week. Another doctor said all I had to do was perform one particular leg-lift exercise that Swedish nurses did, and I'd be fine. One therapist said I should run more; another therapist said I should run less. One said that human beings weren't built to sit as much as I sit; another said people were never meant to stand upright. One thought I would need to keep seeing him for years and years; another criticized me, after a few months, for not cutting the cord. I used to feel that everything I know I learned through my lifelong struggle with stuttering; I now feel this way about my damn back. Gerald Jonas's book about stuttering is subtitled *The Disorder of Many Theories*. Back Theory seems to suffer from the same Rashomon effect: as with almost every human problem, there's no dearth of answers and no answer.

A few days after 9/11, I saw a back doctor who, unlike ninety-five percent of doctors I've ever seen, presents himself as a person rather than as an authority figure; ask him how his day is going and he'll say, "Terrible; no one's getting better." He, too, has a bad back, and when he drops his folder, he'll squat down to pick it up, the way back patients are instructed to do, rather than just lean over, the way everyone else does. When I speak to most doctors, I feel slightly or not so slightly crazy, whereas I feel like myself when talking to Stan Herring (great name—sounds like a figure from my dad's Brooklyn childhood, like a character from a Malamud story). At my first appointment with him, he emphasized how many of his patients with bad backs carve their entire identity out of the fact that they're patients; they'd have no idea what to do with their lives otherwise. The World Trade Center suicide bombers were, to Dr. Herring, similar to professional patients; their entire existence was given structure and purpose by the fetishization of their pain, their victimhood. The message was subtle, but I got it: *Don't let yourself become a suicide bomber.*

Herring recommended that I see a physical therapist with the unlikely name of Wolfgang Brolley, who goes by the name "Wolf" and looks and moves in a rather lupine way as well. As I am, he's bald (with a shaved head) and bespectacled, but he's elfin whereas I'm tall and lanky/clanky. I feel somewhat similar to Herring, who's Jewish and self-deprecating; Wolf is Irish, Chicago-born, passionate, earnest, views himself unself-consciously as a healer, goes to Zen retreats around the globe. I give him an essay I wrote about my adulation of Bill Murray (that death haunt); he gives me an article he read about the international black-market slave trade. Partial to quotations from ancient Chinese philosophers and Christian mystics, he's not my buddy; he's something of a taskmaster. When he measured my hamstrings' flexibility—lack thereof—he couldn't help it: he snorted. One morning, when I called to say I felt too bad to come in for my appointment, he said, "You have to come in; that's what I'm here for," and gave me electronic stimulation and a massage. One of my favorite experiences in the physical world is a massage from Wolf.

I used to throw my back out completely—the classic collapse on the sidewalk and yowl to the heavens—but now, thanks in large measure to the Stan-and-Wolf program, I seem to have it under control to the point that my back never goes out completely anymore. (Knock on lumbar.) I sit on a one-inch foam wedge on my chair and get up every hour to do exercises or at least tell myself I do or at least take a hot shower or apply an ice pack or a heat pad. I sleep on my side, on a latex mattress; upon waking, I don't just sit up but rather first "find my center" (there really is such a thing, I'm pleased to report). Wolf keeps reminding me that neither he nor Dr. Herring has a solution: I have to become my own authority and view my recovery as an existential journey. I reassure him that I do. I see going to the drugstore to get toothpaste as an existential journey.

And what existential journey hasn't been aided by chemistry? I've been in and out of speech therapy all my life, but nothing has mitigated my stuttering as effectively as taking a half milligram of Alprazolam before giving a public reading. The ibuprofen, the muscle relaxants have certainly helped my back, but the Paxil has been transformative. At first I strenuously resisted Dr. Herring's prescription, primarily because my father suffered from bipolar disorder for most of his adult life. In 1956, my mother was pregnant with me, which caused my father to confess his fear that I was going to be too much of a burden for him because he had a history of depression.

"What do you mean?" my mother, who was a young thirty-one, asked. "You get down in the dumps every now and again?"

"I think I'm on the road to having it licked," he said, "but after the war, then again during a brief period of unemployment before we met, I needed a little electroshock to get me through some bad patches."

Living with my bipolar father wasn't like living with a drug addict. It wasn't like living with a funeral. Last December, Laurie received a card that showed the words "Merry Christmas" being manufactured by a bunch of goofy little guys who looked like Santa's sugar battalion. It was more like that: just knowing every lake is man-made and sooner or later needs to be emptied. For several years my father would be fine and funny and athletically buoyant, then one day he'd come back with an entire roll of negatives of the freeway. Once, in Sacramento on behalf of the poverty program, he mailed me an epistle consisting entirely of blank pages—for no real reason that I could make out. Another time, I was looking for some leftovers in the fridge and came across a note Scotch-taped together, sticky with bloodstains, like advertisements for a sympathetic reader. My mother would pack his suitcase, and he would wave shy goodbyes like a boy leaving for camp.

However, Dr. Herring assured me that I wasn't "secretly" being treated for depression: Paxil has apparently been used to treat chronic pain for more than a decade. For the last few years I've been taking one ten-milligram tablet of Paxil a day. I worry a little about becoming a grinning idiot, but I figure I already have the idiocy part down, and I'm so far over on the grouchy side of the continuum that a little grinning isn't going to kill me.

Maybe it's all just the pure dumb rush of selective serotonin reuptake, but now, rather than endlessly rehearsing how my life might have been different, I tell myself how grateful I am for my life—with Laurie and Natalie and our relative health and happiness together. I'm newly in love with Laurie, aware of her weaknesses and accepting of them, because I'm so blisteringly aware of my own. I go to sleep with a night guard jammed between my teeth and a pillow between my legs and a CPAP mask stretched across my face (to eliminate snoring and apnea). I walk around with a ThermaCare heat wrap in one coat pocket and Biofreeze gel and methocarbamol tablets in the other. I'm not exactly the king of the jungle.

I like the humility and gravity and nakedness of this need, because—and this is apparently a lesson I can't relearn too many times—we're just animals walking the earth for a brief time, a bare body housed in a mortal cage. For his fiftieth birthday party, a friend rented a gym around the corner from his house, and I played basketball for most of the night as if I'd somehow been transported back to my twenties. I was, according to Laurie, "running around like a colt," although, of course, a couple of weeks later I tweaked my back and was out of action for a few days. At least I'm now in action ("in action": gambling jargon, a Milchism; having gambled away the hundred million dollars he's made in television, he's now reportedly bankrupt). My back will always hurt a bit, or rather the pain will always come and go. "Pain is inevitable," Dr. Herring likes to say. "Suffering is optional." When I quoted the line to Laurie, she said, "Thank you, Dr. Herring." A while ago, I asked Wolf why I have a bad back. He explained that the ability to walk upright was a key evolutionary adaptation for mankind, but vertebrae that are aligned in the same direction as the force of gravity often become compressed, leading to pinched nerves and ruptured disks. Then he said, "In your case, though: bad attitude." He was joking, but I got it.

MEN AND GAMES AND GUNS

Otto Preminger's movie *Laura* is, as Pauline Kael once said, "everyone's favorite chic murder mystery." Its real subject, though, is how, as a man, to exist in relation to a woman: seeing her as a carnation in your lapel, seeing her as your bank, seeing her as herself. It's an American movie. Guess which angle of vision gets the girl.

Made in 1944, the movie features the baldly symbolic Freudianism of its time; a corollary of this is its use of names as overtly signifying as any that might be found in a story by Nathaniel Hawthorne. A body is discovered in the apartment of Manhattan socialite Laura Hunt (Gene Tierney): target of everyone's search, object of everyone's desire. The corpse is assumed to be Laura, since the body was dressed in her clothes, and the deceased's face has been obliterated by a shotgun blast. Homicide detective Mark McPherson (Dana Andrews), hard-boiled Irish cop, a real guy, a real person, has three suspects: Waldo Lydecker (Clifton Webb), a high-society gossip columnist who virtually "created" Laura and who is closeted—in matters related to lying down with someone, he's lying; Shelby Carpenter (Vincent Price—ludicrously miscast), Laura's hunky fiancé, a rube from

Kentucky); and Anne Treadwell (Judith Anderson), Laura's wealthy, soignée aunt who is attempting to purchase Shelby to serve, essentially, as her gigolo—"I can afford him."

Lydecker is too clever, too-too; when Laura introduces herself to him, interrupting his lunch in order to ask him to endorse a product her advertising firm represents, he says, "Either you have been raised in some incredibly rustic community, where good manners are unknown, or else you suffer from the common feminine delusion that the mere fact of being a woman exempts you from the rules of civilized conduct, or possibly both." Carpenter is not enough; prone to waxing rhapsodic over "lunch, beautiful lunch, day after day," he doesn't "know a lot about anything, but I know a little about practically everything." McPherson is just right: a regular Joe who is both smart and handsome, heterosexual yet clever, verbal but physical, the smallest man in the movie but the only one who lands a punch. It's 1944: there's a war on; the hero can't be an artist or a playboy. He needs to be someone who can simply get the job done.

It takes a while, but the film finally gets around to praising the man of action (and a few well-chosen words) rather than the man only of words (all eloquent or witty) or the man of all brawn and no brain. *Laura* begins with Lydecker, in voice-over, wrapping Laura's story in his own Walter Winchell–esque pseudo-poetry: "I shall never forget the weekend Laura died. A silver sun burned the sky like a huge magnifying glass." The camera pans from a portrait of Laura, in her apartment, to "priceless British and American glassware" in Lydecker's apartment, which—"too exquisite for a man," according to the screenplay—bears a strong resemblance to the Metropolitan Museum of Art. He creates and collects beautiful objects; Laura is only his most prized possession. "She deferred to my judgment and taste," he says. "I selected a more attractive hairdress for her. I taught her what clothes were more becoming to her. She became as well known as my walking stick or my white carnation."

Both as narrator and as actor within the drama, Lydecker overanalyzes the action as it unfolds, often deconstructing the drama before it happens. (In the shooting script, Lydecker is even more manifestly the narrator than he is in the film.) He's Writer Man, Language Man, solipsism incarnate. When McPherson arrives and asks him if he's Lydecker, Lydecker says, "You recognized me. How splendid."

Earlier, he explains to a young Laura, "In my case, self-absorption is completely justified. I've never discovered any other subject quite so worthy of my attention." Though the film's charm rides heavily on his wit—"I don't use a pen; I write with a goose quill dipped in venom"—it must finally reject him, as do so many other narratives that feature introverted narrators contemplating more physically prepossessing specimens: Günter Grass's *Cat and Mouse,* Ford Madox Ford's *The Good Soldier, The Great Gatsby, A Separate Peace.* Writers love-hate that they're writers rather than action figures, so they compose works that celebrate and then desecrate their own word-trapped half-lives.

In Lydecker's case, of course, his queerness, especially in 1944, condemns him even more assuredly to narrative hell. In the film's first scene, McPherson, arriving at Lydecker's apartment to interview him, is greeted by Lydecker, who, naked in the bathtub, asks McPherson to toss him a washcloth and then his robe. McPherson complies with each request but both times does so with a look of utter derision, though it's unclear if it's Lydecker's arrogance or anatomy he holds in contempt. Lydecker says that Laura "would never have thrown away her life on a male beauty in distress [Carpenter]"; tells Laura, "If McPherson weren't muscular and handsome in a cheap sort of way, you'd see through him in a second"; and cautions her, "With you, a lean, strong body is the measure of a man, and you always get hurt." (These are all, of course, the most transparent projections.) When Lydecker shows Laura the dossier of dirt he's gathered on Carpenter, he says, "Look at what Old Mother Hubbard has in the cupboard"; in the screenplay, Carpenter even refers to Lydecker as "Mother Hubbard." Encouraging McPherson to arrest Carpenter, Lydecker says, "Quick, McPherson, the handcuffs," then adds, "You'll look nice in handcuffs, Carpenter." "Why don't you get down on all fours again, Waldo?" Carpenter replies, alluding to Lydecker's fainting earlier. "It's the only time you've ever kept your mouth shut." A clause in Clifton Webb's contract prohibited anyone on the set from referring to his homosexuality. Tierney's memoir, *Self-Portrait,* mentions his "prissiness."

Big surprise, then, that Lydecker turns out to be the killer. Unable to accept that Laura is marrying Carpenter, Lydecker tries to kill her, but in the darkness, by mistake, he kills model Diane Redfern, with whom Carpenter had been having an affair. McPherson, inflamed by a painting of Laura, her letters and diary, and admiring testimonials by all her friends, falls in love with her image. When she returns from a weekend in the country, she assures him that she no longer intends to marry Carpenter; McPherson finds evidence to incriminate Lydecker. Knowing that McPherson is going to arrest him and that she's now in love with McPherson, Lydecker again attempts to murder Laura, but McPherson's fellow detective, McEveety, kills Lydecker, Laura falls into McPherson's arms, and fade to black.

Shelby Carpenter, the un-Lydecker, has no access to any thought other than the trash conventions of the day. He greets every girl with "honey" or "darling." Courting Laura, he says, kiddingly but not too kiddingly, "I cook, I swallow swords, I mend my own socks, I never eat garlic or onions—what more can you want of a man?" He says to her, "The way you talk, you'd think I was in love with you." He also calls her "moon of my delight" and says to her, "I approve of that hat and the girl in it, too." Questioned by McPherson, Carpenter says, almost proudly, "I've spent very little time in observing my own character." Equally blithely, he says, "I can afford a blemish on my character but not on my clothes." When Lydecker and Laura confront Carpenter and Laura's aunt Anne having dinner together at Anne's apartment, Carpenter's only response is, "Hello, darling. I didn't expect to see you tonight." Lydecker's gloss: "In a moment of supreme disaster, he's trite." He is trite: a lummox with no interior life whatsoever, whose charm is precisely that he has no interior life whatsoever. A simple appetite. A walking penis, looking for warm homes to hide in for a while.

If Lydecker is a more effete Fitzgerald and Carpenter is bad Faulkner, McPherson is pretty pure Hemingway—the war correspondent in time of war, the necessary deflator of Lydecker's decadent afflatus, and the swift counterpuncher to Carpenter's lazy, cowardly plodding. Taking Laura's diaries out of her desk drawer to read, McPherson immediately puts them away and wanders around her apartment, looking at her clothes, smelling her perfume, drinking her expensive liquor. He's a word guy but not too much of a word guy, or rather his words are more tied to earthly realities. Asked by Lydecker if he's ever viewed a woman as anything other than a "doll" or "dame," he says he did once, "but she kept walking me past furniture stores to look at parlor suites." Lydecker tries to use this information to lure Laura away from McPherson by telling her that when asked if he's ever been in love, he replied, "A dame in Washington Heights once got a fox fur out of me." Laura says, "That doesn't mean anything. He isn't like that." She understands that it's just a male code (Hammett, Chandler, Hemingway) to which McPherson subscribes and that part of the code is that he's so full of feeling it has to be phrased as anti-feeling, whereas Lydecker is so devoid of feeling ("The sentiment comes easy at fifty cents a word") that he buries his ennui under a bouquet of florid rhetoric. When McPherson says to Laura, "I'd reached a point where I needed to talk to you in official surroundings," she beams, understanding that in McPherson's rhetorical register this is tantamount to a marriage proposal, and she digs the male reserve of it. McPherson shows genuine concern for Laura as a person; virtually the first thing he says to her is to suggest that she change out of her wet clothes so she doesn't catch cold. Later, he buys food with the intention of making breakfast for her—as opposed to viewing Laura as a vector on the grid of his own ego, which is how Lydecker sees her ("the best part of myself, that's what you are").

"Love Calls Us to the Things of This World," as the Richard Wilbur poem has it. Or as John Hawkes says more alarmingly in his novel *The Lime Twig,* "Love is a long close scrutiny." McPherson is vivid concreteness to Lydecker's airy abstraction. When confronted by McPherson with a reference in an old column of his that anticipates the present murder, Lydecker says, "I never bother with details, you know." McPherson, inevitably, says, "I do." Later, Lydecker, feigning regret, says, "I shall never forgive myself for letting Laura become involved with Shelby. It was my fault. I should have stopped it somehow"; McPherson shrugs and says, "Well, it's too late now." Similarly, when Laura tries to blame herself for Diane Redfern's death, since her unwillingness to detach herself from Lydecker indirectly led to the model's fate, McPherson's only response is, "That's nonsense. Forget it." McPherson's philosophy is anti-philosophy: the demand of reality.

McPherson is a guy's guy; his one vice is a taste for the bottle. When Carpenter explains that he didn't know what music was played at a concert because he fell asleep, McPherson accepts the alibi: "I fall asleep at concerts myself." Carpenter is tall, Lydecker is medium height, and McPherson is short, but McPherson is the one who knows how to use his body for something other than fucking—men, in Lydecker's case, or too many women, in Carpenter's case. For no real reason other than that he doesn't like him, McPherson punches Carpenter, who doubles over and, in his last words in the movie, asks for Anne's motherly ministrations.

When McPherson's aides-de-camp are engaged in a shoot-out with Lydecker, McPherson valiantly covers Laura. The details that are real for Lydecker are the details of art—the sound of words, the primitive masks in his apartment. He's Oscar Wilde: art for art's sake; life is a rumor. When it becomes apparent to Lydecker that Laura is falling in love with McPherson, Lydecker says to her, "I hope you'll never regret what promises to be a disgustingly earthy relationship." Lydecker girlishly faints when he sees Laura (whom he thought he had killed) alive again, and explains his fainting by claiming he has epilepsy. When, early in the film, Carpenter asks Laura if she wants to dance, she explains that she's not alone—she's Lydecker's "date"—and Carpenter says, "Oh, him? He's probably still dancing the polka." "Yes, Betsy Ross taught it to me," Lydecker says, dispelling the put-down with wit. His trump card is his mind, whereas Carpenter's is his body, and McPherson's is his perfect equilibrium between mind and body.

McPherson likes sports, games of chance, formalized risk. He asks Anne why, on the day she withdrew $1,500, Carpenter deposited $1,300, then on the day she withdrew $1,700, Carpenter deposited $1,550. Lydecker interjects, "Maybe they were shooting crap." For the first and only time in the movie, McPherson laughs. Throughout the movie, he keeps trying to get three little silver balls into three depressions on first base, second base, and third base in a handheld mini-puzzle called Baseball. The first time Lydecker sees the puzzle, he asks McPherson whether it's "something you confiscated in a raid on a kindergarten." "Takes a lot of control," McPherson replies; "would you like to try it?" "No thanks." When McPherson continues playing with the puzzle, even or especially during the most heightened moments of conflict, Lydecker says, "Will you please stop dawdling with that infernal puzzle? It's getting on my nerves." "I know," McPherson says, "but it keeps me calm." Lydecker dislikes Jacoby, a former suitor of Laura's and the painter of the portrait of her that dominates her living room, because he "was so obviously conscious of looking more like an athlete than an artist." Lydecker asks McPherson if he has ever "dreamed of Laura as your wife in the bleachers"—that is, of taking her to down-market entertainment like a baseball game. The script features a long scene of Lydecker, McPherson, and Carpenter going to a Yankees game, to no particular purpose except to underline that Lydecker is detached from the human parade and, therefore, by his own admission, "vicious"; Carpenter is an athlete, present only physically, and therefore boring, a mere animal; McPherson is the paradox: detached in his detective work (love is a long close scrutiny) but attached to Laura (love is a long close scrutiny), even if she's going to wind up walking him past furniture stores to look at parlor suites.

Another way in which McPherson demonstrates his masculinity is the incredible number of cigarettes he smokes. When he takes McEveety's place guarding Laura's apartment, he shakes a cigarette out of the pack to give to him, thus reminding McEveety that they both have penises and are very heterosexual. A crucial "tell" in McPherson's courtship of Laura occurs when he forgets to light her cigarette for her; he's too smitten. When Laura rejects Carpenter's proffer of a light, the relationship is clearly over. The symbol of Laura joining the boys and rising up the ranks in the ad biz occurs when she's offered a cigarette and expertly tamps down the tobacco. There is, I swear, more smoking in *Laura* than any other movie ever made. In Laura's apartment, perusing her journals and diaries, McPherson builds a veritable pyre of butts. The most interesting thing that happens to the cigarettes in this hilariously psychoanalytical movie (why do you think "McEveety" sounds like "McCavity"?) is that in the last twenty minutes the cigarettes disappear and become guns: the fireworks get bigger. And when Laura inspects with admiration the long shotgun McPherson is holding in his lap, she doesn't need to ask if he's happy to see her. Lydecker, of course, can't control his gun: He kills the wrong girl earlier in the movie, and when he later tries to complete the act, even Laura can outmuscle him, causing him to misfire. He's quickly mowed down by McPherson's boys. There's control (verbal), then there's control (physical). There's language, then there's blood.

The people I've met who most closely resemble Carpenter are my jock friends from high school—dense galoots who are unaware that there's anything to say about anything other than meaningless bromides. In real life, in my experience, the Mark McPhersons of the world don't have deep reserves of feeling beneath their just-the-facts exteriors; their interiors are equally data-based. Lydecker, on the other hand, *c'est moi*. In at least one crucial sense, he's all of us: We're all trapped in our own invention of reality. In the movies, though, we get to banish him, exorcise him, tell ourselves we're not him, tell ourselves a World War II–era fairy tale: she's rich; he's smart; she's beautiful; he's brave; Mark+Laura4Ever. Theirs is the one uncorrupt relationship in a film otherwise populated with "kept" couples: Lydecker and Laura, Carpenter and Anne. The way the movie makes the most sense is if you understand Lydecker's malevolence to be only a more extreme version of the other characters' misbehavior. "We are adrift—alone in the cosmos, wreaking monstrous violence on one another out of frustration and pain," Woody Allen informs us. No punch line. "As history has proved, love is eternal," Lydecker says just before raising his gun and attempting, woefully, to murder his beloved.

LETTER TO MY FATHER

Dear Dad,

After last night's phone conversation—in which you said, apropos of *Dead Languages* and the "uncomfortably close" resemblance between yourself and the character of Teddy, that your pride in my accomplishment was at least matched by your anger and shame at seeing your foibles publicly paraded—I thought I would sit down and try to write to you some of my thoughts and feelings about the relationship between "real life" and "fiction." Your response to all the following may only be (though I hope it isn't) *Methinks he doth protest too much.*

Any novel, no matter how autobiographical (and mine certainly looks plenty so), is a verbal machine that wants only to function, and the writer will do everything he can to get the book to work. More specifically, it seems to me that a writer uses a combination of characteristics from different characters or character types—based on memory, imagination, available archetypes, and his own odd will—to create "characters," who are pieces of language that the author wants to work together in a way that makes a meaningful puzzle. *Yeah, yeah,* I'm sure you're thinking, *but how would he like it if I wrote a book in which all of* his *most embarrassing moments had been resurrected for all to see?*

One of the things I've learned about writing a novel is that once you get certain characters and certain relationships set up, it's virtually impossible to alter these relationships or change these characteristics in any significant way. Once you put a character on a particular path, e.g., Teddy suffers from bouts of manic-depression, that's sort of the path he tends to follow throughout the book. The rhetoric, grammar, and coherence of the book demand that. I mean the portrait of Teddy (of "you") as a sympathetic one, and I hope that comes across—the ferocious identification and empathy between Jeremy and Teddy. Some of my favorite scenes in the book (Jeremy observing his father at the dinner party in the opening chapter, Jeremy buying his father a lime SnoCone, Jeremy going to Montbel to tell his father that Annette has died) are pretty much, so far as I can tell, love letters from me to you.

Novels, at least the ones that I seem to want to write and read, are about failure, and so when I wrote *Dead Languages,* the characters tended to take on the one most problematic quality of members of our family as I remember them from my childhood. The dominant trait of each character in the book—in some ways almost the only trait of each character in the book—is the one that stood most powerfully to me as the symbol or symptom of some sort of tension: my stuttering, your manic-depression, Mom's obsession with political causes, [my sister] Paula's struggles with her weight. (I don't suppose it's any solace that I feel I was much harder on myself than I was on anyone else. I got to control the disclosures.) The imagination—my imagination, in any case—feasts on one attribute, takes that one attribute and can't let go. All good novels are about "complex" characters, and yet there is something, it seems to me, of the cartoon to all memorable characters in fiction.

Maybe it takes an exceptionally talented or experienced or mature writer to create characters who are not only interesting but also not always pained—to show them in their happiness and fullness and glory and yet not sentimentalize them, either. Maybe writers cartoonize what they can't fully understand.

I've tried to cut a subjective swath through my own patch of experience, as any writer must do, and I hope I haven't harmed anyone in the process, particularly you. Because this is a book about inconsolable pain, the portrait of Teddy leaves out many of the wonderful times and good moments and full feelings. I needn't tell you—or maybe I do, but certainly you must know—that I love you with all my heart and soul for all the support you've given me, all the nourishment and encouragement, all the laughs and discussions and insights, all the jokes and games and tears and tribulations, all the complicated, joyful, mysterious legacy handed down from father to son. If I didn't get all this into the book, it's because I'm not a good enough writer yet.

Love,
Dave

II. WOMEN

Like a face crossing a mirror at the back of the room, Eros moves.
You reach. Eros is gone.

—ANNE CARSON

MOTHERHOOD

At the Alaska SeaLife Center, Aurora—a giant Pacific female octopus—was introduced to J-1, a male octopus. They flashed colors and retreated to a dark corner of the center's Denizens of the Deep display. A month later, Aurora laid thousands of eggs. Despite the fact that her eggs didn't appear to develop, and aquarists—animal caretakers—believed the eggs were sterile, Aurora daily sucked in water through her mantle and sent cleansing waves over the eggs, defending them against hungry sea cucumbers and starfish. Even when aquarists, certain the eggs weren't fertile, began draining her 3,600-gallon tank, Aurora sprayed her eggs, which were exposed and drying on rocks. Aurora's eggs hatched exactly ten months after her encounter with J-1 (long since deceased); her baby octopi received food through an electronic, automatic feeder in a rearing tank. Although giant Pacific females usually die about the same time as their eggs hatch, mostly because they stop eating for months and spend their energy defending their eggs, aquarist Ed DeCastro said Aurora appeared invigorated and that "she was still tending the eggs." (She was later euthanized out of concern for her comfort.)

Starting in eighth grade, Natalie loved to criticize Laurie for getting a point of information wrong or having pieces of food caught between her teeth or chewing too loudly or, especially, talking while eating. These were the opening debate topics of the inexorable mother-daughter donnybrook that dominated our house for the next half-dozen years.

My father, who died in 2009, took a dozen medications to combat anxiety, depression, and sleeplessness. A decade ago, he and I visited his psychiatrist to make sure that he was taking them in the right combination. We had a few extra minutes at the end of the session, so I asked my father's very Freudian psychiatrist why teenage daughters are so critical of their mothers. He said, "All that hormonal energy is coursing madly through a daughter's body, and she unconsciously senses the tremendous leverage the onset of her fertility gives her, which causes the family to start treating her with more deference. She's the chance for the family to perpetuate itself. Her mother's leaving this arena just as the daughter's entering it. When researchers study this issue [disputes between mothers and daughters], not only does the father invariably side with the daughter"—I can't remember my father ever doing this with my sister; my mother ruled the roost, regardless—"but so does everybody else. The genes are driving the family to protect the most fertile female. So a good deal of a girl's anger at her mother has to do with the mixture of power she feels with the onset of fertility and the burden she feels at being the designated bearer of children." My dad sat next to me, listening to this, nodding and elbowing me in the ribs at appropriate moments, proud of his shrink's Olympian overview.

The test of a first-rate intelligence is the ability to hold two opposed ideas in the mind at the same time and still retain the ability to function.

—F. SCOTT FITZGERALD

LOVE IS A DOG FROM HELL

DIANE SAWYER: So is Karen Cooper a woman who deserves another chance to prove she can be a real mother, or should her children get to choose the parents they want? She lives here, in a halfway house for recovering mental patients in Cedar Rapids. She's been diagnosed as manic-depressive. There's no cure, but it can be controlled with medicine. And she is determined that the children will live with her again.

KAREN COOPER: Why should they be with me? I'm their mother. I love them. I care about them. I want a chance. I know I've made a lot of mistakes, but I want a chance. Those are my kids and I love them. And I don't think anybody can love them like I love them. I don't care what they say.

SAWYER: But is the Micks' problem that they love them too much? Do you blame them for loving them too much?

COOPER: Do I blame the Micks for loving them too much? I blame the Micks for being so selfish and for not—for knowing that the children loved me to begin with and ignoring that fact.

SAWYER [*voice-over*]: But the children say the Micks never told them not to love their mother.

COOPER'S DAUGHTER ANNA: No one told us not to love her. Everyone told us, "She's your mother. You're going to live with her. You're going to have a happy time." Mom and Dad did that all the time. And yet Mom and Dad are blamed for taking care of us and providing us a happy home and loving us. Lord, I thank you for letting us stay with Mom and Dad as long as we have, and I hope it'll be longer. I love you, Lord. Amen.

SAWYER [*voice-over*]: When Anna, now twelve, and Amanda, ten, learned that they might have to leave the Micks, they went to a store and tried to buy sleeping pills. They say they really talked about suicide. But the younger children have few, if any, memories of what it was like before. Justin was only three months when his mother gave him up; Sarah was just five and Samantha was three.

[*interviewing*] Do you remember the things that they say happened during that period?

COOPER: No, what?

SAWYER: That they were beaten?

COOPER: That's not true.

SAWYER: Anna says that one time you beat her with a chain.

COOPER: I don't know where she got that.

SAWYER: Never happened?

COOPER: Never. No.

SAWYER: She also says one time she was beaten with a board of some kind?

COOPER: That is true.

SAWYER: That's true?

COOPER: Mm-hmm.

SAWYER: What sort of board? How badly beaten?

COOPER: Well, I was at a girlfriend's house and Anna was trying to make cookies, and the other lady's kids ate all the cookies. Well, Anna just flipped out. You know, I mean, she went into a rage. I looked at the lady and I said, "Do you have a belt?"

And she says, "No, use a board. It doesn't leave any marks." I'd never used a board on Anna before, ever. No. Have you ever been hit with a board?

SAWYER: No.

COOPER: It stings.

SAWYER: But you hit her with a board?

COOPER: Yes.

SAWYER: Bruised her?

COOPER: I bruised her leg.

SAWYER: Let me ask you about some of the other things the children have said happened during that time. They say there'd be no food in the house.

COOPER: I don't know about that. I don't remember.

SAWYER: That the clothes were dirty, that the house was dirty.

COOPER: I was washing clothes in the bathtub; the house was dirty. That's true.

SAWYER: Cockroaches and—

COOPER: Yes, we had a lot of cockroaches.

SAWYER: And dogs had gone to the bathroom on the floor.

COOPER: They would do that. That's true.

SAWYER: Anna says, too, that your boyfriend, at least once, threatened her.

COOPER: I wouldn't doubt that.

SAWYER: And beat her.

COOPER: I've never—I didn't know him to beat her. He beat Samantha.

SAWYER: He beat Samantha?

COOPER: Yes, he did.

SAWYER: If you were a child, would you want to go back to it again? Would you want to risk going back to it again?

COOPER: No.

SAWYER: So you understand how they feel?

COOPER: Yes.

SAWYER: Should they be forced to go back to it when they don't know what's ahead? Should they be forced?

COOPER: Forced? Should they give—should they be given an opportunity, as it was planned in the beginning, to let me change? And should I be given a chance?

SAWYER [*interviewing*]: Did you see the scene on television when they left the Micks?

COOPER: Yes, I did.

SAWYER: What did you think?

COOPER: It killed me. It hurt.

SAWYER: What hurt?

COOPER: I guess what hurts the most is that they're not mine anymore.

SAWYER: But someone might say, "If you really loved the children, wouldn't you want to see them happy?" And if they are happy with the Micks, wouldn't that be the greater love?

COOPER: Well, I don't know if they weren't happy with me when I was sick and they lived in a house full of cockroaches. They were happy then, too.

USHER

Natalie celebrated her tenth birthday with twelve of her closest friends at Skate King, where the lights are low, the mirror ball glitters, the music crescendos every thirty seconds, and the bathrooms are labeled KINGS and QUEENS. The girls, wearing rollerblades, seemed preternaturally tall, as if they were wearing high heels. Several of Natalie's friends bought split-heart necklaces: One girl wore one half while her best friend wore the other. There was quite a competition for certain girls. Natalie's best friend, Amanda, asked the DJ to play a Michelle Branch song, and when it came on, Amanda beamed.

Seeing the lights go off, all the younger girls rushed onto the rink. They liked the dark setting, which made them feel less noticeable, and yet Natalie and several of her friends were wearing orange glow sticks. So they didn't want their bodies to be noticed, but they did want their bodies to be noticed. This, I want to say, was the crux of the matter.

The girls skated backward. Then they skated in the regular direction. After a while they did the limbo. The DJ played the standards: "I Will Survive," "Gloria," "YMCA," "Stayin' Alive," Madonna, 'NSync,

Backstreet Boys, Usher. Some of Natalie's friends bought plastic roses for themselves. Two teenage kids were feverishly making out in a far corner. Duly noted by the management—quickly remedied.

As the father of a daughter who was a Skate King devotee, I found the place utterly terrifying. It was about amplifying kids' sense of themselves as magical creatures and converting that feeling into sexual yearning—a group march toward future prospects. For Natalie and her friends, still, just barely, the purpose of Skate King was to dream about the opposite sex without having to take these romantic feelings seriously, let alone act on them. In the dark, Natalie held Amanda's hand and lip-synched to Aaron Carter.

The last song of the afternoon was "The Hokey Pokey," which, the DJ explained to me, "adults don't care for." Of course adults don't care for it; you wind up having to put your whole body in. What—Natalie and her friends were wondering—could that possibly consist of?

GOOKUS EXPLAINS THE ETERNAL MYSTERIES

Although he was fat and ugly and the same age as I was (eleven), the Gookus knew more about it than I did, much more, so I sat on my bed with my back to the wooden wall and my feet dangling over the side of the bed, and listened as Gary—my great Gookus with his Buddha stomach—told me absolutely everything he knew about the subject, waddling around the room, sucking on cigarettes, stuffing dirty clothes into the crack of the door, turning on the overhead light when it got dark in my basement bedroom, the heater when it got cold, the radio when he grew weary of hearing his own high voice. For hours in an empty parking lot, which had just been black-topped and painted and was still wet, he'd kissed Yvonne Rasnick until she cried and shuddered and Gookus didn't know what to do, so he stopped. He'd felt up Teri Schraeder, who, whatever else one might want to say about her, was not flat. He'd already started masturbating; on bad nights he rubbed his skin raw until he bled, but on good nights he was pretty sure he came. He opened his wallet and showed me his rubber. He tried to explain to me too much terminology. He'd found stacks of *Playboy*s in the cabinets of his father's study, and when his father was away, Gookus would go in and not leave until he'd been transfixed by a picture to urge him through the night. He'd seen his mother, walking from the shower to the bedroom, naked.

"What did she look like?" I asked.

"She looked like my mother."

"But naked, I mean."

"Good. Real good."

"Like the women in the magazines?"

"No. Wetter. Older. Fatter. Hairier. But still good, Dave."

"How do you kiss?"

"I used to kiss my mother quickly on the cheek before I went to bed."

"And now?"

"I don't."

"But I mean real kissing. How do you kiss girls?"

"On the lips."

"What do you do?"

"You tilt your head."

"To which side?"

"The left," Gookus explained. "You tilt your head, you close your eyes, then you put your lips on her lips. You open your mouth and make long, wet kisses. You close your mouth and make short, dry, little ones. You put your tongue in her mouth."

"Your tongue? Doesn't she choke?"

"No. She moans."

"Where do your hands go, Gookus, and your legs and the rest of your body? What do you do with yourself?"

"You put your hands in her hair and your legs go behind you."

"I can't imagine it. I can't see it."

"I'll show you."

"What do I do with my nose, Gookus? Won't it bop her in the face?"

"Let me show you."

"What do I do with my stomach—suck it in so she doesn't feel it or puff it out so it rubs against her? I need to know these things. I'm afraid I'll forget."

"Let me show you."

"No."

"Yes."

"Leave me alone," I said.

Gookus put down his cigarette, turned up the volume a little on the radio for background music, and sat down next to me on the bed. Before I knew what was happening, he'd pushed me down and was rolling on top of me, sliding up and down my legs, and laughing. He pressed his thick, rough lips to mine, kissed me on the cheeks, the pimpled nose, the chin. Gookus blew hot air and whispered obscene nothings into my ear. I learned fast: We French-kissed. The first kiss of my life didn't last for long, because when he started fooling around with my zipper, I sat up and tried to hit him in the face, but he caught my fist, twisted my right arm, and shoved me off the bed onto the floor. He pounced on me. All ninety-five pounds of him landed with full force and then he sat on me, bouncing up and down on my chest while he pinned my arms and legs.

"Give," he said.

He pinched my skin.

"Give," he said again.

He twisted my wrist.

"Give," he said one more time.

He kneed me in the groin.

I gave.

Gookus got off and let me up, and I hurried away from him into the bathroom. I looked at my flushed face in the mirror, then dunked my head in a basin full of cold water and dried myself with a towel. Gookus barged into the bathroom to take a piss, flushing before he was through, wiping his hands on his pants—what a Neanderthal. Out of nowhere and down the windowpane crawled a black spider. It wasn't a symbol of this or that; it was just a spider. Gookus tried to smash the poor little thing with my favorite bathroom book, Maury Wills's (ghostwritten) autobiography, but he missed and the spider continued to crawl toward the floor. Before he was able to try again, I grabbed his arm and said, "Don't. Don't, Gookus. Don't kill it. Leave it alone."

"Why?"

"Just leave it alone. It's not hurting anything."

Gookus picked up Maury Wills's autobiography again.

I cupped the spider in my hands and tossed it out the window.

"Why did you do that, Dave? I wanted to kill it."

"Well, I didn't want you to."

"Why not?"

"I don't like killing things. Spiders, bugs, ants, anything. I can't help it."

"You're afraid."

"No I'm not."

"Yes you are."

"No I'm not."

"You are."

"What if I am?"

"You don't want to become a fairy. Girls don't kiss fairies. Fairies kiss other fairies."

I closed the window, turned out the bathroom light, then Gookus and I collapsed, me onto my own bed and Gookus onto the sleeping bag stretched out on the floor. We had trouble falling asleep; through the open air vent we heard raspy breathing coming from my parents' bedroom directly above mine.

"Know what that is?" Gookus asked.

"What what is?"

"That sound."

"Sure."

"What is it?"

"My mother snoring."

Gookus made the sound of a buzzer on a game show indicating the wrong answer.

"Then what is it?"

"Your father doing your mother."

"My father doing what to my mother?" I inquired, mildly alarmed.

"It—screwing."

"No way."

"Uh-huh. You can tell 'cause you can hear the bed squeak."

For a minute or two we stayed extraordinarily quiet but couldn't hear the bed squeak.

"Still, that's what it is," Gookus said.

"I don't believe you."

"Wanna go watch? I'll prove it to you. Or are you too much of a fairy?"

In our pajamas, in the dark, we crept upstairs, took turns looking through the keyhole of my parents' bedroom, and by the night-light watched my mother sleeping on the other side of the bed from my father. She lay on her back with her arms folded across her chest and one foot sticking out of the covers, heaving her entire body with every breath.

"They must have heard us coming and broke it off," Gookus said as he crawled back into the sleeping bag. "Wanna go back and check again? I swear I heard 'em doing it."

"You go if you want."

Gookus, disgusted, gave up and punched the pillow. I remember what exquisite torture it was to know that this dangerous territory, which Gookus already seemed to have thoroughly staked out, was, so far as I was concerned, not yet even on the horizon.

"Well, if they weren't doing it," Gookus wanted to know, "why was she breathing like that?"

"She has cancer."

"Get outta here."

"She's had it for years."

"Get outta here."

If Gookus had sex, I had death; I'd capped him. (Pure invention on my part, but several years later my falsehood turned true.) "She'll probably have it a while longer," I said.

"And then?"

"She'll either get better or she won't."

"Jesus, Dave. I'm sorry. Really I am. I didn't know."

"Yeah."

"Nice face, though. She's got a really nice face."

DESIRE

Toward the end of elementary school, my sister and I would think and talk about *Batman* or *Get Smart* or *The Addams Family*—whatever the show was that year—and on the night of the show we'd make sugar cookies and root-beer floats, then set up TV trays; immediately after the show, we'd talk about how much we hated that it was over and what agony it was going to be to wait an entire week for it to be on again, whereas the show itself was usually only so-so, hard to remember, over before you knew it.

Senior year of high school my best friend and I—both virgins—had to spend at least one night a week hanging around the San Francisco Airport. Why? The dirty magazines they let us flip through at the newsstand and the sexy stewardesses tugging their luggage like dogs on a leash, but more than that it was everybody marching with such military urgency to their destinations, as if everywhere—everywhere in the world: Winnipeg, Oslo, Milwaukee—were to be desired.

In my early thirties, I admired the Boy Scout belt a friend of mine was wearing—I liked the way it was a joke about uniformity at the same time it simply looked good—and when I asked where he got it, he said, to my astonishment, that it was his original Boy Scout belt: he still had it; he could still wear it; he was very skinny, stylish, good-looking. I never made it past the Cub Scouts and even in the Cubs failed to distinguish myself. Slipknots and shiny shoes have never been very high priorities for me. I wanted a Boy Scout belt, though, and thought it would be easy. I stopped in at a Boy Scout office, where I was told that BSA clothing and accessories could be purchased only by scouts or troop leaders. I went so far as to schedule an interview for a troop-leader position until, fearing accusations of pedophilia, I ended the charade. Visits to several stores led me to the boys' department of J. C. Penney, which carried Boy Scout uniforms in their catalogue and told me I could order a belt. They called me when it came in. I wore it once, maybe twice, with jeans, then tossed it into the back of the closet.

Fifty years ago my parents hired a guy named Gil to paint the inside of the house. After he left, my mother discovered the word FUCK etched into the new white paint in the dining room. I'd never seen her so infuriated. Had my parents underpaid or somehow mistreated him, and had this been his underhanded revenge? He adamantly denied it, offering to return to rectify the problem. Had my sister or I done it? We insisted we hadn't, and I'm confident we were telling the truth (in any case, I was; I can't speak for my usually well-behaved sister). Although over time the inscription lost its hold on my mother's imagination, FUCK remained—if faintly—and continued to cast a subtle, mysterious spell over the dining room for the remainder of my childhood.

Is desire, then, a sort of shadow around everything?

REFLECTION IN A ONE-WAY MIRROR

My mother was born in Steubenville, Ohio, which was once mentioned in an episode of *Gr. Smart*. Whenever The Wise Chief and The Dumb Detective had something secret to discuss, they'd enter The Cone of Silence. They'd never be able to understand each other before the "cone" would rise. Steubenville sits on the shore of the Ohio River, and I suppose adorable little Hannah swung over the rim of the river on a rope swing and ran barefoot in the woods in summer and skipped stones across the creek at night, but it would be preposterous to assert that she was ever anything resembling a river rat. I see her instead writing only one word—"Uneventful"—in her diary at the end of each day and reading mysteries under the covers with a flashlight until morning. I see her doing these things because she was never the storyteller my father was; she never liked to talk about her distant past.

Girlhood strikes me as one of life's more unfathomable mysteries, and I haven't the faintest idea what my mother did when her family moved to Los Angeles in 1938. She wasn't sitting in a malt shop wearing a tight pink sweater, waiting to make it big with Paramount, because she always had tiny breasts like wings. And she wasn't falling in love with the star wide receiver because, until her too-late twenties, until she met and married my father, she had a terrible time with pimples. I suppose she was busy hating her father, whom she thought she loved, and envying her brother, whom she thought she admired.

Uncle Justin wound up becoming science attaché to the American ambassador to Japan, but when he was just a kid in LA he was content to wander around the junk shop, fixing whatever his father thought was irreparable. Justin transformed a dark corner of the garage into a lab, where he had an impressively low number of nuclear near-explosions, and every math class he took at Dorsey High he ended up teaching. He received a full fellowship, in physics, to Caltech.

My mom didn't go to Caltech. She went to UCLA. At the time, any girl, if she was able to secure a parking space, could attend UCLA. And my mother wasn't plagued even by this problem, since she was living at home and hitchhiking to school, something that very few other UCLA "coeds" were doing. Something that even fewer of them were doing but that Hannah was doing, with deep, unapproved pleasure, was smoking two packs of Kents a day through a filter, if indeed Kents were in circulation in 1942 and, if not, two packs a day of another equally strong brand through a filter. Something that absolutely no one else in all of Westwood except Hannah was doing was serving as the editor-in-chief of the *Daily Bruin*. She did very little all day other than call up the police station and correct proof sheets, then hitchhike home in the dark.

Although newspapers are meant to be read very quickly and then thrown out, or used to start fires or line trash bins or wrap fish for the freezer, my mother had the *Daily Bruin* from her tenure as editor, 1942 to 1945, bound in green leather. I don't know where those volumes are now—Paula is so very much the archivist she probably has them locked away in a trunk slid beneath her four-poster bed—but when I was a child I used to read back issues of the *Bruin* all the time. I have no idea what I was looking for, since it wasn't like a yearbook in which there would have been black-and-white photographs of my mother at her more immature. It seemed to me like any other newspaper, only a little yellow around the edges, a little more obviously beside the point. Apparently, it was one of the very best college dailies in the country and, in any case, beyond comparison with the cross-town competition, which printed lead editorials in praise of the USC football team.

When FDR died, my mother put on the front page a picture of him puffing a cigarette through a nicotine filter. This wasn't an appropriately glum photo for the president's funeral, and she caught so much flak from the chancellor that she threatened to resign until the entire editorial staff delivered an eloquent letter of support. Frank Mankiewicz (who later became Bobby Kennedy's press secretary, regional director of the Peace Corps, and then the head of NPR, but who at the time was nothing more than sports editor of the *Daily Bruin*) would conspire with the rest of the boys in Sports to write an article that, if you read it linearly, made almost no sense at all but that, if you read it backward and skipped every other line, produced a rather risqué narrative. Every Thursday evening they'd try to sneak these naughty tales past my mom into the Friday edition. I think it would be unfair to say she ever had a particularly dirty mind. She was an amazingly precise proofreader, though, and she never let Frank and the boys' lewd little stories get by her. I feel for Frank and the boys. Growing up, I used to feel *like* Frank and the boys, speaking backward to rebel against her but never making it into her Friday edition, her heart of hearts. She was always the editor, I was always her little cub reporter turning in rough drafts, and she was always sending me back for one more rewrite.

In my senior year of high school, I was the editor of the school newspaper, which the principal thought was being secretly dictated to me by my mother, who in her twenties and thirties had become the West Coast correspondent for the *Nation* magazine. Every other week I wrote what was called "A Satire" but was really an all-out assault upon myself, a sort of suicide note in the guise of covering student government. One night, while I was staying late to work on what I thought was a particularly wicked essay, my mother knocked on the door of the newspaper office, ostensibly to bring dinner but actually to determine whether I was doing justice to the name that meant so much in mass media. Seventeen years old, I hated everything but the sound of the door being closed from the inside, and there she was—on the other side of that door, peering through the glass window, tapping with her key ring, wanting in.

She was wearing her black leather boots (what Paula called "boots not made for walkin' "), her Pacific Ocean–blue business dress, and a weird string of wooden beads. Perfume was apparent, as were lipstick, eye shadow, and rouge. In one hand she held her reporter's notebook in which her mercurial shorthand recorded every word uttered at a press conference whose highlight was Mayor Alioto's denial that he'd ever met his brother-in-law, and in the other she had a sack of food she'd bought for me at A&W on her way home after my father told her I was still at school. While I inhaled the hamburger and French fries, she walked around the office, studying the assignment sheet on the bulletin board, trying out the typewriter (which was missing plastic caps to vowel keys and had a jammed margin release), and flipping through the photo file—dead-black negatives of all twenty-seven candidates for student body president.

In the way that anyone human would have asked how you are doing, she asked, "What are you working on?"

"My column," I said. She wasn't the most loyal fan of my column, but she did think every fifth or sixth effort scored some marvelous sociological points.

"How's it coming along?" she asked, still flipping through the photo file.

"Fine. I just finished."

"Are you happy with it?" For her, this wasn't a question so much as a direct challenge, since she was never happy, at least publicly, with her own work and assumed no one else would cop to pride in his own expressions, either.

"Very happy," I said. I couldn't help it. I liked the column a lot.

"It can't stand any improvement?" she asked, tilting her head to the left. She leaned against my desk, watching me sweep crumbs onto the floor with a ruler.

"No, Mom."

"That's great. It must be very good. I'm eager to read it." *And woe to you if I am at all disappointed.*

I didn't want to let her see it now because I remembered how thoroughly she took the fun out of the city championship by calling my article a "tissue of sportswriting platitudes." The fluorescent lights flickered like melodramatic special effects for a storm scene.

"I won't criticize it, I promise. I'm just curious to see what you've been working on. I wrote three thousand words today on Joseph Alioto's ancestry. You can look at that and laugh. Let me just look at your lead," she said, descending to her most transparent strategy.

This could have gone on forever. Her sincerity was starting to get on my nerves, so I opened my desk drawer, took out my satire, and handed it to her. I figured the least I could do was let her look at my lead, if that was what she really wanted to do, although of course she read the lead, then the paragraph after the lead, then the paragraph after the paragraph after the lead, all the way to the column's sad conclusion. I walked around the office, pretending to clean up, putting away scissors that didn't cut and staplers that didn't have staples, while she brandished her Blackwing pencil—she actually carried a Blackwing pencil with her at all times—and interrupted her reading of the article only twice: at the end of the third paragraph to ask if I wanted a ride home, and at the end of the sixth paragraph to ask for an ashtray. She commenced her attack upon my little column immediately after she finished reading it.

REFLECTION IN A ONE-WAY MIRROR:
A SATIRE
By Dave Shields

I'd like to applaud, with unabashed pleasure and amidst great revelry and excitement, the replacement of windows with mirrors in the principals' offices. Silver, one-way mirrors.

I've been told the windows were replaced because in the sun they caused glare. The reflection of the sun off the windows was disturbing, was discomfiting to passersby, and comfort should be our first consideration.

There were, though, other disadvantages to the windows.

They were, first of all, windows, clear glass panes: people could see in and out. We could stare at one another.

If safety should be our first consideration, then privacy should be our second consideration.

Also, the windows revealed ugliness. I often found evidence of fingerprints and dust and dirt and rain and mud on the glass. If safety should be our first consideration; and privacy, our second; then cleanliness should be our third consideration.

The silver, one-way mirrors, on the other hand, appear spotless and reveal no smudges. They are easier to clean, too.

As to privacy, there's now a sense of security, even peace, for students needn't know whether there's anything recognizably human behind the mirror. All we can see is our own reflection in black shadows of silver. This is how it should be.

It's not clear to me how the principals are to see out without being seen, for I'm not a scientist, but rest assured they can see out.

Lastly, as to comfort, the silver mirrors dull the sun's glare: What's seen isn't the reflection of the sun but the glossy image of ourselves. I'm pleased that I no longer have to avert my eyes as I walk by the windows.

I cheer for the new mirrors.

I guess now I can admit that the irony is heavy-handed, the last few paragraphs are dominated by overwrought figures, the prose is repetitious in a coy, anachronistic sort of way, the basic idea is needlessly Manichaean, but at the time I thought it was killingly good, and when my mother lit into it I wanted to scream. She said one of these days I really must begin to take into account the objective world of reality. She said I'd better learn how to write a "straight news story" that "tumbled down cleanly," if I ever wanted to amount to anything as a journalist. She said there was editorializing and there was editorializing, but this was psychosis. She said there might be a "decent four-inch filler of a factual story" buried somewhere in the "piece" and, if I wanted, she'd stay late "digging it out." I imagined a night of the two of us sitting next to each other at a wobbly desk and giving the thing a much closer reading than it deserved. I asked her to stop smoking and told her I didn't need a ride home; I'd walk. She said if I couldn't take constructive criticism I was a baby. With that, somehow, I fell apart. I ran around in a crazy circle, yelling, "Get out, please get out," and tearing up the satire, only to spend the rest of the night on the floor piecing it, then taping it, together, although the next morning I decided not to print it, anyway. Not enough space.

That was the way my mother ran a newspaper. That was the kind of chaos she could create so quickly. It's a wonder to me that Frank and the boys didn't lock her up in the ladies' lav until she promised to be less imperial, but she served her reign without a whisper of insurrection. On the Monday after commencement, which her father didn't deem a signal enough event to attend, she started working as the editor of the "house organ" for the ACLU, which have always been interesting initials to me in that *ACLU* is an anagram of *UCLA*, as if wherever she went my mother, in contradistinction to her disfluent son, changed the language to suit her own needs.

Satire is what closes Saturday night.

—GEORGE S. KAUFMAN

SATIRE

Renée, who was one of the paper's assistant editors, wanted to become the editor next year. As the outgoing editor, I recommended—actually, chose—my successor. Renée was aware of this.

The office itself was an odd mix of desolation and faux fashion. Renée thought I designed it that way, but in truth I never gave a second thought to the room's color scheme and furniture. A green chalkboard, with cracks down the middle, was nailed to the wall. A cork bulletin board framed the assignment sheet. I scribbled the story assignments in pencil, which smeared, so no one could read my writing. In one corner of the room, near the door, was an enormous black leather chair in which Renée always sat (with her platform shoes kicked under the chair, sweater draped across the headrest, bare feet tucked into the crevices). I don't remember her ever sitting in any other chair.

Late one night, in May—after the parking lots and swimming pools and playing fields were emptied—Renée and I were counting the newspapers to be distributed in the morning. We divided the fifteen hundred newspapers into sixty rolls, each of which we wrapped with a rubber band. She was moving her lips as she counted the papers. Helpfully, I pointed this out to her.

"You made me lose track," she said.

The late sun cast light into the room through the windows. Her face was faintly shadowed on the wall. The heater sputtered. The lights flickered, then died; I hit the wall and they came back on.

"It makes you look like a slow reader," I said.

"What?"

"Moving your lips makes you look like a slow reader."

"I'm not reading; I'm counting."

"I know, but if you want to be editor next year . . ." Power corrupts; absolute power etc.

I counted sloppily and probably inaccurately while Renée continued to whisper numbers to herself, intermittently licking the forefinger of her right hand. I suddenly began counting aloud in Latin, with great seriousness, as if I were chanting Mass.

"Stop it," she said. "Please."

"It shouldn't bother you. If you want to be editor next year, you can't let little things bother you."

"Enough about—"

"Anyway, I thought you were taking Latin."

"But I can't think in Latin or try to count in English while you're counting in Latin. I mean, I'm only in second year."

"Do you prefer Horace or Juvenal?" I asked.

"What do you mean?"

"Haven't you been reading any Horace or Juvenal?"

She played with a rubber band, stretching it until it snapped. "Just sentences here and there," she said.

"Well, whom do you prefer?" Latin taught me proper grammar, which I loved to flaunt.

"I don't know. They're both all right. What's the difference?"

She made me feel much older than I actually was. Not even little children made me feel as lifeless as Renée did. Her loyalty was to questions, and mine, sadly, was to answers. But the difference between Horace and Juvenal meant, at that time, everything to me. I wanted desperately for her to see and feel, quite like nothing else, this difference. I had, in fact, waited all year to illustrate this very thing to her, and I got up from my chair and stood over her. She responded, quite naturally, by putting her feet out as a barrier.

"They were both satirists," I said, stepping back. "I was the only person in the class who liked Juvenal. I love Juvenal. Horace loved the people he wrote about, but Juvenal couldn't. The poor man hated everybody."

"You're terrible. Juvenal must have hated himself."

"Even greater consistency!"

"I pity you, I really do."

"Pity won't get you the editorship."

Renée's folders and books were on the table. The Latin book I had studied two years earlier was on top. The cover showed a Roman soldier's profile against a green background. The lettering was orange. Toward the bottom of the front cover was written *Laudatus sum:* "I have been praised." I did not want to be praised. I did not want to praise anyone else. I was not worth praising. Neither was anyone else. I did not want to write constructive editorials.

Renée had attached paper clips to many pages and highlighted important rules in pink. The margins of the pages were filled with questions and reminders and doodles she'd written to herself. Her handwriting was sweeping, immaculate, breathless.

"How far are you?" I asked, turning the pages of her book, trying to find a certain sentence of Juvenal's.

"I've counted out all but the senior homerooms."

"I mean, how far are you in Latin?"

"Third-conjugation verbs."

"This verb's third conjugation," I said, handing the book to her and pointing to the Juvenal quotation.

Renée put the book down on the chair and mouthed the words to herself. She read it aloud, slowly, awkwardly, pronouncing the words as if they were Spanish. "'*Difficile est saturam non scribere.*' That's easy," she said. "'It is not difficult to write satire.'"

"Close."

"'Difficult satire is not to be written.'"

I shook my head.

She curled her hair behind her ears. "'Satire is not written difficultly.'"

I shook my head again.

"'It is satire which is difficult to write for nobody.'" It was such a short sentence, but she still didn't seem to get Juvenal's sentiment. I laughed a little—what an asshole.

"What, then?"

" 'It's difficult *not* to write satire.' "

"What?"

"Don't you see? Juvenal found it difficult to do anything but write satire. Horace probably could have written anything but only decided now and then to write satire. Juvenal had to. He had no choice."

"Well, what's so great about doing what comes naturally?"

"Juvenal didn't rein in any of his hate. He despised the fools around him. He refused to love them. He simply couldn't. I love him."

A drop of sweat from Renée's forehead spilled onto her lips. She rubbed her hand on her face, streaking newsprint across her cheek, then straddled the chair and stood up, tipping over the small stack of newspapers that remained. On her tiptoes, in her bare feet, she pulled down the camera case from the cabinet. The lights went out and she banged the wall to get them to stay on. She took the lens cap off and fidgeted with the dials. I disliked quite a lot being photographed; Renée knew this, knew I couldn't stand the pseudo-truth of a "candid" portrait. She attached the flash, pressed her nose to the back of the camera, and pointed it at me, then pressed the button.

I still have the photograph, and what's striking to me now about it is its amazing generosity. I was awful to Renée, but the picture—a sort of out-of-focus X-ray of my eyes—shows how badly I wanted to learn how to love her. It shows this while refusing to judge it. Although of course I couldn't hear it in time to do anything about it because I wasn't listening, I had been praised.

ODE TO THE DONNER PARTY

With my sister and me away at college, my mother and father took long hikes in the woods together and went to chamber music concerts and treated each other to dinner when either of them could afford it. They still fought, of course—one night she kicked him out of the house and didn't let him back in until the weekend was over—and she was still getting used to buying two little bags of groceries rather than four full ones, but that would change. He'd fall asleep early, snoring in the living room with a magazine folded across his chest, and awake at sunrise to run around the block a few times before he went to work. She'd stay up late, watching PBS and writing letters—to me, to my sister, to historians at Stanford, Berkeley, and UCLA who corrected errors in the articles she now wrote for the state historical society's monthly magazine. My parents would see each other at dinner, though, and often had long and heated conversations about philosophy or politics or money, which usually ended in both of them leaving the house and stomping around the front lawn until it got dark.

She saw no point in going to all the bother of making a lavish dinner for just the two of them, so she'd bake a few blintzes or scramble some eggs or warm up leftovers and he would say, "This is dinner?" He'd throw down his napkin and, according to my mother, drive to the most expensive restaurant in town, where, while correcting page proofs for the suburban weekly he edited, he'd wolf down the specialties of the house and charge it to his business account. Or, if he stayed and they didn't argue, they'd stare at their plates and nibble their food. Hardly a word would pass between them: only the sounds of chewing and swallowing, the dog padding through the house, coughs filling the silence, the cold clank of utensils doing their routine work. After dinner they'd fight like siblings about who would clean the table and who would scrape the dishes. Who would rinse? Who would stack? Who would take out the garbage? Who would wipe the table? Who indeed? And every night this absurdity was enacted.

Weekends they'd rake, water, and mow the lawn and trim the hedges, but he'd always leave the water running and flood the lawn, or he'd cut the grass so unevenly that it looked like an aerial shot of the midwestern states. My mother would march onto the front lawn and say, "See, Milt, this is how you rake. It's very simple. You rake the leaves off the lawn into a pile in the gutter, then you put them in a barrel. Any idiot can do it." Or she'd drag the hose from the backyard, attach it to a spigot underneath the front porch, and placing her thumb over the nozzle, spray the water low and full through the top of the grass so the lawn looked cool and fresh. "See, honey," she would say, "is this so hard? Why is this so difficult for you?" He never had any answers, so they'd swear at each other or shake their heads or shake each other. Sometimes, my father said, they'd fall to their knees together and pound the earth, tearing out grass.

All day Saturday, she'd clean the house and he'd track mud across a carpet she'd just vacuumed. She'd scatter newspapers—often copies of *his* newspaper—across the waxed linoleum, and he'd be very careful to walk in the spaces in between the pages. Never would he think to come in the back door or notice that the kitchen floor had been mopped and was wet. Sometimes she'd get so mad she'd throw the mop at him. Sometimes she simply screamed.

Saturday nights they'd disagree about which movie to see and then disagree about the movie. He'd get lost driving there, then park on the wrong side of the street. After going to the bathroom, he'd lose his ticket stub and forget to zip up his zipper. He'd walk up and back in the aisle because he wouldn't be able to find the row and she'd have to whisper, "Over here, Milt." He'd squirm in his seat, ask her questions about the plot, play with his false teeth, hold his head when he got tired. "Milt," she'd say, "do you have to do that? Would your head really fall off if you didn't hold it?" If he liked the movie, she'd find it manipulative and sentimental; if he disliked it, she'd think it was original and provocative.

Or if they didn't go to a movie, they'd go to a party, where my father would back into a corner whomever he could and talk about the Rosenbergs or Alger Hiss or Sacco and Vanzetti or Alfred Dreyfus or the Hollywood Ten. If he got drunk enough, he'd tell stories in Yiddish, but no one would listen because this was my mother's crowd. These weren't recent Eastern European immigrants; these were American Jews who had made it a long time ago—lawyers and journalists and professors and psychiatrists who didn't want to hear about the old country. My mother would laugh and gossip, and my father would wander away from the crowd and collapse on a bed in the guest room with Paul Goodman's *Growing Up Absurd* at his side. She'd wake him when the party was over, and driving home, she'd accuse him of being socially illiterate, which was an exaggeration with some basis in fact: he had a way of standing very close to you and talking very loud and poking his finger into your chest to make sure you got the point.

Sunday, though, provided a respite from all this ugliness. She'd make a big breakfast for him and he'd let her have the sections of the newspaper she most highly prized. Then they'd change into their tennis whites. She'd wear a big, floppy hat to protect her skin from the sun, and he'd wear a tight cap to cover his bald head and prevent the sun from blinding him when he hit overhead smashes. Hand in hand they'd walk to the park, where they'd reserved a court, and they'd rally back and forth to get warmed up. She could neither bend low nor move more than a few flat-footed steps in any direction, but put a ball waist high and in front of her and she could sock it, so he'd try to hit the ball directly at her, and if he hit it a few inches too high or half a step out of her way, she'd wave at it with her racket and glower at him. Usually they'd play mixed doubles against another couple, and he would want to win so badly he'd rush onto her side of the court to take shots away from her. Whenever this happened, she would take extraordinarily long water breaks.

My father would send me every issue of his weekly newspaper, which I was supposed to read thoroughly, mark up with my comments, and mail back to him. His paper consisted almost exclusively of advertising, and what few stories he wrote were usually features about local merchants who were not yet advertising. He wrote long windy sentences that recalled, he said, early Mencken. For instance: "With the city fathers giving their official blessings—and some 250 mothers and fathers seated in the bleachers, giving their partial blessings and vociferous cheers—the city soccer players launched their season on Saturday with a bang or, more accurately, a boot." He'd take photographs for the paper with his Polaroid camera, but he never learned how to roll on the gloss or when to peel off the backing, and the pictures always turned out fuzzy and faded, like very late Mencken.

My mother didn't send me the articles (which were always odes to the Watts Towers or John Steinbeck or the Donner Party) that she wrote for the historical society magazine. Instead, she'd type up passages from novels she was reading and mail them to me. The passages would always be extremely pejorative summaries of a male character who reminded her of my father; this paragraph from Wallace Stegner's *The Spectator Bird* is a perfect example: "Joe Allston has always been full of himself, uncertain, dismayed, dissatisfied with his life, his country, his civilization, his profession, and himself. He has always hunted himself in places where he has never been; he has always been trying to thread some needle with a string that was raveled at both ends. He has always been hungry for some continuity and assurance and sense of belonging, but has never had ancestors or descendants or place in the world. Little orphan Joe, what a sad case."

Paula, a sophomore at Berkeley, and I would write letters to each other in which we expressed our pity for people such as our parents who thrived on chewing up the furniture; our determination to avoid similarly disastrous entanglements in our own lives; and our certainty that our correspondence would someday be valuable because both of us were destined to become famous in the fields of politics and literature, respectively. What did we know? We were twenty and nineteen, respectively, and knew nothing yet of love.

REBECCA'S JOURNAL

From the sound of things, the girl who lived next door to me my sophomore year of college was having problems with her boyfriend. One night Rebecca invited me into her room to share a joint and told me she kept a journal, which one day she hoped to turn into a novel. I said, "Kafka believed that writing in a journal prevents reality from being turned into fiction," but as she pointed out, Kafka did nothing if not write in a journal. I liked the way she threw her head back when she laughed.

The next day I knocked on her door to ask her to join me for lunch. Her door was unlocked; she assumed no one would break into her room and, in any case, the door to the dormitory was always locked. Rebecca wasn't in and neither was her roommate, who had all but moved into her boyfriend's apartment off campus. Rebecca's classes weren't over until late afternoon, I remembered, and I walked in and looked at her clothes and books and notebooks. Sitting down at her desk, I opened the bottom-right drawer and came across a photo album, which I paged through only briefly, because underneath the album was a stack of Rebecca's journals. The one on top seemed pretty current and I started reading: the previous summer, she had missed Gordon terribly and let herself be used on lonely nights by a Chapel Hill boy whom she had always fantasized about and who stroked her hair in the moonlight and wiped himself off with leaves. When Rebecca returned to Providence in the fall, she knew she wanted romance, and after weeks of fights that went all night and into the morning, she told Gordon she didn't want to see him anymore.

Me, on the other hand, she wanted to see every waking moment of the day and night. As a stutterer, I was even more ferociously dedicated to literature (the glory of language that was beautiful and written) than other English majors at Brown were, and I could turn up the lit-crit rhetoric pretty damn high. She loved the way I talked (my stutter was endearing); her favorite thing in the world was to listen to me rhapsodize about John Donne. She often played scratchy records on her little turntable (this was 1975), and when I said, "The *Jupiter* Symphony might be the happiest moment in human history," her heart skipped a beat. Toward my body she was ambivalent: "Simultaneously attracted and repelled" by my strength, she was afraid I "might crush" her. These are, I swear, verbatim quotes.

I finished reading the journal and put it away, then went back to my room and waited for Rebecca to return from her classes. That night we drove out to Newport, where we walked barefoot in the clammy sand and looked up at the lighted mansions that lined the shore in the distance. "The rich, too, must go to sleep at night," I said, offering Solomonic wisdom. We stood atop a ragged rock that sat on the shoreline; the full tide splashed at our feet. The moon made halos of our heads. I put my hands through her hair and kissed her lightly on the lips. "Don't kiss hard," she said. "I'm afraid I'll fall."

Tuesday and Thursday afternoons—when she worked in the development office—I'd go into her room, shut the door, lock it, and sit back in the swivel chair at her desk. She always left a window open. The late fall wind would be blowing the curtains around, and the *Jupiter* Symphony would always be on the little red record player on the floor. She often left wet shirts hanging all over the room and they'd ripple in the wind eerily. On the floor were cracked pots of dead plants. On the wall were a few calligraphic renderings of her own poetry. Her desk was always a mess, but her journal—a thick black book—was never very difficult to find.

I was nineteen years old and a virgin, and at first I read Rebecca's journal because I needed to know what to do next and what she liked to hear. Every little gesture, every minor movement I made she passionately described and wholeheartedly admired. When we were kissing or swimming or walking down the street, I could hardly wait to rush back to her room to find out what phrase or what twist of my body had been lauded in her journal. I loved her impatient handwriting, her purple ink, the melodrama of the whole thing. It was such a surprising and addictive respite, seeing every aspect of my being celebrated by someone else rather than excoriated by myself. She wrote, "I've never truly loved anyone the way I love D. and it's never been so total and complete, yet so unpossessing and pure, and sometimes I want to drink him in like golden water." *You* try to concentrate on your Milton midterm after reading that about yourself.

Sometimes, wearing her bathrobe, she'd knock on my door in order to return a book or get my reaction to a paragraph she'd written or read. She'd say, "Good night," turn away from me, and begin walking back to her room. I'd call to her, and we'd embrace—first in the hallway outside our doors, then soon enough in my room, her room, on our beds. I hadn't kissed a girl since I was twelve (horrific acne throughout high school), so I tried to make up for lost time by swallowing Rebecca alive: biting her lips until they bled, licking her face, chewing on her ears, holding her up in the air, and squeezing her until she screamed.

In her journal, she wrote that she'd never been kissed like this in her life and that she inevitably had trouble going to sleep after seeing me. I'd yank the belt to her bathrobe and urge her under the covers, but she refused. She actually said she was afraid she'd go blind when I entered her. Where did she learn these lines, anyway?

Shortly before the weather turned permanently cold, we went hiking in the mountains. The first night, she put her backpack at the foot of her sleeping bag—we kissed softly for a few minutes, then she fell asleep—but on the second night she put her backpack under her head as a pillow. Staring into the blankly black sky, I dug my fingers into the dirt behind Rebecca's head and, the first time and the second time and the third time and the fourth time and probably the fourteenth time, came nearly immediately.

From then on, I couldn't bring myself to read what she'd written.

I'd read the results of a survey in which forty percent of Italian women acknowledged that they usually faked orgasms. Rebecca wasn't Italian—she was that interesting anomaly, a southern Jew—but she thrashed around a lot and moaned and screamed and if she was pretending I didn't want to know about it. She often said it had never been like this before.

Every night she'd wrap her legs around me and scream something that I thought was German until I realized she was saying, "Oh, my son." *My son?* She had her own issues, too, I suppose. We turned up the *Jupiter* Symphony all the way and attempted to pace ourselves so we'd correspond to the crashing crescendo. I was sitting on top of her and in her mouth, staring at her blue wall, and I thought, *My whole body is turning electric blue.* She was on top of me, rotating her hips and crying, and she said, "Stop." I said, "Stop?" and stopped. She grabbed the back of my hair and said, "Stop? Are you kidding? Don't stop."

By the end of the semester, packing to fly home to San Francisco to spend the Christmas vacation with my family, I suddenly started to feel guilty about having read Rebecca's journal. Every time I kissed her, I closed my eyes and saw myself sitting at her desk, turning pages. I regretted having done it and yet I couldn't tell her about it.

"What's wrong?" she asked.

"I'll miss you," I said. "I don't want to leave."

On the plane I wrote her a long letter in which I told her everything I couldn't bring myself to tell her in person: I had read her journal, I was very sorry, I thought our love was still pure and we could still be together, but I'd understand if she went back to Gordon and never spoke to me again.

She wrote back that I should never have depended on her journal to give me strength, she would throw it away and never write in it again, and she wanted to absolve me; she wasn't God, although she loved me better than God could. Anything I said she would believe because she knew that I would never lie to her again. She loved me, she said; she'd known and loved me all her life, but she had just now found me. Our love, in her view, transcended time and place.

Well, sad to say, it didn't. The night I returned from San Francisco, she left a note on my door that said only "Come to me," and we tried to imitate the wild abandon of the fall semester, but what a couple of weeks before was utterly instinctive was now excruciatingly self-conscious, and the relationship quickly cooled. She even went back to Gordon for a while, though that second act didn't last very long, either.

It was, I see now, exceedingly odd behavior on my part. After ruining things for myself by reading her journal, I made sure I ruined things for both of us by telling her that I had read her journal. Why couldn't I just live with the knowledge and let the shame dissipate over time? What was—what is—the matter with me? Do I just have a bigger self-destruct button, and like to push it harder and more incessantly, than everyone else? Perhaps, but also the language of the events was at least as erotic to me as the events themselves, and when I was no longer reading her words, I was no longer very adamantly in love with Rebecca. This is what is known as a tragic flaw.

THE SHEER JOY OF AMORAL CREATION

I've tried very hard to imagine what that night was like for my mother and father, since the evidence is so strong it had been a night tinged with not a little romance, and yet I experience considerable difficulty when I try to visualize the embrace that brought about my birth. I never saw them so much as kiss except at a California Democratic Council New Year's Eve fund-raiser, 1966, when my father drank so many vodka and sodas without the soda that at midnight he threw confetti at the clock and said, "Pull me in, sweet," locking his lips with hers and rubbing the back of her head until 1967 held very definite promise of things to come. My childhood bedroom had been directly below theirs, but even when—post-Gookus—I stood on top of my desk and listened to the open air vent for the creak of the bed, I rarely heard anything much more than the sound of one or both of them sighing. *They never hold hands,* I remember thinking, *they never touch.*

Three weeks before she died—in 1977, of breast cancer that spread quickly via her lymph nodes to her spine, lungs, skull, and adrenal glands—my mother slipped off the commode and her gown caught on the aluminum side bar, which left me looking at her naked from the navel down: skinny white legs stretched into a V and vibrating until I lifted her up off the floor. One winter many years earlier, she swam with me every week at an indoor pool as I rehabbed a broken leg, and every week an old lady wearing blue goggles and fins asked if we were brother and sister. Another winter my mom got tired of walking around city hall with wet feet and bought a pair of black leather boots with two-inch heels; so many of her fellow reporters asked what she was doing tonight that she threw the boots in the closet and never wore them again. I showed a color photograph of her to my junior-year girlfriend, Rachel, who said, "I didn't think she'd be so good-looking." Although I didn't think of my mother as particularly good-looking, I wondered why Rachel didn't think she would be. In the photograph, taken at a party in the hospital, my mother looked much more beautiful than she ever had before: thin, delicate, admirably self-contained.

On the anniversary of her death, my father visited me in Providence. While Rachel slept wrapped in wool pajamas and kneesocks next to an electric heater burning orange coils on the floor near the head of the bed, I walked around in the snow with my dad, who said, "I've been more active this year with Evelyn than I'd been the previous twenty-five with your mother." I slipped on ice; he threw a snowball at a tree (missing) and said (quoting someone or other, for he was always quoting someone or other), " 'I like the horse I ride; I like my freedom.' " I like/liked neither horses nor freedom, since the only horse I've ever ridden shook me out of the saddle, very nearly stomping me to death, and freedom—distance from Rachel—seemed exciting for about six hours until I'd convinced myself she was a saint.

When my mom died, my dad decided to sell the house, but she'd divorced him the year before she died, altering her will so that Paula and I would get everything she owned, which included her half of the house. I said, "Sell it." Paula, who had always loved things (a glass case of Japanese dolls our uncle brought back from the war and gave her, a rocking chair that the antiques dealer said could not be later than 1835 and might be as early as late eighteenth century, although it did have new runners) and who later insisted upon saving every article of clothing our mother had ever worn, sat on the living room floor and dusted off first editions. I stood over my dad in the den and told him not to stop and read every article about Cesar Chavez his ex-wife had ever written, wondering aloud what it was like to finally be free of your lifelong antagonist until he said, "There were periods, Dave, there were long stretches of time that I thought would never end, when I failed with your mother." That was what I wanted to hear, and now that I'd heard it, I didn't want to hear any more, but my father thought he needed to explain, and after a few minutes his confession became so clear that he cried into the large wastebasket, using his ex-wife's old articles as so many hankies.

I can understand how he might have lost his lust for his then wife; I remember her as having short black hair, blue veins popping through white skin, and boyish hips. I know she couldn't possibly have had red eyes, and yet—on the basis of one photograph, which was shot with too much flash—I remember her eyes as the frenzied red eyes of an angry mouse. I know she'd been a sturdy five foot seven, but I'm unable to remember her other than as an impossibly light, frail being whose bones were collapsing and whose flesh was falling off as she slowly became less visible and then vanished. I imagine her in bed with her back against the headboard, smoking a cigarette and editing a book about the condition of farmworkers in Salinas. And then I imagine her untying her bathrobe, lifting her nightgown, pulling back the covers, and, as she'd done all day, advising her husband what to do. He could pretend to sleep and snore for only so long. He would try once and try again; he would fail and say, "I'm so sorry, sweet," and cry into her arms until she'd fallen asleep.

My mother often used to reminisce about how she and Milt and Paula lived in a nice little duplex in Hollywood on Orange Drive; shortly after I was born, they left Hollywood for a ranch house in Griffith Park. Once, when Rachel and I traveled cross-country partly in order for me to scrutinize the prelapsarian apartment I'd heard so much about, we could find no such address (the only true paradise is lost paradise), and my main impression of Orange Drive was of a quiet tunnel between the prostitutes on Sunset Boulevard and the massage parlors on Melrose. I was forced to imagine what it had been like, and I couldn't. It wasn't in me. I tried, but I couldn't.

Shortly after my mom's death, I hoped to find somewhere in all her papers at least one thing that contradicted the completely stoical persona she'd presented to the world, since at the time I didn't believe in heroes or heroines. Her last will and testament had a handwritten note stapled to the back of it:

> In the event of my death, I would like to have my body cremated and the ashes disposed of in the simplest way possible. My first choice would have been to donate my heart, kidneys, and corneas for transplants, but it is not possible to donate the organs of someone with cancer. I realize that cremation is not in accordance with Jewish law, but I think it is the most sensible method of disposing of a lifeless body. Although I do not want a religious memorial service, I hope it is helpful for family and friends to have an informal gathering; people can draw strength from one another. I leave this world without regrets or bitterness of any kind. I have had a good life. May the future be kind to each of you. Shalom.

To me, there was something unnatural, almost spooky about her matter-of-fact tone. She had apparently started a journal a few months before dying but never got back to it after this first, formal entry:

> Of one thing I'm sure: I don't want to live if I can't function, make decisions for myself, and take care of myself. I hope that if I reach that point I'll have the courage to take my life. I feel very strongly that life is a very precious gift and that one should always choose life, but to me life is being able to function. Maybe I'll be able to express this better and more clearly as time goes on.

At the time I was quite cowardly when it came to the contemplation of my own mortality, and if I admired my mom's sentiments, I also had trouble truly understanding them. I wanted to find one thing about her I understood, instinctively. She had an entire broken suitcase full of scraps of papers on which her employers had paid her professional compliments: "I enjoyed this issue very much." "The layout really had movement." "Your patience, concern, and insight are most noteworthy." "You are, without the slightest reservations as to character, ability, or personality, the finest newspaperwoman I have ever had the pleasure of working with." I'd been doing essentially the same thing with my professors' comments as my mother did with her bosses' little bouquets of praise, but I'd been impressed with my mother my whole life; I was dying to come across a piece of paper that attacked my heart.

All the condolences were only more journalistic encomia: "She always brightened the city room with her sparkle and excellent ideas." "It was a delight and privilege to work with her all these years." ". . . my deep respect for her professionalism, intelligence, and capability . . ." These people didn't seem, to me, to be talking about a real person; they were describing some cardboard cutout of Lillian Hellman. I needed to get past the cartoon and clichés to someone who wasn't a ghost, who was physical. "She was a talented professional, a remarkable woman."

Save for the first paragraph, she'd written even her own obituary, which recounted her jobs with more than a dozen progressive newspapers, magazines, and organizations: coordinator of public information, researcher, writer, correspondent, editor, managing editor. The final sentence of the obituary read, "Mrs. Shields requested that friends make a memorial gift to the United Farm Workers." I couldn't help but laugh a little; maybe there really was nothing about her that wasn't public-minded and altruistic. About twenty copies of the obituary had been photocopied (by my dad, I supposed), and I threw them up in the air. A fragment of completely yellowed paper slid out from the obituaries as they fluttered back down. It was a poem—"I Need Not Tell You Why," by Thomas Emmet Moore—that looked like it must have been snipped from her college textbook:

> I did not dream you could forget,
> I could not know that love may die;
> I only know my eyes are wet,
> And that I need not tell you why!
> I need not tell you why, dear heart—
> Your cold lips would deny;
> But well I know that love is fled,
> I need not tell you why!
> You smile, and kiss me, and I hear
> You say your love is strong and true
> As when you wooed me; yesteryear,
> To leave my world and follow you!
> You say my hair is as the foam

That crowns a cup of amber wine;
But though you've called me to your home,
Your love, dear heart, is now not mine!
Nay, do not fold me to your breast,
You well should know you give but pain;
For aching hearts there is no rest
Till love hath healed their wounds again!

I'd never heard of Thomas Emmet Moore, so I went through some of my mom's reference books until I discovered that Moore was an Ohio lawyer, editor, and poet who was born in 1861 and died in 1950. He was born and he died and he lived and he loved and he lost and he wrote at least one really bad poem. Which didn't matter, because the poem was a revelation. Never had I considered even the possibility that my mother could harbor such helpless, primitive, irrational feelings; never had I considered the possibility that it would be permissible for *me* to feel such feelings, since so much of dinner table conversation had centered on the intersection of political activism and journalistic ambition. I remember, at that moment, wishing and wishing and wishing that on the night of my conception (and on subsequent days and nights) my mother and father had communicated to each other (and thus to me) not that the body was moral, which it isn't, but that it's mortal, only mortal, and that the act of love isn't one more good deed but a riot of feelings, for if they had, if they only had, I might have become (who knows?) a more imaginative person than I am now.

Fathers and teachers, I ponder, "What is hell?"
I maintain that it is the suffering of being unable to love.

—DOSTOEVSKY

A BRIEF SURVEY OF IDEAL DESIRE

Galleons laden with jewelry and threatened by pirates sailed through treacherous seas in the gold-on-blue design of my rabbit-feet pajamas. I would hold the strap attached to my rocking horse's ears and mouth, lifting myself onto the little leather saddle. One glass eye shone out of the right side of his head. His mouth, once bright red and smiling, had chipped away to a tight-lipped, unpainted pout. His nose, too, was bruised, with gashes for nostrils. He had a brown mane that, extending from the crown of his head nearly to his waist, was made up of my grandmother's discarded wigs glued to the wood. Wrapping the reins around my fist, I'd slip my feet into the square stirrups that hung from his waist. I'd bounce up and down to set him in motion, lean forward, press my lips to the back of his neck, and exhort him to charge. (Infantile, naïve, I thought I could talk to wooden animals.) When he pitched forward, I'd scoot up toward the base of his spine, and when he swung back, I'd let go of the leather strap and lean back as far as he could. I'd make him lurch crazily toward the far wall by squeezing my knees into his sides and jerking my legs forward. Then I'd twist my hips and bounce until it felt warm under me, bump up against the smooth surface of the seat until my whole body tingled. I'd buck back and forth so it hurt, in a way, and I wouldn't know what to do with this ache.

From age eleven until fifteen I did little else but play basketball all afternoon and evening, and when it grew too dark to see the rim, I played by the light of the streetlamp. I played on school teams, on temple teams, in pickup games, for hours alone, with friends, against friends, with people I'd never seen before and never saw again, with middle-aged men wearing college sweatshirts who liked to keep their hands on my ass as they guarded me, with friends' younger brothers who couldn't believe how good I was, with Stanford starters keeping in shape during the summer who told me I might make it, with coaches who told me the future of their jobs rested on my performance, with the owners of a pornographic bookstore who asked me if I wanted to appear in an art film, with my father, who asked me whatever happened to the concept of teamwork. I wore leather weights around my ankles, taking them off only in bed, so my legs would be strong and I'd be able to jump as high as my black teammates could. I read every available book on technique, every biography of the stars. I jumped rope: inside, around the block, up stairs, walking the dog. I played on asphalt, in playgrounds, in gyms, in the street, in the backyard, in my mind, in rain, in winds that ruled the ball, beneath the burning sun.

I ascended two flights of cement stairs, then knocked on the door, which had an engraving of Venus straddling an aqueduct. A large blond lady, wearing high heels made of glass, opened the door. "Hello," she said, aspirating heavily, "and welcome to A Touch of Venus." She handed me a glass of white wine and a piece of paper, which was encased in plastic and which said,

A TOUCH OF VENUS—THE MOST IN MASSAGE

1. *The Basic.* Masseuse fully clothed. No oils, no scents. 1 drink. Access to billiard table. Very relaxing. Fifteen minutes. $20.

2. *The Rubdown.* Masseuse clothed in underwear. Oils, no scents. 2 drinks. Access to billiard table, whirlpool, shower massage. Highly sensitizing. Twenty minutes. $30.

3. *The Total Massage.* Masseuse clothed in black underwear. Oils, scents. 3 drinks. Access to billiard table, whirlpool, shower massage, screening room, Jacuzzi. Extremely refreshing. Thirty minutes. $50.

4. *A Little Bit of Heaven.* Masseuse topless. Asian oils, Parisian scents. Unlimited drinks. Access to billiard table, whirlpool, shower massage, screening room, Jacuzzi, lemon creme facial. Quite exciting. Forty-five minutes. $75.

5. *Ecstasy.* Masseuse topless and bottomless. Asian oils, Parisian scents. Unlimited drinks. Access to billiard table, whirlpool, shower massage, screening room, Jacuzzi, sauna, lemon creme facial. Hot towel wrap. Champagne bubble bath. Discount card for return visits. Fulfilling. One hour. $100.

I was astonished that so many of the details with which I'd conjured up this scenario proved to be accurate: black leather couches, thick red carpet, low lighting, disco music, shiny wood paneling, coffee tables on which were spread recent copies of *Penthouse.* "So," my hostess said, "what'll it be—Ecstasy, A Little Bit of Heaven, Total Massage . . ." Her voice trailed off. It seemed clear that anything short of Ecstasy was mere flirtation. "Ecstasy," I said. I paid her with money from my work-study job as a proofreader, and she took me on a tour of the building, which used to be the fire department, she said, before it was converted. I thought back to a time when big, happy men were polishing trucks and waiting around to be heroes. She held me by the arm and walked me through the lounge, in which the other masseuses were watching a faded color film of four people fucking, then gave me a white bathrobe and a key to a locker and told me to change into—the phrase was meant to be incredibly erotic, and it was—"something more comfortable." The sauna, the whirlpool, the shower massage (whatever that was), the Jacuzzi, the champagne bubble bath, all this stuff was in the basement of the ex-firehouse; I was instructed to slide down the golden pole and amuse myself for a while and come upstairs when I was ready. I was ready right then, of course; I hadn't paid a hundred dollars to take a bath by myself, and as I climbed into the sauna and sat on the wooden bench, I tried and failed to imagine anything worse than being in the basement of this converted fire station on Sunday morning. I consoled myself with the thought that before I left, at least I would have sinned. When I went upstairs, I sat in a director's chair, watching the movie and thumbing through magazines, and one by one the employees offered themselves to me. My hostess asked me to play pool with her, a short redhead sat next to me and watched the movie for a couple of minutes, and a skinny woman with black hair wrapped high around her head like tangled snakes brought me a drink. I was supposed to give a little ticket that I held in my hand to the woman of my dreams, but instead I got up and gave the ticket to the only masseuse who was not in any way appealing or exciting or terrifying. She was shy, and I had to force the ticket into her hand to get her to look up. She led me into a room and told me to take off my bathrobe. I lay facedown on a table in the middle of the room, where she rubbed me from head to toe. I stared at a large mirror positioned on the floor in such a way that I could see her. Most of what she did tickled, so I thought about other things to keep from laughing. It wasn't arousing, and after a while I flipped over on my back, sat up, and complained. She said this was a legitimate massage parlor and they didn't do that kind of thing here. "We'll be quiet," I assured her and offered her a twenty-dollar tip, but she said no. I lunged toward her; she stepped back and hurried out the door before I could stop her. I ran out of the room and down the stairs to my locker, changed into my clothes, then left by the back exit. The rest of the money in my wallet was gone. When I got outside and into the sunlight, I felt the same way I'd felt upon leaving the theater after seeing a pornographic movie for the first time: sentimental, thrilled by the mundanity of stoplights and flowers, and repelled by the prospect of physical love.

Rachel and I had remained in bed until three o'clock in the afternoon, which was twenty minutes after I was supposed to have boarded a Bonanza bus to Logan Airport, because Rachel, wearing only socks and mittens, wanted to wrap her legs tightly around my back so I'd feel like I was being devoured by a lioness and return as quickly as possible and think of no one and nothing else while I was away.

Every time she got even near me, I started sneezing, and unfortunately I was one of those boy-undergraduates who, rather than make a quick little ka-choo into a handkerchief, not only neglected to carry a handkerchief but also tended to blow coagulations of snot onto whatever was around them at the moment. What was around me at the moment was Rachel's bedsheet, which she'd just washed and dried so that she and I would have a clean white surface to slide around on on our last night together. She was so disgusted by the way I shook the snot off my hands into the wastebasket that she got out of bed, standing with her mittens on her hips and her stockinged feet on the floor next to the electric heater, and quoted back to me the analogy I liked to make between the itch in the nose and desire. "It really empties you out, right?" she said. "Tell me, sweetheart, does it also make you feel sad?" I thought I was sneezing because I'd finally developed an allergy to Rachel, whereas Rachel, who'd learned all about psychosomatic disorders when she was in analysis, assumed I was sneezing because I'd developed an allergy to my family, whereas it turned out I'd developed an allergy to the dust I'd encountered the night before, searching for my suitcase in the basement. While I stuffed the suitcase with what few articles of light clothing I still owned, she started the car, an old Peugeot the color of pool water, which her father had given her after the mechanic said he'd never be able to stop the ping in the motor; she drove ten miles an hour faster than anyone else on 95 North all the way to the airport. We made it in plenty of time. "I'll miss you—I love you," I said to reassure Rachel, who had started glowering when I glanced at the cover of *Club International* in the gift shop before doing whatever was the opposite of deplaning. "You love your free detachable calendar of Miss Cunt of the Month," she said, and kissed me goodbye until I started sneezing again.

"I can see why you're a Miss Nude USA regional finalist," I imagined writing the woman whose ad was placed in the back of *Club*. "You have beautiful long silky blue-black hair, a perfect pout, and a gorgeous body. Please send me the color photos you mentioned of yourself in fur, leather, lingerie, garter belt, and heels. Thank you. Payment enclosed."

·　　·　　·

The ending of James Joyce's story "The Dead" is usually interpreted as Gabriel Conroy's unambiguous, transcendental identification with universal love and human mortality, but to me—when I was twenty-two—it seemed more plausible to read the last page or so as an overwritten passage that conveyed emotional deadness taking refuge in sentimentality. "Generous tears filled Gabriel's eyes. He had never felt like that himself towards any woman, but he knew that such a feeling must be love." Gabriel is thinking about the passion of his wife's ex-suitor, but to me the word "generous" appeared to suggest Gabriel's confusion of self-pity with selfless love. I figured that if Joyce had meant the last sentence of the story to be truly beautiful, he wouldn't have used "falling faintly" and "faintly falling" within four words of each other. This repetition created discord at the very climax of the rising hymn; even as Gabriel believed he was liberating himself from egotism, his language for compassion was self-conscious and solipsistic. Neither in memory nor fantasy was he capable of imagining union, completion, or even shared intimacy. That was my interpretation.

LOVE IS ILLUSION

The most dramatic sexual experience of my life was a yearlong relationship with a woman whose entire philosophy, or at least bedroom behavior, was derived from the sex advice columns of racier women's magazines. She wore extremely tight jeans tucked into catch-me/fuck-me boots, and she applied lipstick and eye shadow in such a way as to create the effect that she was in a perpetual state of arousal. Once, as I walked several paces ahead, she told the couple we were walking with that I had a great ass (I do!—or at least I did). In the missionary position, she would whisper, "Deeper," and wrap her legs tightly around me. When she was on top, she would rub her breasts together, lick her lips, and run her hands through her hair, encouraging me to pull, hard, on her gold choker. When being penetrated from behind, she would suck on my thumb and look back at me with googly eyes, as if to prevent herself from losing consciousness.

Before performing fellatio, she'd moan, "Give me that big thing." Although my equipment is only standard, she called it "Porno Penis." (The first time we had sex, I'd just masturbated, imagining her, and I was at half-staff; she nevertheless said I was "the perfect size," which is *Cosmo* 101.) She would kneel, gaze up at me as if with reverence, swallow, and, at the end, wink. She'd slurp my semen as if it were maple syrup atop pancakes, which she made one Sunday morning in her underwear. Whenever I went down on her, she'd wrap her fingers—with brightly lacquered nails—around my hair, tug, and pretend to come almost immediately, thanking me profusely afterward. Once, when I licked her from behind, she exclaimed that she'd never been anywhere near this intimate with anyone before. Anal sex, with requisite screams. Her voice occupied a middle register exactly halfway between Baby Doll and Dominatrix. At dinner parties, she would mouth *I love you,* and look at me as if I were the president. I'm not making this stuff up.

Her goal seemed to be to burn images of herself into my retina forever. Mission accomplished: I could never tell how much genuine feeling there was in her brilliant performance, and yet I still have quite specific sense-memories of these events, which occurred more than thirty years ago. Humankind cannot bear very much reality.

POSTCARDS FROM RACHEL, ABROAD

Hi, David. Here I am in Geneva. The Swiss have the second-largest standing army in the world. They can mobilize their entire force in less than 30 minutes. All men 18 and older serve one week per year in the army, running drills and practicing shooting (I'm sure you'd love that!), or doing paperwork when they get older (more your style). They all have loaded rifles and pistols at home in their closets. I guess they want peace at any cost. They made me wait in a crowded room for my physical exam just to be allowed into the country. I had my chest X-rayed for tuberculosis. Sitting there, I realized that everyone around me was from somewhere else: Senegal, Lebanon, Turkey. I feel like the only one of my kind here. I feel like the outsider.

I'm sitting on the Quai Wilson during the Fêtes de Genève (the annual carnival). To my left is a group of young women dressed in full Muslim garb. One of them thinks I don't see that she's staring at my naked skin—bare legs, bare feet, bare arms, neck, hair being free. I assume that she's hot under her black robe and that she wishes she could be as free to choose as I am. It's only when they turn to leave and our eyes meet that I realize what I see on her face is not jealousy but pity. I miss talking to you about stuff like this.

Went out with my friends last night in Geneva. We went dancing at L'Usine. "Black Night" or "Nuit Black," as my young friends call it. (Are you starting to feel old now, too?) Most of them are from Senegal and Ethiopia and know nothing about PC. They celebrate their differences in language and culture, and they know that here the Arabs and the Portuguese are "below" them (in the Swiss's opinion). "At least we speak French" is what they say. I didn't realize the Swiss hated anyone openly. I'm learning a lot. I feel colorless with them. It's nice.

On the bus on my way to work today in downtown Geneva, I saw a group of banner-carrying Serbs smash the glass bus shelter right in front of the UN. They were burning into the grass a word I didn't recognize. Our bus driver took one look at them and lowered the arm to the electric cable, taking an alternate route. When I came back after work, the only sign of it ever having taken place was that the grass had been mowed to a new, short length and the burnt parts sprayed with what I guess is some sort of Astroturf paint. There was nothing on the news that night. If a word is written, and no one reads it, does the word exist? Is this the sort of esoterica you're still interested in?

Got strip-searched in Tel Aviv while trying to leave the country. I'm sure it seemed suspicious—two young Americans, holders of UN travel cards, coming to Israel for a four-day vacation—but that's what it was. (My friend Matthew took me on this crazy trip before his move to Hungary.) They examined our bags first, X-rayed my shoes, and ripped the film out of my camera, before making me stand in my underwear while the inspector checked me out (jealous?). I guess being white and female doesn't always mean you're above suspicion. Matthew thinks it's his fault: he's sure they could tell he's gay.

·   ·   ·

I'm in the Zurich train station, waiting for the train to Berlin. Next to me is a large family—Romanian? Hungarian?—with trash bags and battered suitcases. Their whole lives are jammed into these bulging cases. When they begin speaking, I lean in to hear what they're saying. It's yet another language I don't speak. When will I know enough languages? When will I be more than just an American woman?

Matthew's boyfriend, Nicholas, wants me to marry him. Not how it sounds. He's French and holds a C permit (next best to being a Swiss citizen) and I, of course, have the almighty green card behind me. It's tempting to imagine offering my future children all of these passports—all of these opportunities. Knowing me and my great guilt, I doubt it'll happen. And besides, Matthew would kill me. Um, why didn't you and I ever get married? Because being with each other we scared ourselves. (Nearly wrote "scarred," which is true, too.)

Things the Merrill Lynch lawyer told me about Swiss work-permit renewals: (1) I can stay for two separate periods of three months after it expires (with 24 hours somewhere else in between). For this I'll need to go to the *contrôle des habitants* with *annonce depart* and get a *visa touristique*. (2) I can stay as a student and work 80 hours a month. I'd need to get a new permit. (3) I can try to get a job with the UN (I won't need any permit to work for them). The lawyer hates this idea—of course, he's Swiss. (4) If I marry a Swiss or a person with a C permit, I'll get a C permit immediately. This is illegal. Guess I'll apply to the UN.

Not one but three offers: the first with the International Organization for Migration, the second with World Intellectual Property, and the third with the World Health Organization. I think I'm going to take the IOM job. I'll be working with a team of people creating a database and statistical reports that track immigration and refugee movements. If I stay long enough, I could get sent to work at one of the missions—Africa, Hungary, Thailand, Haiti. I'll actually be having an effect on people's lives. I'm sure this seems hopelessly idealistic to you, but the world is a real place, monsieur.

. . .

I found out today that the man I rent a room from goes to Thailand twice a year for the prostitutes. While cleaning the living room, I found some photographs of beautiful young Thai girls and I asked him about them. He told me if he weren't "sleeping" with them, someone else would be and at least he's disease-free, nonviolent, and generous with his tips and gifts. I'd heard this sort of thing happened, but I never knew anyone who actually did it. He's not bad looking—he's a dead ringer for that guy (Patrick?) we used to go to movies with in LA—and he's young enough and interesting enough to get a woman over here, or so I thought. He said the girls are young, sometimes virgins, and they always ask him to marry them. Well, no kidding, I said. He's Swiss and, in their eyes, he offers them a freedom they've never known. He says he's even considering it. They don't even speak his language. I think he just wants a sex slave. (Now, if he only wanted to *be* a sex slave . . .) He's really highly ranked in the Swiss army and—get this—his name is *Christian.* Perfect. Time to look for a new apartment.

Went to L'Escalade and watched people run through the windy streets in the cold. The race is run every year to symbolize the retreat of the Duke of Savoie's army. They run through Geneva's steep streets and climb its many flights of stairs. Matthew bought me a marmite (a chocolate cauldron filled with brightly colored marzipan vegetables). It's a symbol of the Mère Royaume housewife who killed an invader with a hot cauldron of vegetable soup when the Duke of Savoie was trying to take over Geneva. She defeated him and the city remained free. Europeans turn all of their attacks and wars into holidays.

I love the winter holiday season in Geneva. Mont Blanc and Le Salève (local mountain) are white-capped, and the air is crisp and cold. The city is decorated in old-timey lights and ribbons, and everywhere I go are vendors selling roasted chestnuts. I wait for the tram, holding the warm cone of nuts in my hands, smelling their richness, and watching the Swiss. They stroll past, hand in hand, red-cheeked and smiling. I don't know how, but they remain sweetly childlike in their fascination with holidays. *Très* kitsch, but I am chock-full of longing and envy; I'm sure you can relate.

Szia! See ya! That's how you say the Hungarian word for hello. I've been in Budapest, visiting Matthew for a few days now, and I couldn't understand why everyone was telling me goodbye right when I met them. This place feels so steeped in history and yet so modern. Young Hungarian women wear such short shorts that there's not much left to the imagination. They mostly have great bodies and they dress as if they're waiting to be discovered by *Vogue.* And yet they all live at home; families of 10 or more people share 3 rooms. It's hard to reconcile the fact that Hungary was shuttled back and forth between the Germans and the Russians with the fact that Hungarians remain such gentle and open people. It makes sense only when I see that all of the Communist stars—on bridges, buildings, statues—haven't been removed, merely covered with a thick canvas. Nothing is permanent.

In Budapest, foreigners must carry Hungarian money at all times. If the police stop you and you can't show them the money, they kick you out of the country. This is their solution to "squatters." Last week a friend of mine got caught and thrown in jail. After he'd gotten back to Romania, I didn't hear from him for a week. He'll sneak back in soon; he needs to find a job to support his family. I told him I'd give him some money to carry in his pockets. He said that wouldn't help; he's a tzigane (gypsy) and looks like a tzigane and will always be forced to leave: *See ya!*

Driving through northern Italy with friends. The beauty of this area amazes me. Mountains and water—so green and blue that only Italian could describe them. And the black-gray of the tanks that appear quickly as we move through the switchbacks. Europe never lets you forget that you are fragile, you are different from everyone else on the planet, and this difference is both lovely and awful. Ah, but you already knew this. We knew this together, didn't we, sweetheart? Love, Rachel

ECONOMIES OF DESIRE

In the first of the eight interlocked stories or chapters of *Butterfly Stories: A Novel,* William Vollmann tells "what happened to the child," establishing the psychic interconnection—for the butterfly boy—between solitude, beauty, loss, pain, and punishment. The lyric catalogue of childhood humiliations in the first story yields, in the seven stories that follow, to litanies of the butterfly boy (who as an adult is called first "the journalist," then later "the husband") re-enacting—with a lesbian traveling companion, the son of a former SS officer, a sybaritic and amoral photographer, and especially with a Phnom Penh prostitute named Oy—the sadomasochistic scenarios of his childhood.

Vollmann begins *Butterfly Stories* with an evocation of war torture by the Khmer Rouge. On the next page, he writes, "There was a jungle, and there was murder by torture, but the butterfly boy did not know about it. He knew the school bully, though, who beat him up every day." Vollmann thus makes absolutely explicit the link between the butterfly boy's childhood and his adult experiences in Thailand and Cambodia. The butterfly boy thinks about the school bully, "The substance that his soul was composed of was pain," but this is at least as true of the butterfly boy, who "was not popular in the second grade because he knew how to spell 'bacteria' in the spelling bee, and so the other boys beat him up." One evening, a monarch butterfly lands on the top step of his house, squatting on the welcome mat and moving its gorgeous wings slowly. Then it rises in the air. He never sees it again; he remembers the butterfly the rest of his life.

Butterfly Stories is told in more than two hundred very short sections, many of which deal with the economies of desire: "A middle-aged midget in a double-breasted suit came down the alley, walked under one girl's dress, reached up to pull it over him like a roof, and began to suck. The girl stood looking at nothing. When the midget was finished, he slid her panties back up and spat onto the sidewalk. Then he reached into his wallet."

In the middle of the novel, Vollmann appends to the conclusion of several sections the words "The End," as if to suggest the cease-lessness of the butterfly boy's capacity for self-inflicted punishment. After acting out "endless" scenarios of humiliation and loss, "the husband," who may have AIDS, returns in the final chapter to San Francisco, self-consciously trying—and failing—to play his spousal role: "Sometimes he'd see [his wife] in the back yard gardening, the puppy frisking between her legs, and she'd seem so adorable there behind window-glass that he ached, but as soon as she came in, whether she stormed at him or tried desperately to please him, he could not feel. *He could not feel!*" Reading this extraordinarily intimate book about the butterfly boy's incapacity for ordinary intimacy, I couldn't iden-tify more closely with him if I crawled inside his skin.

The greatest poverty is not to live
In a physical world, to feel that one's desire
Is too difficult to tell from despair.

—WALLACE STEVENS

DESPAIR

Pornography is not, in my experience and opinion, a substitute for closeness; it's a revel in distance.

Our fifth-grade social studies teacher had supposedly once appeared in *Playboy*. This rumor could never be confirmed or denied, but for the only time in my life I got a C: no one in that class—boys or girls—could concentrate on anything except Miss Acker.

"Petite Nancy Spiess," "a bunny of Detroit," "a motorcycle buff," was the first figure in a magazine to whom I ever masturbated. Those silver fingernails, that green bikini bottom—I couldn't stop imagining her in the buff, on the back of a motorcycle.

In high school, I couldn't keep looking at a girl once she'd seen me looking at her—that is, looked back. This wasn't a lot of help to me on the dating scene. Saturday nights, during my adolescence, were exhausting: first Sally Struthers, then Mary Tyler Moore, then Suzanne Pleshette—all on CBS. By 10:00 p.m. I was relieved *Mannix* was on.

In a college literature class, the professor asked us what scenes represented genuine desire—the scenes of the main character going to pornographic movies or the scenes of the main character making love with his wife? "The scenes of the main character going to pornographic movies," I said.

In my twenties, I was particularly partial to the ink screens covering certain words and certain body parts in ads for films and phone sex in porn magazines. It was the most transparent ruse, but it always worked. Once, flipping through the pictures in a dirty magazine, I noticed, on one woman's leg and back, a couple of blotches marked with grease pencil circles, which, rather than being responded to by the photo retoucher, had, through negligence, remained, like a critique of false premises.

I went through a Seka phase—did any straight American man not, in the early eighties, go through a Seka phase?—until I noticed that, in group shots with other women, Seka was granted the rare privilege of not having to make eye contact with the viewer; even for me, this seemed too remote a spot from which to worship the goddess. The fantasy was that she disdained you until you fucked her into loving you.

In my local convenience store, cigarette ads with openmouthed women are hung just inside the door at, I never fail to notice, crotch level.

When the man behind the counter at the blue-movie store asked if he could help me find anything, I said, "Just browsing." He replied, "That's what I said four years ago, and look at me now."

Roger Fanning: "Then the boy replays a porno film paid for/a quarter at a time, bad milk spilled in a booth."

Porn star Nina Hartley: "They're masturbating and they can't mask their eyes. You can see their trepidations. They come to me with their expectations and their desires, and they're very fearful. Their eyes are filled with a mixture of erotic energy, openness, hope, and fear. Vulnerability. But some of them are completely comfortable with the whole thing. They're the funnest."

I kept asking a woman in a peep show to do this, mouth that, look a certain way, until she finally said, "What do you want, a girlfriend or a show?"

Immediately after the breakup of a relationship, I became a fan for a while of a massage parlor called Misfits. I never went there, but I enjoyed looking at their ad in the phone book; calling and hanging up; thinking about the perfect pun of their name: Miss/Fits—a little relief in a tight spot for the alienated man.

When I was a little kid, I read in the *San Francisco Chronicle* that the stripper Carol Doda was "statuesque." I didn't know what the word meant, but in one important feature my babysitter resembled Carol Doda, so I asked her whether she was statuesque. She said she didn't know what that meant, but we could look it up.

I was a very good Little League baseball player, but I actually preferred to go over to the park across from our house, sit atop the hill, and watch kids my age (or younger) play for hours. "What's the matter with you?" my father would ask me. "You should be out playing. You shouldn't be watching." I don't know what's the matter with me—why I'm adept only at distance, why I feel so remote from things, why life feels like a rumor—but playing has somehow always struck me as a fantastically unfulfilling activity.

MASK OF MASKS

Women wear glasses on chains, like metal dogs on a leash. They whip them around in the air like a lasso. They bite the earpiece of the temple, than which simply nothing is more suggestive. They lay their glasses down on the table, allowing the whole world to go fuzzy on them, while they rub their eyes. They crawl around on the floor, looking for their glasses, which they can't find because they're not wearing their glasses. They find their glasses and hug you in a frenzy of unblurry relief. They clean their glasses with your T-shirt. They read in bed. They place their glasses on top of their head like deep-sea divers emerging from the deep sea. They push them halfway down their nose so they can neither see you nor not see you, so you can neither see them nor not see them. They remove their glasses, exposing the little red indentation across the bridge of their nose. They smash their glasses while making love to you. They tuck their glasses carefully in a case, like putting a baby to bed.

A woman recently riding the crosstown bus struck me as extremely beautiful, if in a rather traditional, all-American way. Without glasses, she would have been a statue, a mannequin, a doll, a cartoon; her beauty would have been too-too. Her simple red tortoiseshells eroti-cized her to an almost intolerable degree. They drew me in and stood me off. They said, *You can look at me all you want, but you can't see me in public. You have no idea what I look like or am like. You have no idea how interesting things get when I take these off. I'm so sexy I need to wear these as a buffer.*

The way her glasses worked against her beauty was exactly what made her more beautiful: more human. Glasses insist upon the con-stant simultaneity of body and mind; the beauty of a woman's face is deepened and complicated by the antiglamour scholasticism of her eyewear. Superman without Clark Kent would be perfect, completely unconvincing, boring.

Glasses have the spectacular virtue of suggesting that there's every-thing left to imagine: Only someone in special circumstances will see the veil removed, the gate opened, the cage unlocked—her naked eyes. Only I get to see her without her glasses; only I get to see the beauty behind the barrier. Glasses make completely explicit the rela-tionship between eyes and I, between love and trust. Glasses, mask of masks, allude to the difference between how a person appears in public and how the same person might perform in private, and thus suggest the bedroom. The arrogance implied in believing that one's beauty can afford to be concealed is entrancing. By contrast, peo-ple not wearing glasses sometimes seem preposterously accessible, uncomplicated, unmysterious, trampy.

What's so sexy about glasses is that they block the male gaze and return it redoubled; they transform the woman from viewed to viewer, from looked-at to looker. *Men seldom make passes at girls who wear glasses*—Dorothy Parker's aphorism tells us much more about her particular brand of self-loathing than it does about eyewear. *Smell me, touch me, but don't look at me:* needless to say, this is a tantalizing message to send.

When a woman wears glasses, she is—to me, anyway—displaying her woundedness. (In the wild, a wounded animal doesn't get courted.) She seems both very vulnerable—I could remove her glasses, causing her to be disoriented—and very brave, choosing not to conceal her defect in the most vital of the five senses. One sense is diminished; another sense—touch? taste?—must, in order to com-pensate, be particularly acute.

In high school I read Philip Roth's *Goodbye, Columbus,* which begins, "The first time I saw Brenda she asked me to hold her glasses. Then she stepped out to the edge of the diving board and looked foggily into the pool; it could have been drained, myopic Brenda would never have known it." Immediately I was deep into Brenda.

"Now what can you do?" I once asked a lover who, in bed, had just removed her glasses and who without glasses was legally blind. I thought I meant, *How well can you function without your glasses?* but my question clearly implied another question—concerning mattress acrobatics. I wanted her to put her glasses back on so I could tear them off.

Is anything more unnerving than to be asked, in the middle of a lovers' quarrel, "Why won't you look at me?" The eyes, as the Renaissance never gets tired of telling us, are the windows of the soul. What glasses say is *My soul is not so easily accessible.*

The terms for frame parts are about the distance between me and you, between here and there—rim, bridge, hinge, shield. Some temple parts: bend, shaft, and, um, butt portion. Is everyone aroused by looking at diagrams of glasses, or is that only me? I love how the long thin temples screw into round liquescent lenses. In the interest of full disclosure: absolutely nothing could possibly be more erotic to me than the subservient-yet-unreachable paradox embodied by a woman performing fellatio while wearing glasses.

I must acknowledge that some things about glasses just don't work. All sunglasses, for instance, which are striving so strenuously to be mysterious that they have zero effect on me. So, too, the cat's eye, which is much too obvious in its female = feline, Catwoman = bitch-goddess equations. Movie stars at the Academy Awards wearing horn-rims in order to read the teleprompter don't suddenly seem deeper and more widely read. Pornographic photos—intended to excite the bookish gentleman—in which glasses are perched on the tip of the model's nose as a totally alien accessory aren't very exciting. Glasses can't be a self-consciously sexy accoutrement; the joke can't be explained; the contradiction can't be resolved in favor of overtness: glasses are sexy precisely to the degree that a woman's sexiness appears to emerge despite her attempt to hide it.

Laurie needs glasses only to drive at night and read subtitles in movie theaters. As often as possible, I tell her I'm not sure I know the way home—would she mind driving? As often as possible, I suggest that we sign up for, say, the Fellini retrospective at the Grand Illusion.

And yet, finally, no one, as I've learned all too well, wants to hear, "I love how you look in your glasses; I think you look even better with them on." The sexiest thing about glasses is that they come off. The sexiest thing about glasses is that the first time you kiss, she lets you take them off and then blinks once, trying to focus.

DELILAH

Hi!" Delilah says. "Welcome aboard. I'm so glad you found us. If you're a newcomer to this show, you're probably wondering what in the world this is all about. Well, it's not about politics. It's not about wars going on around the world. It's not about national trials and tribulations. It's about you. It's about your heart. It's about what in the world is going on in your world. We are here for you—to take your calls about family, friends, sweethearts, that special someone you met over the internet, falling in love, having your heart broken by love, babies, and graduations. And then we mix those stories together with your favorite love songs. Thank you for finding us. You're listening to *Delilah.*"

When a caller named Helen mentions having a baby with her fiancé, a soldier who's stationed in the Middle East, Delilah says, "When are we getting married?"

Helen replies, "We haven't set a date yet, but we're going to start planning as soon as he gets home." Delilah plays Selena's "Dreaming of You."

To a young woman who is still stuck on her ex-boyfriend, Delilah says, more than once, "I hate it when that happens."

Delilah—who, as any icon seeking goddess status must do, goes only by one name—discusses how your kids can drive you crazy, especially during the summer; it's important, she says, to step back and remember how much you love them.

Kirsten calls and says about her son, "Our little guy's a special-needs guy."

"Aren't we all special needs in one way or another?" Delilah says, before playing Whitney Houston's "Greatest Love of All."

Delilah advises Kathy, who's shy about approaching the former security guard she's in love with, "What happens if you don't follow through with this and he gets away again? Say 'Thank you for alerting me to the fact that my headlight was broken. I owe you my life. Here's a plate of cookies and my phone number at home. And my cell phone and my pager number and my fax number and my email address.' Come on, Kathy. Shoulders back. Be bold. Be brave." Then she plays Mariah Carey's "Dreamlover."

Delilah takes five calls and plays about ten songs an hour—adult-contemporary soft rock: Whitney Houston, Michael Jackson, Jason Aldean, Journey, Foreigner, Sarah Bareilles, Bon Jovi, Cher.

Asked what her three most requested songs are, Delilah responds, "'Wind Beneath My Wings,' 'Wind Beneath My Wings,' 'Wind Beneath My Wings.'"

Delilah, which is recorded live in Delilah's home studio in the Seattle area and is broadcast up to seven nights a week between seven and midnight in most markets, has eight million listeners on about one hundred forty stations in forty-three states, covering most of the country, even though the show isn't on in several major cities, such as Philadelphia, Atlanta, Phoenix, and San Francisco. Many of *Delilah*'s affiliates are number one with women ages twenty-five to thirty-four, including stations in Cleveland, Miami, Boise, and Dallas.

According to Compendia Media, one midwestern law firm had to withdraw its commercial from Delilah's show because it couldn't handle the business its ad drummed up. In 2002, fans at a bookstore in Louisville wouldn't let Delilah leave, even after she'd spent five hours signing copies of her first book, *Love Someone Today.* Delilah has also released several themed-compilation CDs: *My Child,* three volumes of *Love Someone, The Wedding Collection,* and *Love Someone at Christmas.* In 2008, she released the book *Love Matters: Remarkable Love Stories That Touch the Heart and Nourish the Soul.* When she endorsed Bissell vacuum cleaners in 2000, Bissell outlets across the country were besieged by customers. Bob Carlisle's father-daughter ballad, "Butterfly Kisses," was getting very little airplay except on Christian radio; in 1997, Delilah put the song into heavy rotation, causing the album to go double platinum.

Dick Fennessy, onetime program director for WFPG in Atlantic City, says that *Delilah* had an "unbelievable" impact on his station when he worked there: "In every female demographic, we doubled the numbers. We were number one in women twenty-five to thirty-four and number one in thirty-five to sixty-four. Need I say more?" The show gets a hundred thousand call-in attempts and more than a thousand email messages a night; three hundred calls get through to a screener; twenty-five calls make it on the air.

Who are these people, and why are they all calling Delilah?

"Every one of our affiliate stations was established and exists to reach women twenty-five to fifty-four," Delilah says. "I have mammary glands. I lost a grandmother to breast cancer. My executive producer"—Jane Bulman—"has two sisters who have been diagnosed with breast cancer. We're single parents. We understand the frustration of having to get up at three a.m. because your child is puking their guts out, plus you have to fix breakfast at seven for the other kids, get them to school, take care of the pets, and get yourself to work. We shop at Target and Walmart. Janey and I are that audience." Delilah lives "the remote-location farm life" on forty-nine acres in South Kitsap, near Puget Sound.

Delilah says that she's the anti–Howard Stern; she's also the anti–Rush Limbaugh, extremely female in a male-dominated medium and genre. Reyn Leutz, onetime senior partner at MindShare, which bought advertising on *Delilah* for Sears, Kimberly-Clark, and other blue-chip accounts, says that many of their clients were looking to reach women in a medium that tends to skew male. Premiere Radio Networks' online media kit claims that Delilah is the "most-listened-to woman on the radio."

Delilah's listeners are overwhelmingly female, modestly educated, and as much as I can judge from listening to the show for a couple of months, politically middle of the road. She also said that "it seems as if half my callers are single moms." Unlike, say, Oprah (who had twenty-one million viewers a week), Delilah only infrequently accompanies the sugar pill with harsh-tasting medicine.

To a young man ambivalent about continuing a relationship with a woman because he doesn't want the responsibility of caring for her two young children, Delilah posts this message on her website: "She deserves far better than you have to offer, I am afraid. She deserves a man who has a spine—a man who is not afraid of the challenges that lie ahead and who will stick around when the going gets tough. Someone who will love those babies as his flesh and blood, not a child in a man's body who says one thing one minute and then changes his mind the next. You are playing with her heart, and with the hearts of two very precious children. God warns us that it would be better for a person to have a millstone tied around their neck and be thrown into a lake than to hurt a child. You are hurting two children." This admonition seems to have been written with not only her addressee but also an ex-husband in mind, one with whom (as Delilah suggested to me when I interviewed her) she has had a less-than-amicable relationship.

On air, she says, "If you're a parent, love your children. If you're married, honor your spouse instead of looking on the internet for love in all the wrong places. I'm talking about real relationships, not false intimacies. To show love for people—that's what the show is about." Each caller is, briefly, famous, her solitary life turned into a national narrative. Girls' night out, lonely hearts club, universal pain association. *Delilah* is a relentless valentine for and about the struggling class, a trump card for those holding an empty hand. Delilah offers the possibility of ordinary American female life redeemed by . . . by what? The sugar rush of over-the-moon sentiment. In five hours at her house one day, I ate pancakes and syrup for breakfast, cookies for lunch, and ice cream for an afternoon pick-me-up. The hungry heart will be cured by sweetness itself. Delilah wants every call to end on an "audio hug" of empathy and recognition, and it does, it does. Inevitably she lifts us up where we belong—where the eagles fly, etc.—even as her own life remains obdurately earthbound.

"I made just about every mistake a person could make before God came into my heart," Delilah told me. "If some of those painful experiences can help someone avoid the same mistakes I made, then perhaps my heartache was not totally in vain."

Delilah Rene Luke, the second of four children, was born in North Bend, Oregon, on February 15, 1960. When I asked if, as a divorced mother of twelve, she attached any symbolism to being born one day after Valentine's Day—missed it by that much?—she shrugged and said that the only significance is that if she'd been born a day earlier, she would have been named Valerie. In seventh grade, she won a speech contest by reciting the Gettysburg Address. The judges of the contest owned the local radio station, and she soon had her own show, *Delilah Luke, on the Warpath*—school news and sports. In high school she had a part-time position at the station, writing and reading afternoon newscasts. After working as a DJ and newscaster on two small stations in Eugene, Oregon, she moved to Seattle, where she did traffic, rock, and jazz. She worked for stations in Boston, Philadelphia, and Rochester, then in 1996 started doing *Delilah After Dark*. The show was originally broadcast in three cities and expanded to more than two hundred in four years.

A caller named Jan says, "Thank you for allowing the world to know that music has no color. I appreciate that."

Delilah knows what Jan means, but she plays dumb: "Music has a myriad of colors, actually. It's passionate reds and bright yellows and bluesy blues."

Jan: "Let me rephrase that. When I say 'color,' I mean—"

Delilah: "Prejudice?"

Delilah is white; most of her children—three biological, nine adopted—have African American, African, or Hispanic ancestry. She's thrice-divorced.

In 1982, when she brought her African American husband home to meet her parents, her father "freaked out and jumped up and ran to the gun closet. He chased me off with a shotgun." Her father disowned her, and when he was dying, he refused to allow her to visit.

By 1986, Delilah and her first husband had divorced. ("He was the love of my life I will love until I die," she told me. "He's charismatic and sexy and sweet, and we had a wonderful love." Delilah worried about his capacity to stay faithful.) Her brother, Matthew Mark Luke, and his wife had died in a plane crash. She had been fired from a radio station. She said that one night she thought, *God, if You exist, I need to know;* the next day, when she went shopping, she found something stuck beneath the windshield wiper of her car. "I got nearer and saw that tucked under my wiper was a tiny book—a Bible. Inside someone had written, 'Jesus Loves You.'"

She views her success as divinely inspired: "It is because of God's faith in me that my show is successful. It is the only reason that my show is successful. God wants people to know that He is real, that He cares, that He listens. He wants people to experience the deep joy that comes from an intimate relationship with Him."

A disproportionately high percentage of callers are raising two or three children without the father, who has left or was never there. Asked what kind of man she's attracted to, Delilah says, "You've got to be quick, bright, funny—and a mass murderer. I could walk into a crowd of five thousand men and pick out the two biggest jerks. Ever since I was a teenager, I'd pick out a guy that would break my heart. Because my father was so passionate and smart and so brilliant and so emotionally not available—that, I guess, is what I'm attracted to." Delilah and the show are father-fixated, redressing the absent or dead or distant father by positing an all-knowing, all-loving God.

Delilah embodies the ambivalence her audience feels toward competing definitions of being female. Her voice is half-tease, half-hug, which is what she looks like: ex-bombshell/mother of the year. When I met her, she was wearing a low-cut blouse, which emphasized her décolletage, but she tended to pull up her blouse and cross her arms over her chest. Espousing self-esteem to her listeners, she nevertheless confided to Bulman, "My legs are the only part of myself I like." In most photos, she appears to be an all-American blonde, but she frequently reminds her listeners that her hair color comes from Kmart.

Donna calls to say, "Unfortunately, not long after my daughter Cassandra was born, her dad decided he didn't want the responsibility and left. Needless to say, I was devastated and didn't know what to do, but my mom was there for me. She helped me get through the roughest time in my life. She was my voice, my shrink; she was my everything." *She* is always everything to everybody; *he* is inevitably null and void. If *Delilah* offers feminism lite/feminism late, it needs to do so in an extremely traditional, even conservative context, so it tucks its delinquent-dad demolition into an ode to family.

When I asked Delilah whether she thinks of herself and the show as feminist, she replied, "I don't consider myself a feminist, and I don't consider myself not a feminist. I am a woman who works hard. I am a woman who deserves the same opportunities as any other person who is trying to make it in this business. The fact that I don't have a penis should not mean that I don't have the same opportunities, or that I should put up with prejudice or obstacles. It is a shame that I work in a format that is for and about women, and yet it is controlled almost completely by men, and women have little, if any, input. I am not a feminist in that I don't subscribe to a lot of their philosophies. I believe abortion is killing an unborn child."

Bulman responded to the same question by saying, "Delilah and I have many different political views but always a common goal. The *Delilah* show is, without a doubt, pro-woman. We want this show to make women—and men—feel better about themselves."

In *Love Someone Today*, Delilah writes, "I had romantic notions playing in my head of a midnight dance under the spectacular sky. I found him"—her last husband, when they were still married—"sleeping soundly in our bed. (He is less friendly when he is sleeping.) I tried to wake him. After several unsuccessful attempts, I gave up and walked out. I felt angry and rejected, my feelings hurt that he wouldn't jump up and enjoy my romantic fantasy with me. I zipped up my coat and headed out to the backyard again. I stood there, frozen in the beauty of the moment, yet still feeling a bit sorry for myself. I uttered a small prayer of praise, thanking the Almighty for this wonderful scene. And then, in a voice that was so clear it was almost audible, I heard God speak to my heart. 'I didn't create this moment for you and Doug,' He seemed to say. 'I created it for you and me.' And together we danced in the moonlight."

The world is a beautiful place, in other words, but men are oblivious, hopeless; as solace, *Delilah* presents romantic ballads about idealized lovers, narratives about children as cherubim, praise hymns about our Lord, our Father.

Mary calls to reminisce: "Mama's Nativity had a music box in it that played 'Silent Night,' but it was very old. I think she bought it before she and my father met. Some of the chimes were broken, so our 'Silent Night' was very strange, but we all liked it."

Delilah laughs and says, "It was nearly silent."

Mary says, "No, it wasn't nearly silent. It just was—you missed a lot of the melody and you got a lot of the accompaniment, and it just made it very unusual. My dad did woodworking as a hobby. One summer he got a catalogue that had music boxes, so he ordered a 'Silent Night.' Without telling anybody, he got out the Nativity scene, changed the music box, and threw away the old broken music box."

Delilah: "And it was never the same."

Mary: "And it's still not the same. Every one of us can still sing that old 'Silent Night' that played on that music box for so many years. When we wound it up and heard that it was correct, we all just really attacked him. He didn't know. He thought he was doing us a favor. And we were like, 'Oh, Daddy! How could you do that to us?' But we all still can sing that 'Silent Night,' that unusual version of it."

Delilah: "Let me hear it."

Mary: "Well, there's no words, but . . ." She hums the tune.

Once, a long time ago, something happened. It's never been the same since. It was Dad's fault. We'll forgive him and sort of not forgive him. What sustains us is religion and ritual and the broken music box, which Dad inevitably tries to fix and isn't fixable and is us.

KAREN

Karen Shabetai, dead at forty-four.

When you were around her, you sometimes felt like a bit of a jerk, because you knew you weren't as good a person as she was. You weren't as generous, as kind, as civilized, as communal, as energetic, as fun (Karen riding the elevator seated atop her bike with her helmet still on). She gave the best parties in Seattle, at least the Seattle that I know. She made belonging to part of something larger than yourself—a discipline, a city, a religion—seem like a possibility. She had the most and best tips for what school to send your children to, what summer camps, where to travel (Rome, Rome, and Rome, apparently), what to see, what to read.

Once, masquerading as a scholar, I applied for an NEH fellowship, and I swear Karen spent more time on the application than I did (still no luck!). Having her students in my creative writing classes was a distinctly mixed blessing: They were inevitably among the most well-prepared students in the course, but they expected me to be as dedicated a teacher as Karen was. She believed in the continuity of culture in a way that I pretend to but don't, and one of my most luminous memories is of her daughter, Sophie, playing the violin at a birthday party for Karen.

It's important to remind myself that Karen was sweet but not too sweet; the loving and challenging contentiousness between Karen and Ross was and is to me a model of a successful marriage. One night, Laurie and I and Karen and Ross saw *Il Postino,* and afterward we went out to dinner at an Italian restaurant. The waiter at the restaurant was so Italian, so obviously an extra who had somehow (*Purple Rose of Cairo*–like) escaped from *Il Postino,* that Karen and I virtually—no, not virtually: literally—had to stick napkins in our mouths every time he came by to inquire about us. Laurie and Ross were considerably more composed, but Karen and I were beyond rescue.

A FABLE

One summer, a friend of Laurie's worked as a graphic artist in a T-shirt shop in Juneau, Alaska. Cruise ships would dock, unloading old passengers, who would take taxis or buses a dozen or so miles to Mendenhall Glacier, which is a hundred square kilometers—twenty-five thousand acres—and whose highest point rises a hundred feet above Mendenhall Lake. Once, a tourist said about the glacier, "It looks so dirty. Don't they ever wash it?" On their way back to the boat, one or two ancient mariners would invariably come into the shop and ask Laurie's friend if he would mail their postcards for them. Able to replicate people's handwriting exactly, he would add postscripts to the postcards: "Got laid in Ketchikan," "Gave head in Sitka," etc.

What do I love so much about this story? I could say, as I'm supposed to say, "I don't know—it just makes me laugh," but really I do know. It's an ode on my favorite idea: language is all we have to connect us, and it doesn't, not quite.

III. ATHLETES

*The gulf between an onlooker and a boxer is as vast
as the one between a man and a woman.*

—ZOË WEISS

ANOTHER FABLE

The kicker made the field goal, and as the game went to commercial, the kick was shown again in slow motion. The camera was positioned in such a way that the ball kept spinning higher into the upper-right-hand corner of the screen. At the end of the replay the ball was out of view, and for a held moment the screen showed only black, on a Monday night, November 6, 1989, in San Francisco, three weeks after the earthquake. For a second, there was just the night in all its elegiac beauty. The shot conveyed terror, but only for a moment. Then graphics came up.

WORDS CAN'T BEGIN TO DESCRIBE
WHAT I'M FEELING

'll be honest with you: I'm here to tell you: The big key is: The bottom line is:

There's no question about it. There's no doubt about it. You got that right. I couldn't agree with you more. Obviously, the statistics speak for themselves.

He's a highly touted freshman. Last week was his coming-out party. He has all the makings of a great one. He has unlimited potential. He's a can't-miss prospect. You'll be hearing a lot from him. He can play at the next level. He can play on Sundays. He's got his whole future ahead of him. He's a youngster who bears watching. He's being groomed for a future starting job. The team is really high on him. He's going to set the world on fire. He's a rookie phenom.

He moves well for a big man. He's sneaky-fast. He has lightning-fast reflexes. He has great lateral mobility. He can pick 'em up and put 'em down. He has speed *and* quickness. He's a cutter and a slasher. He has speed to burn. He's fleet-footed. He's a speed merchant. He can fly. You can't teach speed.

He's a unique physical specimen. He has a low center of gravity. He plays bigger than his size. He's built like a brick outhouse. He's a stud. He's a warrior. He's a bulldog. He has a linebacker mentality. He's fearless. He's a physical player. He's an impact player.

He's a tough, hard-nosed player. He's their spark plug. He's their role player. He understands his role on this team. He lets the game come to him. He's the consummate team player. He's an unselfish player. He's a real throwback. He plays with a lot of emotion. He has a passion for the game. He always gives 110 percent. He plays for the name on the front of the jersey, not the name on the back of it.

He's their playmaker. He's their field general. He's their floor general. He's a good table-setter. He's the glue that holds this team together. He makes the players around him better. He's a stand-up guy. The team looks to him for leadership. He's a leader on this team. He's a leader on and off the field.

He's a true professional. He's a professional hitter. He just goes out there and gets the job done. I was just doing my job. I was just hoping I could make a contribution in whatever way they needed me.

He's some kind of player. He's the real deal. He's legit. He can flat-out play. He's as good a player as there is in this league. He's one of the best in the business. He's a franchise player. Players like that don't come along very often. He's in a league of his own. He's a future Hall of Famer. He's a first-ballot lock. You can't say enough about him.

He's got ice water running through his veins. He's got the guts of a burglar. He thrives under pressure. He always comes through in the clutch. He always comes through at crunch time. He's their go-to guy when the game's on the line. He's money. He can carry the team on his shoulders. He can take them to the promised land.

He's shooting well from downtown. He's making a living behind the arc. He's getting some good open looks. He's shooting the lights out. He's in a zone. He's feeling it. He's in a groove. He's lighting it up. He's on fire. He's hot. He's locked in. He's unconscious.

He blew 'em away.

They pay him to make those catches. That pass was very catchable. He's usually a sure-handed receiver. He usually makes that catch. He heard footsteps. He's become a little gun-shy. He's got all the skills—he just needs to put them together. He needs to bulk up in the off-season. He needs to elevate his game. He's playing out of position. He lacks the killer instinct.

He's only played sparingly this season. He's the subject of trade rumors. He's being shopped around. He's on the trading block. He's bounced around a lot. He's a journeyman. He's the player to be named later. He's lost a step. He's their elder statesman. He has a new lease on life. I just want to give something back to the community. He's a great role model. He's a winner in the bigger game of life. I just want to be able to take care of myself and my family.

He doesn't have that good fastball today. He's getting by with breaking stuff. He took something off that pitch. He's getting shelled. He's getting rocked. They're teeing off on him. Stick a fork in him—he's done. They need to pull the plug. He hits the showers. Today I didn't have my plus-stuff. Regardless of what kind of stuff you have on a given day, you just try to go out there and pitch to the best of your ability and give your team an opportunity to win.

He got hung out to dry on that play. That was blown coverage. That was a missed assignment. They're playing in the shadow of their goalposts. He couldn't turn the corner. They're looking at third down and forever. They have to establish the running game. They have to air it out more. They have to take care of the football. That missed extra point could come back to haunt them. You gotta hit the holes they make for you. You gotta follow your blockers out there. He's been quiet so far—they need to get him some more carries in the second half. This is their deepest penetration of the half. They've got to punch it in from here. They can't cough it up here. They need to just go out and make football plays.

He has all the time in the world. He has all day back there. He has all kinds of time. He has an eternity. He threw into double coverage. He threw up a prayer. He'd like to have that one back.

We just couldn't execute. We weren't able to sustain anything. They got us out of our game plan early. They took us completely out of our rhythm.

We got beat like a gong. They beat us like a drum. They outplayed us. We ran into a buzz saw. Turnovers absolutely killed us. We didn't get any calls. Sometimes this game just comes down to the way the ball bounces. We didn't get any breaks. They were the better team today. Give them credit. We just didn't get the job done. We weren't mentally prepared. For some reason they've just got our number. We didn't come to play. They stepped up and made football plays. Football players make football plays. They wanted it more than we did.

This was a wake-up call. I tip my hat to them. We beat ourselves. We only have to look in the mirror. I don't want to point any fingers. We came up a little short. We had our chances. They outplayed us in every phase of the game. They just made the big plays and we didn't. We dug ourselves a deep hole. We have to put this loss behind us. It's going to be a long plane ride home.

The coach is on the hot seat. His head is on the chopping block. Unfortunately, there are days like this. We're in the business of winning. It's the nature of this business. It's time to move on. We have to look forward. We need a change of direction. We need a clean slate. We need someone who can take us to the next level.

I feel the time has come for new leadership of this ball club. Everyone has to be held accountable. It's all about winning and losing. I take the blame. I'm not going to stand up here and make excuses. Obviously, I'm disappointed things didn't work out. This is my responsibility and I feel badly I haven't been able to get us where we should be. I want to thank our great fans. I'm looking forward to the next chapter in my life. First I'm going to spend more time with my family.

I'm excited about this opportunity. I'm looking forward to the challenge. I have high expectations for this team. This franchise has a great winning tradition. We've got a good solid foundation to build on. We're going to right the ship. We're going to get things turned around. This is a great sports town.

They stumbled coming out of the gate. They got off on the wrong foot. They're finally showing signs of life. They need a late surge. It's been an up-and-down season. It's a marathon, not a sprint.

This team is starting to make some noise. They've finally gotten off the schneid. The players have bought into the system. He's got them headed in the right direction. He's a players' coach. He's more of a people person than an X's and O's guy. These guys have been busting their tails for him. He gets the most out of his players. They've turned the corner. They've raised the bar. They've gotten over the hump. They're loaded this year. They're stacked. They have a strong supporting cast. There's no I in "team." They've added a new wrinkle to their offense. They're finally getting the respect they deserve. They're for real. They're here to stay. They're playing with newfound confidence. They've got great team chemistry. This team is like a family.

Everything's clicking. We're starting to gel. Everybody's on the same page. We're hitting on all cylinders now. Everybody's contributing.

We've got the league's best offense against the league's best defense—something's gotta give. We've got an intriguing matchup. This is a pivotal game. This game is for the bragging rights. These teams flat don't like each other. There's no love lost between these two teams. There's bad blood between these two teams. It's gonna be a war out there. When these two teams get together, you really *can* throw out their records.

You have to respect their athleticism. You have to respect their quickness. They have tremendous leaping ability. They can put up big numbers. They do a great job defensively. They play tough D.

They're feeling each other out. Here's the payoff pitch. He chased a bad pitch. Tough to lay off that pitch. Three up, three down. This is shaping up to be a real pitchers' duel. That ball should be playable. It's a can of corn. The ball took a bad hop. Strike-'im-out, throw-'im-out double play. Inning over. He got a good jump. That brings the tying run to the plate. He hits 'em where they ain't. He's a long-ball threat. He hit a solo shot back in the fifth. He's seeing the ball real well. He wears them out. He made good contact. He hit that ball squarely. He hit that ball on the sweet spot. He knocked the cover off the ball. In any other ballpark, that's a home run. Chicks dig the long ball. He's sitting dead red. He got all of it. He went yard. He hit it into the cheap seats. He flat jacked it. He went deep. He went downtown. Going, going, gone. It's outta here. See ya later. Goodbye, baseball. Kiss it goodbye. Aloha means goodbye.

It's been all theirs to this point. It's theirs to lose. They're not play-ing to win—they're playing not to lose. They're putting the ball in the deep freeze. They've gone four corners. Now's the time to run some clock.

Looks like we've got some extracurricular activity going on out there. Let's hope cooler heads prevail. They're mucking it up in the corner. He stood him up on the blue line. That's gotta hurt. He was mugged. He's gonna feel that one on Monday. Looks like we've got a player shaken up. Looks like he got his bell rung. That hit really cleaned his clock. He ran into a brick wall. He was literally run over by a freight train. He was blindsided. He's slow getting up. He was really clotheslined. They can ill afford to lose him. Their locker room must look like a MASH unit. X-rays are inconclusive. He left the field under his own power. We hate to speculate on the nature of the injury.

There's a flag on the play. It depends on where they spot it. Terrible call, terrible call. We got hosed. We got jobbed. We got robbed. Highway robbery. We knew it was going to be tough going up against the other team—I didn't know we were going to have to play the guys in the striped shirts as well. They're the best refs money can buy. The refs should just let them play. Bad calls even out over the course of a season.

It ain't over till it's over. As Yogi said, it ain't over till it's over. It ain't over till the fat lady sings. They won't go quietly. We've still got plenty of football left. No need to panic—there's plenty of time left.

You can feel the momentum shifting. Big Mo. They're going for the jugular. They can smell blood in the water. They're within striking distance. *Now* we've got a football game. It's a whole new ball game. This team shows a lot of character. This team shows a lot of poise. This team shows a lot of resiliency. This team shows a lot of heart.

It all started out with good field position. They've marched down the field. That was a goal-scorer's goal. He lit the lamp. He went high to the top shelf. He put the biscuit in the basket. He found the twine. He went upstairs. He nailed the buzzer-beater. She really stuck the landing. He hit pay dirt. Nothing but net. This should be a chip shot for him. The kick splits the uprights.

What an incredible turnaround.

We found a way to win. A win is a win. It wasn't pretty, but we'll take it. I'm really proud of the way our guys hung in there. This is always a tough place to play. We're just glad to get out of here with a *W.* We're happy we could pull this one out at the end. They're tough competitors. They gave us all we could handle. They're a class act. Give them a lot of credit. I tip my hat to them. There are no easy games in this league. The game was a lot closer than the final score indicates. They weren't going to come in here and just lie down for us. We're going to use this as a building block. We'll use this win as a stepping-stone to the next level.

What a difference a week makes.

We were really on our game. We took them out of their game.

We really came to play. We brought our A game. We knew what we had to do and went out and did it. We answered the call. This team has finally learned how to win. It was a total team effort. Obviously, this was a great win for us. It was a big win for us. We came to play. We stuck to the game plan. We wanted to make a statement. We sent a message. We came through when it counted. We're going to savor the victory tonight, then tomorrow morning we'll start looking at film.

The only thing that matters in the Stanley Cup playoffs is the man between the pipes. You can't win an NBA championship without a dominant big man. You can't win in the NFL without establishing the run. Offense puts fannies in the seats—defense wins championships. You've got to have pitching if you're going to make it through the postseason.

We just need to go out there and take care of business. It all just comes down to execution. You can't leave anything on the table. We have to go out and leave it all on the ice. We need to bring it. We need to dig deeper than we've ever dug before. We just gotta go out tomorrow and have fun.

They've battled back from the brink of elimination. They're down but not out. They're in a must-win situation. They need a win to stave off elimination. Lose and go home. Go big or go home. There's no tomorrow. I know it's a cliché, but we just have to take it one game at a time.

We gotta stick to the basics. We need to remember what got us here. You gotta dance with who brung you. This is it. This is for all the marbles.

They need to keep up their intensity. They have to stay focused. They have to get after it. They have to rise to the occasion. They've got tremendous mental toughness. They're a blue-collar team. They're overachievers. They've come out of nowhere. They're a real Cinderella story. They have to stay hungry. They're loaded for bear.

The city has rallied around this team. We've got die-hard fans. We feed off the energy of our fans. Our fans are our twelfth man. We've got the greatest fans in the world.

We're happy to be in the postseason and now we want to go out there and do some damage. We're capable of going deep in the postseason. We're not just happy to be here. This team has a chance to do something special. Hopefully, we can steal one on the road. In the playoffs, anything can happen.

Game time.

The fans are on their feet. This crowd is going wild. This place is a madhouse. This place is pandemonium. You can feel the electricity. Ya gotta love these fans. Ya gotta love this game.

HEAVEN IS A PLAYGROUND

I'm a sucker for sports movies. Netflix must think I'm training to coach high school football and basketball. Although she'd never expressed the slightest interest in it, I insisted on taking Natalie, at nine, to see *The Rookie* (we loved it!). Why do I have such an affinity for sports movies? Not good sports movies, though, such as *Bang the Drum Slowly,* or melancholy sports movies, such as *North Dallas Forty,* or great sports movies, such as *Raging Bull,* but the pure sugar solution itself. *Hoosiers. Angels in the Outfield. Rookie of the Year. Field of Dreams. For Love of the Game. Ladybugs. Mr. Baseball. Rudy. Rocky. The Natural. The Air Up There. Hardball. Karate Kid. Major League. The Replacements.* Why, despite knowing how formulaic these films are, am I invariably moved when watching them, often to the point of tears? What story are they telling that appeals—at least to me—on such a primitive level? And how can the same story get told—why does the same story need to be told—over and over and over?

In *For Love of the Game,* Kevin Costner plays a character named Billy Chapel. In *Downhill Racer,* Robert Redford is David Chapellet. In *Hoosiers,* the player who saves the team is named *Jimmy Chit-*

wood. In *He Got Game,* Denzel Washington's son is named Jesus. Sports movies, which need to convince the viewer to care about fictional contests between nonexistent teams, borrow the grammar of resurrection and salvation. Something has to be at stake in the game other than the final score; the script inevitably moves in the direction of religious iconography.

Major League begins by informing the viewer that Cleveland last won the World Series in 1948. *Rookie of the Year* opens with similar information about the Chicago Cubs (last World Series win: 1908). The overture of *Field of Dreams* is the voice-over narrator's ode to his dead father, who nearly made it to the bigs. In *Hoosiers,* we immediately learn that the Indiana high school team Gene Hackman coaches last won the state championship in 1951. Walter Matthau, now a Little League coach in *Bad News Bears,* was once a major-league pitcher. So was Tom Hanks, now coaching a women's team, in *A League of Their Own.* Rocky, as a photo of him on his dresser makes evident, was once a happy kid with light in his eyes; he takes the photo off the mirror and holds it up, comparing what he was to what he's become. Costner, in *For Love of the Game,* was earlier in his career an All-Star pitcher—"golden, one of the giants." The first, crucial gesture many sports movies make is for the protagonist to say, sub rosa or not so sub rosa, to the viewer, *We once strode the earth as gods.*

An alternative scenario is that long ago, in the primordial past, the hero fucked up. History is a nightmare from which he is—all of us are—trying to awake. He gets a second chance to come back to life; he better not blow it. In *The Best of Times,* Robin Williams drops a pass in the big game against the high school down the road. He spends the rest of his life being pummeled for this failing and finally gets a chance to redeem himself. In *The Replacements,* Keanu Reeves has never recovered from his mysteriously awful performance in the 1996 Sugar Bowl, but he now gets an opportunity as a replacement player for the striking pros. Paralleling Reeves's transformation, the disco hit "I Will Survive" goes from locker room joke to oddly moving anthem of personal redemption and team solidarity.

In either version, we get evicted from paradise. We're lost in a vast desert. *Major League* begins with a vast desert, literally. The team's training camp is in Arizona; a lizard crawls among the cacti just outside the field. The Indians' roster, in *Major League,* features a voodoo worshipper, one player who can't hit the ball fair, another who can't throw it straight. The play-by-play man is a drunk; the color man never says a word. It's a freak show. In *Field of Dreams*, the wounded warriors on the yellow brick road are a blocked writer, a player who got into only one game and never had an at-bat, a man who never made it to the major leagues, and a melancholy soul unfairly tarnished by scandal. In *Bad News Bears*, the Little League team is sponsored by Chico's Bail Bonds, and the players include a black kid, a Hispanic kid, a Jewish kid, a fat kid, a shy kid, a bookworm, and a kid who's been abused by his parents, all of whom are mocked by the WASP kid. The dramatis personae of *The Replacements*: a deaf guy, a sumo wrestler, a couple of bodyguards, an insane SWAT team cop, a wide receiver who can't catch, a thief. We're living in the land of the damned.

The team is, needless to say, losing. Some of this is simple narrative typology: A romantic comedy can't begin with the lovers in a happy embrace. This goes beyond that, though. It's a plague of losing streaks. We're losing. We're losers. We're bums. We're in a state of infinite regress, of existential failure. In the land of opportunity, we are antimatter. In *Slap Shot*, the players are trapped in Pennsylvania's Federal League; in *Bull Durham*, it's minor-league A-ball; in *The Replacements*, they're scabs replacing the real NFL players; in *Field of Dreams*, we're in Iowa, with players forever shadowed by the 1919 Black Sox scandal; in *Rocky*, the setting is South Philly; *Hardball* takes place on the South Side of Chicago; in *For Love of the Game*, we're with the Detroit Tigers, a team that has an illustrious past but hasn't won in decades. And they're playing the Yankees, who figure in many baseball films as the Goliath whom David must slay or die trying. These films are, by definition, obsessed with the underside of the American Dream—the detritus of Yankee triumphalism. As a corollary, movies such as *Paper Lion, Lucas, Tin Cup, Rocky, Bad News Bears, A League of Their Own,* and *Rudy* are odes to perpetual losers who succeed by the force of their trying; they fail, but their failure is noble, because, determined to succeed but overpowered by forces of economics, personal psychology, and body type, they nevertheless get their groove back. We can identify: our body types might not be so ideal, either.

The owners in sports movies are eleven kinds of asshole: They're money-obsessed; they want to fire the hero; they want to sell the team; they want to move the team to Miami. Why, in so many movies, Miami? It's both heaven (paradisal retreat from the workaday world of, say, *Slap Shot*'s Pennsylvania rust belt) and hell (retreat and descent from, say, *Slap Shot*'s Pennsylvania rust belt, which gains a heavenly aura once the balm of athletic glory has been applied to it). If the player often becomes a Christ figure, the owner is clearly a stand-in for the Pharisees, the Roman officers, the Jewish priests, the money changers. Athletes are in touch with the gods—that's why we love them—but the only god the owner is in touch with is Midas. In movie after movie, the owner's younger, voluptuous wife pours alcohol down her throat or stuffs her face with food or stuffs her yappy little dog's face with food, because hubby-made-of-money doesn't satisfy in the sack. She wants, implicitly or (in a few films) explicitly, the players, who are "real," or a particular player, who is particularly "real," the irony being that this player is always Paul Newman or Keanu Reeves or Nick Nolte or Kevin Costner or Robert Redford. He's real, but he's a movie star. "He's an animal," as *The Babe* has it; "No, he's a god."

This suits-versus-jocks animus is the narrative tension of many sports movies, for these films frequently return to the opposition between the social (which is corrupt) and the body (which is miraculous). The three-act structure of every studio-produced American movie mandates that Plot Point A occur right around the twenty-seven-minute mark. The next hour is then devoted to the complications arising from Plot Point A. Twenty minutes before the end, Plot Point B occurs, which spins the action downward to its conclusion. In many sports movies—*The Natural, Angels in the Outfield, Rookie of the Year, Field of Dreams, Like Mike*—Plot Point A is the discovery of the protagonist's inexplicable athletic prowess; in many other sports movies the magic element is introduced at exactly this same point, but the magic is more figurative. The next hour consists of a debate between various forces of social corruption and the force of this mysterious power, and then at the end of the film the magic is triumphant. The magic, though, is no longer supernatural ability—which has usually dissipated by now (Plot Point B)—but the redemptive power of love.

And so the son plays catch with the father, resurrected (in *Field of*

Dreams). Our hero pitches a perfect game (in *For Love of the Game*). We win. We win. We win the big game. We reconcile generations, races, the war between the sexy sexes. We win the pennant. We make it to the majors. We get to play in the big game. We're finally on the interstate; we're no longer trapped on the service roads. We hit the home run. We save the team from bankruptcy, departure, ignominy, collapse. We defeat the bully opponent (the Yankees, the fascistic karate coach). We come together as a team, especially that; we're now all pulling on the same oar. In *Field of Dreams,* Ray's brother-in-law, that Pharisee, that money changer, tells Ray, "Just sign the papers. Sell now or you'll lose everything. You're broke. When the bank opens in the morning, they'll foreclose." James Earl Jones thunders back, "Ray, people will come [to the baseball field Ray has imagined into existence in his backyard]. They'll come to Iowa for reasons they can't fathom. They'll turn up your driveway, not knowing for sure why they're doing it. They'll arrive at your door, as innocent as children longing for the past. And they'll walk off to the bleachers, sit in shirt-sleeves on a perfect afternoon, and they'll find they have reserved seats somewhere along one of the baselines where they sat when they were children and cheered their heroes, and they'll watch the game, and it will be as if they dipped themselves in magic waters."

"Magic waters": baptism, one of the seven sacraments of the Catholic Church, is frequently called the "first sacrament," "the door of the sacraments," and the "door of the church." *Field of Dreams* isn't about Ray Kinsella (Costner) sacrificing his body—he's not an athlete—but baptism is a good way of understanding the movie's signature line, "If you build it, they will come." Ray is building a baseball field, but he's also building a door of the church. Does James Earl Jones die when he walks into the cornfield? The players who show up, including Ray's father, are most certainly dead, but here they are, playing catch. In baptism, we're "buried with Him into death," but it's also a "likeness of His resurrection": an immersion, followed by an emersion. "Is this heaven?" Ray's father, John, asks Ray. Ray says, "It's Iowa." "Iowa?" John says. "I could have sworn this was heaven." "Is there a heaven?" Ray asks. "Oh yeah," John replies. "It's the place where dreams come true." Ray, watching his wife play with their daughter on the front porch, says, "Maybe this is heaven." Paradise regained: Heaven is a playground. The movie—any sports movie—becomes a praise song to life here on earth, to physical existence itself, beyond striving, beyond economic necessity. G. K. Chesterton: "Earth is a task garden; heaven is a playground."

In *Ladybugs,* Rodney Dangerfield protests to his type A boss, "'The best, the best'—that's all I keep hearing. You want to be the best [have him coach the boss's daughter's soccer team to the championship]. Well, let me ask you this: What good is being the best if it brings out the worst in you?" What shall it profit a man if he gain the world but lose his soul? This is the semi-interesting middle path that nearly all of these films try to walk—finding a way for the protagonist to be successful without the film endorsing a bland Ben Franklin/Jay Gatsby/Horatio Alger/Little Engine That Could ethos of dogged American striving. The films need to be critiques of win-at-all-costs relentlessness and at the same time figure out a way for their heroes to succeed. In *Remember the Titans* and *For Love of the Game,* respectively, Denzel Washington's and Kevin Costner's Achilles' heel is shown to be workaholism; by the end of the film, they learn to give a little, to discover the *homo ludens* gene hidden somewhere still in their psyche, to learn to depend on themselves a bit less and others a bit more, to cut others some slack; supporting players aren't made of the same stern stuff as the hero, after all. In *Breaking Away,* Dave Stohler doesn't cheat, as the Italian bikers do, but he wins the race with a little help from his friends. In *Mr. Baseball,* Tom Selleck learns from his Japanese teammates that in some circumstances what's called for isn't the Americanish long ball; it's the Japanese-style bunt. In *Hoosiers,* Gene Hackman is, as the town elders are not, willing to let the team lose for the sake of a principle; this very principledness is the source of his and the team's salvation. In *Karate Kid,* Mr. Miyagi teaches Daniel not how to focus monomaniacally on winning the karate tournament (as the opposing coach, a Vietnam vet, does with his charges) but how to think seriously and truly about karate; Daniel also wins the tournament, of course. In *Bad News Bears,* Walter Matthau isn't prepared to go all out to win the big game; it doesn't matter anymore, because the Bears are now bad news to the opposition rather than to themselves. Exactly the same thing happens in *Hardball*: Keanu Reeves's charges lose the final game. Who cares? They're alive again, despite or perhaps because of their saintly teammate Jarius's death. In *Democracy in America,* Alexis de Tocqueville writes, "A democracy finds it difficult to coordinate the details of a great undertaking and to fix on some plan and carry it through with determination in spite of obstacles. It has little capacity for combining measures in secret and waiting patiently for the result. Such qualities are more likely to belong to a single man or to an aristocracy." These movies solve the dilemma of democracy—the difficult negotiation between individual striving and egalitarian community—by praising the ragtag team but really praising the charismatic leader who galvanizes the team. Who wouldn't want to be on that team, led by that leader?

Hell is not, then, as it is in the Euro version, other people, but self, and heaven is team. In Al Pacino's speech to the troops as the coach in *Any Given Sunday,* he says, "We're in hell right now, gentlemen, believe me. And we can stay here—get the shit kicked out of us—or we fight our way back into the light. We can climb out of hell one inch at a time. And I know if I'm going to have any life anymore it's because I'm still willing to fight and die for that inch. Because that's what living is: the six inches in front of your face. Now, I think you're going to see a guy who will sacrifice himself for this team, because he knows, when it comes down to it, you're going to do the same for him. That's a team, gentlemen, and either we heal now as a team, or we will die as individuals. That's football; that's all it is. Now what are you gonna do?" Our "flaws"—we're selfish, we're drunks, we're divorced, separated, we're hotheads, we're kleptomaniacs, we're superstitious, we're drug addicts, we can't throw, can't catch, can't field, can't shoot, can't run, are afraid, are headstrong, are too big, too small, we're women, we're Jewish, we're black, we're fat, we're kids, we're nearsighted, we're poor, we're hicks, we're Americans—are not just overcome; they define us and beatify us, sanctify us. And yet where would the Tin Woodman, the Scarecrow, and the Cowardly Lion be without Dorothy? Still in Kansas. This team needs a strong—a very strong—leader. And who is this leader? "Ah, buddy. Ah, buddy," as Salinger's Zooey would or, actually, does say. "It's Christ Himself. Christ Himself, buddy."

In *For Love of the Game,* Costner moves from person to person, healing their wounds and absolving them of their sins, not to mention fixing their cars, offering sage advice, dispensing gentle witticisms, and tipping megagenerously. This debt is repaid in full at the end of the movie, when the veteran catcher comes out to the mound in the ninth inning of Costner's perfect game and tells him, "Chappy, you just throw whatever you got left. The boys are all here for you. We'll back you up. We'll be there. We don't stink right now. We're the best team in baseball right now, right this minute, 'cause of you. You're the reason. We're not going to screw that up. We're going to be awesome for you right now. Just throw." Athlete as alms giver. Christ and his twelve—in this case, eight—apostles. A shepherd and his sheep. Bathing the team in his love, he makes us better. He loves us into loving ourselves again. Many movies create a nimbus of moral light around the hero, but the pattern here is so insistent as to establish a mini-subgenre: sports movie as Passion Play. In *Field of Dreams,* Costner (again) must "ease his pain." Whose pain? His father's, but also Shoeless Joe Jackson's, Moonlight Graham's, Terrence Mann's, and ours, ours. Rocky loves people to death or, rather, out of their spiritual death; by the end of the film he has remade his shy girlfriend, his bitter coach, his unemployed friend. The first image of *Rocky* is of Christ holding a wafer at the Last Supper; Christ says, "This is my body, which will be given up for you." In the very next shot, Rocky is getting the shit beat out of him. In other movies, athletes sacrifice their bodies by playing with injuries *(Major League, Slap Shot)* or actually dying *(Hardball, Pastime).* The last image of *Rocky* is of Rocky in a close approximation of the *Pietà.* The athlete's bloodied body, given in battle for us, is the crux.

"And a little child shall lead them." Not only the Christ-hero but also the lowliest of us needs to come through as well. In *For Love of the Game,* Billy Chapel's best bud, the guy riding shotgun, the journeyman catcher, needs to come through with a big hit in the top of the ninth before Costner completes his perfect game in the bottom of the inning. *Hardball*'s Jarius, the littlest of the little, proves his mettle before being shot by drug runners and in whose honor they play the championship game. At Jarius's funeral, Keanu Reeves says, "With our hopes dwindling, he hit a shot down the first base line and we won the game. And watching him raise his arms in triumph as he ran to first base, I swear I was lifted in that moment to a better place. I swear he lifted the world for that moment. He made me a better person even if just for that moment. I am forever grateful to Jarius [Jesus?] for that." Even Merle, in *Hoosiers,* the blonde cherub, turns into Merlin and magically hits two free throws to propel Hickory into the state championship. Rudy, in *Rudy*, is a boy among men, but he shows the boy-men how to be men. So does Lucas in *Lucas*. The last shall be first.

And yet nearly every sports movie tends to elide the Big Moment. Weirdly, it often seems to just slide by. In part, this is because the structure of the movie is usually based on the rhythm of a season, so the climax of the film is making it to, say, the World Series; the World Series is a kind of heaven on earth, and since the movie can't show heaven on earth, it shows the ascension. The movie got you there: The viewer can imagine the rest (it's better that way). Watching *Field of Dreams*, we really want to know what's on the other side of the cornfield, but we're never fully enlightened.

What these films' endings aim to do instead is to extract from the relevant sport the perfect sports metaphor and dilate that. In *Karate Kid*, Daniel assumes the Crane Posture, which Mr. Miyagi had taught him early on and the value of which Daniel never understood; using it now, in the final moments of the karate championship, he seems to have gathered all that Mr. Miyagi has taught him and not only absorbed it as philosophy but used it as winning strategy. So, too, in *Personal Best*—a film about two female track stars, Chris and Tory, who become friends, lovers, antagonists, and friends again; at the end of the film, Chris sacrifices herself by running out to a lead too early and then creating an opening, a gap, a space (a female space), through which Tory can pass and thus join her friend in qualifying for the Olympics. The movie doesn't show the Olympics; it shows the striving. Sports movies are often very good at dramatizing this intersection of public and private realms: the body politic.

"Adrian!" Rocky shouts. "Adrian! Adrian!" Surrounded by admirers after he has lasted fifteen rounds with Apollo Creed, Rocky wants only to see his beloved. The ending of innumerable sports movies replicates this moment: The applause of the crowd must be there, but once there, it's deemed inconsequential, background noise. This is a metaphor for being in a movie audience and wanting to be with that audience, needing the human heat of a crowd, but also needing to commune with the screen in a private, rhapsodic way, just you and the star. You and the crowd; then you and the star. Also, you and your sweetheart, and you and the world. Agape and Eros. You want the world to love you, but then you want someone to be there to love you while the world is loving you, so the two of you can tell yourself the world's admiration doesn't matter. Which it does and which it doesn't.

So far I've tried, I suppose, to maintain a certain exegetical distance toward the mythic structure of feel-good sports movies, but listen to this: Thirty-plus years ago, the actor Craig T. Nelson bought the rights to my first novel, *Heroes,* and hired me to adapt the book into a screenplay, though the movie never got made. Over the decades, I kept tinkering with the script, at one point reducing it to a twenty-page treatment. I just pulled it out of a drawer, and whaddya know? The losing team, the town in the toilet. The shepherd leading his sheep to the Land of Oz. Becoming successful but rejecting winning at all costs. And a little child shall lead them. The elision of the big moment. The perfect sports metaphor. The praise song to existence here, now, on earth, beyond worldly care. Virtually every sports-movie motif that I've tracked in this essay I found in full force in my synopsis, written many years ago. And yet I'd never particularly gone to school on these movies, until now. Which suggests that (a) I've watched way too many sports movies over the years; (b) I have or had an embarrassingly formulaic imagination; or (c) this narrative is simply out there in the culture and we (men, especially, since men don't give birth; women already suffer physically to give life to us all) will forever be drawn to it—a lullaby of salvation told by and about the body.

LIFE IS NOT A PLAYGROUND

There has always been some strange connection for me between basketball and the dark. I started shooting hoops after school in fourth grade, and I remember dusk and macadam combining into the sensation that the world was dying, but I was indestructible.

One afternoon I played H-O-R-S-E with a third grader, Renée Hahn, who threw the ball over the fence and said, "I don't want to play with you anymore. You're too good. I'll bet one day you're going to be a San Francisco Warrior."

Renée had a way of moving her body like a boy but still like a girl, too, and that game of H-O-R-S-E is one of the happiest memories of my childhood: dribbling around in the dark but knowing by instinct where the basket was; not being able to see her but smelling her sweat; keeping close to her voice, in which I could hear her love for me and my future life as a Warrior opening up into the night. I remember the sloped half-court at the far end of the playground, its orange pole, orange rim, and wooden green backboard, the chain net clanging in the wind, the sand on the court, the overhanging eucalyptus trees, the fence the ball bounced over into the street, and the bench the girls sat on, watching, trying to look bored.

The first two weeks of summer Renée and I went steady, but we broke up when I didn't risk rescuing her in a game of Capture the Flag, so she wasn't around for my tenth birthday. I begged my parents to let Ethan Saunders, Jim Morrow, Bradley Gamble, and me shoot baskets by ourselves all night at the court across the street. My mother and father reluctantly agreed, and my father swung by every few hours to make sure we were safe and bring more Coke, more birthday cake, more candy.

Near midnight, Bradley and I were playing two-on-two against Jim and Ethan. The moon was falling. We had a lot of sugar in our blood, and all of us were totally zonked and totally wired. With the score tied at eighteen in a game to twenty, I took a very long shot from the deepest corner. Before the ball had even left my hand, Bradley said, "Way to hit."

I was a good shooter because it was the only thing I ever did and I did it all the time, but even for me such a shot was doubtful. Still, Bradley knew and I knew and Jim and Ethan knew, too, and we knew the way we knew our own names or the batting averages of the Giants' starting lineup or the lifelines in our palms. I felt it in my legs and up my spine, which arched as I fell back. My fingers tingled and my hand squeezed the night in joyful follow-through. We knew the shot was perfect, and when we heard the ball (a birthday present from my parents) whip through the net, we heard it as something we had already known for at least a second. What happened in that second during which we knew? Did the world stop? Did my soul ascend a couple of notches? What happens to ESP, to such keen eyesight? What did we have then, anyway, radar? When did we have to start working so hard to hear our own hearts?

As members of the Borel Junior High Bobcats, we worked out in a tiny gym with loose buckets and slippery linoleum and butcher-paper posters exhorting us on. I remember late practices full of wind sprints and tipping drills. One day the coach said, "Okay, gang, let me show you how we're gonna run picks for Dave."

My friends ran around the court, passing, cutting, and screening for me. All for me. Set plays for me to shoot from the top of the circle or the left corner—my favorite spots. It felt as if the whole world were weaving to protect me, then release me, and the only thing I had to do was pop my jumper. Afterward, we went to a little market down the street. I bought paper bags of penny candy for everybody, to make sure they didn't think I was going to get conceited.

The junior varsity played immediately after the varsity. At the end of the third quarter of the varsity game, all of us on the JV, wearing our good sweaters, good shoes, and only ties, would leave the gym to go change for our game. I loved leaving right when the varsity game was getting interesting; I loved everyone seeing us as a group, me belonging to that group, and everyone wishing us luck; I loved being part of the crowd and breaking away from the crowd to go play. And then when I was playing, I knew the spectators were out there, but they slid into the distance like the overhead lights.

As a freshman I was the JV's designated shooter, our gunner whenever we faced a zone. Long-distance shooting was a way for me to perform the most immaculate feat in basketball, to stay outside where no one could hurt me. I'd hit two or three in a row, force the other team out of its zone, and then sit down. I wasn't a creator. I couldn't beat anyone off the dribble, but I could shoot. Give me a step, some space, and a screen—a lot to ask for—and I was money in the bank.

The JV coach told me I had to learn to take the ball to the basket and mix it up with the big guys underneath. I didn't want to because I knew I couldn't. I already feared I was a full step slow.

That summer I played basketball. I don't mean that I got in some games when I wasn't working at A&W or that I tried to play a couple of hours every afternoon. I mean the summer of 1971 I played basketball. Period. Nothing else. Nothing else even close to something else. All day long that summer, all summer, all night until at least ten.

The high school court was protected by a bank of ice plants and the walls of the school. Kelly-green rims, with chain nets, were attached to half-moon boards that were kind only to real shooters. The court was on a grassy hill overlooking the street; when I envision Eden, I think of that court during that summer—shirts against skins, five-on-five, running the break.

Alone, I did drills outlined in an instructional book. A certain number of free throws and lay-ins from both sides and with each hand, hook shots, set shots from all over, turnaround jumpers, jumpers off the move and off the pass, tip-ins. Everything endlessly repeated. I wanted my shoulders to become as high hung as Warriors star Nate Thurmond's, my wrists as taut, my glare as merciless. After a while I'd feel as if my head were the rim and my body were the ball. I was trying to put my body completely inside my head. The basketball was shot by itself. At that point I'd call it quits, keeping the feeling.

My father would tell me, "Basketball isn't just shooting. You've got to learn the rest of the game." He set up garbage cans around the court that I had to shuffle-step through, then backpedal through, then dribble through with my right hand, left hand, between my legs, behind my back. On the dead run I had to throw the ball off a banked gutter so that it came back to me as a perfect pass for a layup—the rest of the game, or so I gathered.

Toward the end of my sophomore year—Mother's Day, actually—I went to the beach with my mother. After a while she dozed off, so I walked along the shore until I was invited to join a game of Tackle the Guy with the Ball. After I scored three times, several of the other guys ganged up to tackle the guy with the ball (me) and down I went. Suddenly my left leg was tickling my right ear, the water was lapping at my legs, and a crowd of a hundred people gathered around me to speculate as to whether I was permanently paralyzed.

The summer between my junior and senior years of high school, my father tried to work with me to get back my wind and speed after the long layoff due to my broken leg, but he gave up when it became obvious my heart wasn't in it. I realized I was now better at describing basketball and analyzing it than playing it. To my father's deep disappointment, I not only was not going to become a professional athlete; I was becoming, as he had been on and off throughout his life and always quite happily, a sportswriter. I was pitiless on our mediocre team and the coach called me *Ace,* as in "ace reporter," since I certainly wasn't his star ballhawk. I could still shoot when left open but couldn't guard anyone quick or shake someone who hounded me tough. I fell into the role of the guy with all the answers and explanations, the well-informed benchwarmer who knew how zones were supposed to work but had nothing to contribute on the floor himself.

That same summer, I went to the San Mateo County Fair with Renée Hahn, who had finally forgiven me for not rescuing her in Capture the Flag. Her knowledge of basketball hadn't increased greatly over the years, but she did know she wanted a pink panda hanging from a hook near the basketball toss.

The free-throw line was eighteen rather than fifteen feet away, and the ball must have been pumped to double its pressure, hard as a bike tire. My shot had to be dead on or it would bounce way off. I wasn't going to get any soft rolls out of this carnival. The rim was rickety, bent upward, and was probably closer to ten feet six inches than the regulation ten feet. A canopy overhung both sides of the rim, so I wasn't able to put any arc on my shot. With people elbowing me in back, I could hardly take a dribble to get in rhythm.

I won seven pandas. I got into a groove, and sometimes when I got into a groove from eighteen feet straightway, I couldn't come out of it. Standing among spilled paper cups and September heat and ice and screaming barkers and glass bottles and darts and bumper cars, Renée and I handed out panda bears to the next half-dozen kids who walked by. This struck me then, as it does now, as pretty much the culmination of existence: doing something well and having someone admire it, then getting to give away prizes together. Renée wound up working with me on the school paper that fall; I don't think I ever saw her happier than she was that afternoon.

I still like to roam new neighborhoods, checking out the courts. In Cranston, Rhode Island, there's a metal ring that looks like hanging equipment for your worst enemy. In Amherst, Virginia, a huge washtub is nailed to a tree at the edge of a farm. Rims without nets, without backboards, without courts, with just gravel and grass underfoot. One basket in West Branch, Iowa, has a white net blowing in the breeze and an orange shooter's square on the half-moon board. Backboards are made from every possible material and tacked to anything that stands still in a storm. Rims are set at every height, at the most cockeyed angles, and draped with nets woven out of everything from wire to lingerie. From Port Jervis, New York, to Medford, Oregon, every type and shape of post, court, board, and hoop.

I once felt joy in being alive and I felt this mainly when I was playing basketball and I rarely if ever feel that joy anymore and it's my own damn fault and that's life. Too bad.

44 TATTOOS

A tattoo is ink stored in scar tissue.

Archaeologists believe, based on marks they've seen on mummies, that human beings had tattoos as early as 4000 to 2000 BCE in Egypt. Around the same time or perhaps even earlier, tattooing developed in Japan and spread from there to Myanmar.

In 1998, thirty-five percent of NBA players had tattoos. Now, well over eighty percent have tattoos. Twenty percent of American adults have tattoos.

Asked by *Playboy* what he'd like people to know, NBA star Allen Iverson, now retired, said, "Tell them not to believe what they read or hear. Tell them to read my body. I wear my story every day, man." At the very end of the interview, Iverson said, "The minister at [his close friend] Rah's funeral said to look at your life as a book and stop wasting pages complaining, worrying, and gossiping. That's some deep shit right there."

In "contact" sports, such as basketball or football, there's a much higher percentage of tattooed players than in more "cerebral" sports, such as baseball, golf, or tennis.

While watching a basketball game on TV, Dakkan Abbe, founder of Fifty Rubies Productions, came up with the idea of NBA players selling space on their bodies to plug products with temporary tattoos. Abbe wanted someone with "bad boy" appeal, so he approached Rasheed Wallace, who once set an NBA record for the most technical fouls in a season, about a candy-bar tattoo. Wallace's agent, Bill Strickland, said there's "nothing in any basic agreement [between the players' association and the league] that forbids advertising on the human body." An NBA spokesman said, "We don't allow commercial advertising on our uniforms, our coaches, or our playing floors, so there's no reason to think we'll allow it on our players." Abbe said, "The NBA is defining tattoos as part of the players' uniforms, but a player's skin is not part of his uniform. I find it offensive that the league would not allow something on someone's skin. Whenever the topic of tattoos comes up, the league says things like, 'We prefer if players didn't have tattoos.' The very nature of tattoos is disturbing to the NBA. The league is a little bit out of touch with the players and fans. Tattoos are a very explicit example of that. They just don't understand what tattoos are about." Strickland said, "Being a lawyer, I thought it presented some interesting free speech issues," but he finally decided not to press the case. Stephon Marbury, who used to play in the NBA and now plays for the Beijing Ducks, asked if he'd wear a tattoo advertisement, said, "Depends on how much money they'd pay. If they're paying the right money: yeah." Selling, say, his left shoulder to a shoe company, would Marbury be losing control over his body or exerting control over capitalism?

·　　·　　·

In the *Tattoo* magazine supplement to the New Orleans tattoo convention, an inordinately buxom but somehow slightly demure-looking blonde is on the cover, wearing a sailor hat, fishnet stockings, a short red skirt, white gloves, a bra top, and a couple of tattoos. Behind her in black shadow is a dark-haired woman dressed in a leopard costume. The function of the blonde's tattoo is to portray her in the process of being transfigured from sailor girl to jungle cat and back again (and to portray as well the Eros of this tension between civilization and savagery; "Eros," as Anne Carson says, "is a verb").

"As for the primitive, I hark back to it because we are still very primitive. How many thousands of years of culture, think you, have rubbed and polished at our raw edges? Probably one; at the best, no more than two. And that takes us back to screaming savagery, when, gross of body and deed, we drank blood from the skulls of our enemies and hailed as highest paradise the orgies and carnage of Valhalla."—Jack London

According to a third-century account of the Scythians' defeat of the Thracians, Scythians tattooed symbols of defeat upon Thracian men, but as a way of turning "the stamp of violence and shame into beautiful ornaments," Thracian women covered the rest of their bodies with tattoos.

On my thirtieth birthday, under my then girlfriend's influence, I got my left ear pierced and bought a diamond earring. I wore various earrings over the next ten years, but wearing an earring never really worked for me, and on my fortieth birthday, under the influence of Natalie, who thought it made me look like a pirate, I took out the earring I was then wearing—a gold hoop—and haven't worn an earring since. Earrings forced me to confront the nature of my style, or lack of style. I'm certainly not macho enough to wear an earring as if I were a tough guy, but neither am I effeminate enough to wear an earring in my right ear as if I were maybe gay-in-training. Instead, I'm just me, muddling through in the middle, and the earring forced me, over time, to see this, acknowledge it, and respond to it.

.   .   .

Marcus Camby's first name is tattooed on his arm; Kirby Puckett, who died of a stroke in 2006, also had his first name tattooed on his arm. Scottie Pippen has small tattoos on his biceps and legs. Michael Jordan has a horseshoe-shaped fraternity tattoo. Dennis Rodman's tattoos include a Harley, a shark, a cross (the loop of which encircles his pierced navel), and a photo of his daughter. Mike Tyson has tattoos of Che Guevara on his abdomen, Mao on his right upper arm, Arthur Ashe on his left shoulder, and a New Zealand Maori tribal design on the left side of his face. Shaquille O'Neal has a Superman tattoo on his left shoulder. Ben Wallace has a tattoo of the Big Ben clock tower on his right bicep, with basketballs for clock faces; he also has two tattoos of Taz, the Tasmanian devil from *Looney Tunes.*

"Human barcodes are hip," declared the *Wall Street Journal,* that arbiter of hip. "Heavy-metal band Slipknot has a barcode logo, with the stripes emblazoned across their prison-jumpsuit outfits. Barcode tattoos are also big, says New York tattoo tycoon Carlo Fodera."

Who owns these words?

In Galatians 6:17, Saint Paul says, "From this time onward let no one trouble me; for, as for me, I bear, branded on my body, the scars of Jesus as my Master."

"Since a tattoo to certain levels of society is the mark of a thug, it becomes also the sign of inarticulate revolt, often producing its only possible result: violence."—Amy Krakow

In order to demonstrate their corporate loyalty, many Nike employees wear on their leg a tattoo of a swoosh.

.   .   .

The Greek philosopher Bion of Borysthenes (circa 300 BCE) described the brutally tattooed face of his father, a former slave, as "a narrative of his master's harshness."

Philadelphia 76ers guard Jason Richardson says, "If you're a good basketball player, you've got to have some tattoos to go with the package. Basketball players have tattoos; that's the way it is. It's a way of showing who I am."

Asked what his tattoos mean, Iverson replied, "I got CRU THIK in four places—that's my crew, that's what we call ourselves, me and the guys I grew up with, the guys I'm loyal to. I got my kids' names, Tiaura and Deuce [Allen II], 'cause they're everything to me. I got my wife's name, Tawanna, on my stomach. A set of praying hands between my grandma's initials—she died when I was real young—and my mom's initials, Ethel Ann Iverson. I put shit on my body that means something to me. Here, on my left shoulder, I got a cross of daggers knitted together that says ONLY THE STRONG SURVIVE, because that's the one true thing I've learned in this life. On the other arm, I got a soldier's head. I feel like my life has been a war and I'm a soldier in it. Here, on my left forearm, it says NBN—for 'Newport Bad News.' That's what we call our hometown of Newport News, Virginia, because a lot of bad shit happens there. On the other arm, I got the Chinese symbol for respect, because I feel that where I come from deserves respect—being from there, surviving from there, and staying true to everybody back there. I got one that says FEAR NO ONE, a screaming skull with a red line through it—'cause you'll never catch me looking scared."

Aaron McKie, a former NBA player who is now an assistant coach at Temple University, said, "A lot of guys get tattoos because they think they look nice and sexy wearing them, but I don't need them. One reason is because of my old college coach, John Chaney. He didn't allow players to wear tattoos or earrings or stuff like that. The other reason is because I guess I'm old-fashioned. I don't see any good reason to pierce or paint my body. I'm comfortable with my natural look."

"The publication of *International Archives of Body Techniques* would be of truly international benefit, providing an inventory of all the possibilities of the human body and of the methods of apprenticeship and training employed to build up each technique, for there is not one human group in the world that would not make an original contribution to such an enterprise. It would also be a project eminently well fitted to counteracting racial prejudices, since it would contradict the racialist conceptions which try to make out that man is a product of his body, by demonstrating that it is the other way around: man has, at all times and in all places, been able to turn his body into a product of his techniques and his representations."—Claude Lévi-Strauss

What Lévi-Strauss means, I think, is this: Before we started, she said she needed to tell me something. She had herpes. Madly in love with her witchy bitchiness, I found occasional enforced celibacy insanely erotic, the way a chastity belt glamorizes what it locks out. We wound up living together, and as we fell out of love with each other, her herpes became a debate point between us. She suggested that we just get married, and then if I got it, I got it, and who would care? I suggested she at least explore some of the possibilities of which modern medicine avails us. For a multitude of reasons, the two of us didn't belong together, but what interests me now is what, for a lack of a better term, a free-floating signifier the virus was. When I was in love with her, it eroticized her. When I wasn't, it repelled me. The body has no meanings. We bring meanings to it.

Ex–NFL fullback Brock Olivo, who has only one tattoo—an Italian flag, on his back, to honor his ancestry—said, "That's my last tattoo. No more. I don't want to scare my kids or affect things in the business world by having all kinds of crazy stuff on me."

·　　　·　　　·

According to *Rolling Stone,* Paul Booth is "the tattoo artist of choice for rock stars who love death, perversion, and torture." His "black-and-gray tattoos of blasphemous violence echo the same nihilist madness of the metalheads he inks," musicians from Slipknot, Mudvayne, Slayer, Pantera, and Soulfly. His East Village shop features cobwebs, rusty meat hooks, a moose head, a mummified cat, medieval torture devices, a gynecologist's black leather chair with silver stirrups, a human skull given to him by a Swedish gravedigger, a note from a customer written in blood. His arms are covered in tattoos, his face is studded with silver loops, and he's enormously fat. Some of his most popular tattoos are "weeping demons, decapitated Christ figures, transvestite nuns severing their own genitals, cascading waves of melting skulls, muscled werewolves raping bare-chested women." He has a two-year waiting list. His clients—including the "hardcore-metal elite"—come to him "because they share his frustration and rage, his feelings of anger and alienation. He understands those emotions and brings them to the surface with his needle. His gift lies in transforming the dark side of his clients—their hurt, their torments—into flesh." Evan Seinfeld, the bassist for Biohazard, says, "We're all trying to release our negative energy, our frustration with the world. Through our art and our music, we're getting it all out." Shawn Crahan of Slipknot says, "I have a lot of dark ideas in my head. Paul develops these same emotions in very powerful pieces." Booth says, "If I woke up one day and became happy, I probably wouldn't tattoo anymore, because I wouldn't see a need to do it. I would lose my art if I became happy."

"In Samoa there is a legend that tattooing was introduced there by the goddesses of tattooing. They swam to Samoa from Fiji, singing on the way their divine message, 'Tattoo the women but not the men.' With constant repetition the message became confused and twisted. When the goddesses finally arrived on the Samoan shore, they found themselves singing just the reverse, and so, says the legend, the tattoo became the undeserved prerogative of the men and not the women."—Albert Parry

·   ·   ·

Who owns these paragraphs?

Revelation 17:5 says of the Scarlet Woman, "And upon her forehead was a name written, MYSTERY, BABYLON THE GREAT, THE MOTHER OF HARLOTS AND ABOMINATIONS OF THE EARTH."

Former NBA player Jud Buechler said that Michael Jordan wanted "me and Steve Kerr [Jordan's then teammates, both of whom are white] to get tattoos" after the Bulls won their fourth championship in 1996. "I thought about it but didn't do it because I knew my mom, wife, and mother-in-law would kill me."

"The human body is always treated as an image of society."—Mary Douglas

"By the early seventeenth century [in Japan], a generally recognized codification of tattoo marks was widely used to identify criminals and outcasts. Outcasts were tattooed on the arms: A cross might be tattooed on the inner forearm, or a straight line on the outside of the forearm or on the upper arm. Criminals were marked with a variety of symbols that designated the places where the crimes were committed. In one region, the pictograph for 'dog' was tattooed on the criminal's forehead. Other marks included such patterns as bars, crosses, double lines, and circles on the face and arms. Tattooing was reserved for those who had committed serious crimes, and individuals bearing tattoo marks were ostracized by their families and denied all participation in the life of the community. For the Japanese, who valued family membership and social position above all things, tattooing was a particularly severe and terrible form of punishment. By the end of the seventeenth century, penal tattooing had been largely replaced by other forms of punishment. One reason for this is said to be that at about that time decorative tattooing became popular, and criminals covered their penal tattoos with larger decorative patterns. This is also thought to be the historical origin of the association of tattooing with organized crime in Japan. In spite of efforts by the government to suppress it, tattooing continued to flourish among firemen, laborers, and others at the lower end of the social scale. It was particularly favored by gangs of itinerant gamblers called Yakuza. Members of these gangs were recruited from the underworld of outlaws, penniless peasants, laborers, and misfits who migrated to Edo in the hope of improving their lot. Although the Yakuza engaged in a variety of semi-legal and illegal activities, they saw themselves as champions of the common people and adhered to a strict code of honor that specifically prohibited crimes against people, such as rape and theft. Like Samurai, they prided themselves on being able to endure pain and privation without flinching. And when loyalty required it, they were willing to sacrifice themselves by facing imprisonment or death to protect the gang. The Yakuza expressed these ideals in tattooing: because it was painful, it was proof of courage; because it was permanent, it was evidence of lifelong loyalty to the group; and because it was illegal, it made them forever outlaws."—Steve Gilbert

"You put a tattoo on yourself with the knowledge that this body is yours to have and enjoy while you're here. You have fun with it, and nobody else can control (supposedly) what you do with it. That's why tattooing is such a big thing in prison: It's an expression of freedom—one of the only expressions of freedom there. They can lock you down, control everything, but 'I've got my mind, and I can tattoo my body, alter it my way as an act of personal will.'"—Don Ed Hardy

Didn't American slave owners brand slaves so they could be identified, like cattle? I've always thought there was a connection between the gold jewelry worn by rap artists and the chains of slavery—transformation of bondage into gold, escape from slavery, but not quite. . . .

During the early Roman Empire, slaves exported to Asia were tattooed with the words TAX PAID. Words, acronyms, sentences, and doggerel

were inscribed on the bodies of slaves and convicts, as both identification and punishment. A common phrase etched on the forehead of
Roman slaves was STOP ME—I'M A RUNAWAY.

Peter Trachtenberg, the author of *Seven Tattoos: A Memoir in the
Flesh,* told me, "The most obvious reason African Americans didn't
get tattooed until relatively recently was that the old inks didn't show
up on black skin. Newer, clearer pigments didn't come into use until
the mid-eighties, which coincides with the introduction of tattoos
into the African American community. I also wouldn't be surprised if
tattooing's association with working-class culture—redneck culture
in particular—made it unpopular with African Americans. You don't
come across many black country-music fans, either. (Charlie Pride's
fan base is entirely white.) My guess is that there were two principal
routes of diffusion: the first from rap, the second from black college
fraternities (some of which also used branding as an initiation rite).
Starting in the late eighties, a number of gangsta rappers adopted
tattoos, most notably Tupac Shakur, who had THUG LIFE tattooed
in block letters down his torso. It would be interesting to go back
through magazines of that period and see if photos of tattooed rappers predate those of tattooed ballplayers." They do, by a lot. "Also, to
find out what percentage of NBA players belonged to black college
fraternities." Some, but not a high percentage. "The tattoos mark their
wearers as gangstas or gangsta wannabes, and one of the hallmarks of
black gangsta rap is its appropriation of white organized-crime terminology, for instance, BLACK M.A.F.I.A. and admiring references to
John Gotti in several songs."

A decade ago, Charles Barkley, explaining why NBA attendance was
down, said, "White folks are not going to come see a bunch of guys
with tattoos, with cornrows. I'm sorry, but anyone who thinks different, they're stupid."

In 1999, the shoe company And1 created a controversial advertisement in which Latrell Sprewell, who was suspended from the NBA

for a year for choking his coach, said, "People say I'm America's worst nightmare; I say I'm the American Dream." In the background, a blues guitar played "The Star-Spangled Banner" in imitation of Jimi Hendrix's version of the anthem (And1 couldn't afford the rights to the original). Seth Berger, the cofounder of the company, said that MTV created a youth market in which blacks and whites are indifferent to color: "It's a race-neutral culture that is open to endorsers and heroes that look different. These people are comfortable with tattoos and cornrows."

Who owns these statements—the people who said them or the people who wrote them down or the person who has gathered them together here or the person who reads them?

Concerning the people who are featured in the book *Modern Primitives*, and who are devoted to body modification, mutilation, scarification, and tattoos, *Whole Earth Review* said, "Through 'primitive' modifications, they are taking possession of the only thing that any of us will ever really own: our bodies."

In the 1890s, socialite Ward McAllister said about tattooing, "It is certainly the most vulgar and barbarous habit the eccentric mind of fashion ever invented. It may do for an illiterate seaman, but hardly for an aristocrat."

Upon being told that the NBA's *Hoop* magazine had airbrushed his tattoos off the photograph of him on the cover of the magazine, Iverson responded, "Hey, you can't do that. That's not right. Who gives them the authority to remake me? I personally am offended that somebody would do something like that. They don't have the right to try to present me in another way to the public than the way I truly am without my permission. It's an act of freedom and a form of self-expression. That's why I got mine."

·   ·   ·

When John Allen was a high school star in Philadelphia, he said, "I think that on the court, if I didn't have as many tattoos as I do, people would look at me as—not being soft—but people would look at me as average. When they see me come in with my tattoos and the big name that I've got, before you even play a game, it's like, 'Whoa, this guy, he must be for real.'"

In the nineteenth century, Earl Roberts, field marshal of the British Army, said that "every officer in the British Army should be tattooed with his regimental crest. Not only does this encourage *esprit de corps* but also assists in the identification of casualties."

I recently had the pin removed from my left leg, for no particularly compelling reason other than it spooked me to think of one day being buried with a "foreign object" in my body (for one thing, it's a violation of Jewish law). Not that I'll be buried; I'll be cremated. Not that I'm religious; I'm an atheist. Still, leaving the pin in seemed to me some obscure violation of the order of things. As one tattoo artist has said, "The permanence really hits other people, and that is linked to mortality. And that is why skull tattoos really ice it."

Who owns this body, this body of work?

WHITE BRONCO

On a visit to Los Angeles, I was sampling two new flavors at the Brentwood Häagen-Dazs when in walked O. J. Simpson with two very young guys in excellent shape. Seniors, say, on the USC football team. O.J. wasn't in excellent shape, not even in good shape, not even close. He was no longer a senior on the USC football team. The air-conditioning was on.

I had liked O.J. since I was a kid, because my mom, the UCLA alum, rooted, in a gloating, ungracious manner, against USC. None of us said anything now to O.J. There was shyness to our behavior, but there was also a smidgen of self-respect. There were maybe six or eight people in the store other than me and O.J. and his friends. Part of the tension was the sheer surprise of seeing O.J. ordering ice cream; I'd never thought of him doing something so mundane and unhealthy. In a curious way, he was unwelcome or at the very least not wholly embraced; he was intruding a little, maybe, by participating in our slovenliness.

Gallantly (so I first thought), O.J. sought to purchase a woman's ice cream for her. She suddenly looked much prettier to me than she had before. O.J. winked at the two seniors on the USC football team, applied pressure to the crook of her arm, recommended rum raisin. I remember thinking, very specifically, *O.J.'s kinda tarnishing his reputation here;* this was many years before he took the Bronco out for a spin on I-5.

The woman smiled a smile that went exactly so far and no further, and said, "Thank you but no," looking at me, trying to get me in on this. I couldn't, though. I didn't. Suddenly I was just standing there.

O.J. persisted, reiterating his desire to buy an ice-cream cone for her. It was like watching a famous suicidal accordion fold in on itself: O.J. kept nudging the woman up to the counter while she, impressively, impassively, kept saying, over and over, "No thanks, O.J. That won't be necessary. I haven't quite decided yet."

Finally, when O.J. refused to relent, she pointed at me and said, "My boyfriend's treating."

"Your boyfriend?" one of O.J.'s minions muttered, in O.J.'s defense. "*That* man's your boyfriend?"

One day, we had a discussion in class. They asked me, Where did they go? The trees, the salamander, the tropical fish, Edgar, the poppas and mommas, Matthew and Tony, where did they go? And I said, I don't know, I don't know. And they said, Who knows? and I said, Nobody knows. And they said, Is death that which gives meaning to life? And I said, No, life is that which gives meaning to life. Then they said, but isn't death, considered as a fundamental datum, the means by which the taken-for-granted mundanity of the everyday may be transcended in the direction of—

I said, Yes, maybe.

They said, We don't like it.

—DONALD BARTHELME

BEING RANDOM IS THE KEY TO LIFE

Asked to cite the best advice she's ever heard, then University of Washington women's basketball player Loree Payne said, "Live in the present: you can't change the past, and the future has enough worries of its own"—which bears absolutely no relationship to how she actually lives her life. She seems to have been born with an ongoing nostalgia for parting, a sense that "life is precious, and your time is short." As a graduating senior, she said, early in the 2002–03 season, "I know that the games are getting limited, as far as how many I have left. I know the seniors are all starting to feel that way, so we're going to play every game like it's our last, because pretty soon it's going to be. There's definitely a sense of urgency to this season. You think about it every time you step on the floor, how this year is winding down." She frequently mentioned being aware of the last time she'd take certain road trips, play in certain arenas, perform particular routines, do particular drills. She's a hypersensitive seismograph attuned to the earthquake of loss.

Payne said, "I kind of like everything-works-out movies"—*Top Gun, Notting Hill, You've Got Mail*. Her then head coach, June Daugherty, who is now the head coach at Washington State and who survived cardiac arrest in 2007, called her a "perfectionist." She can't abide the emptiness of chaos, which she fills with faith. Her pregame ritual was to "relax and pray, giving the game to God." She wore a wristband that said SISTERS IN CHRIST. When she was asked who the most influential person in her life is, she replied, "Jesus." When she was asked to name three people she would like to invite to dinner, she named Jesus, Job, and Paul. The quotation at the end of her emails was, "You will seek Me and find Me when you seek Me with all your heart (Jeremiah 29:13)." Another favorite quotation was, "Do not trust in your own understanding; in all your ways acknowledge Him and He will direct your path." All of her favorite singers and bands were Christian contemporary: Jennifer Knapp, Third Day, Jars of Clay, SoulJahz, Priesthood. Basketball court: Heaven.

Asked, at the beginning of the season, to name her funniest teammate, Payne named her best friend, "Kayla Burt, because she's the most random person I know." Another player, Kirsten Brockman, said, "My funniest teammate is Kayla. She brings out the five-year-old in me and everyone." Kristen O'Neill answered, "Everyone can make me laugh, but Kayla is definitely the biggest spaz." Nicole Castro said, "My funniest teammate is Kayla, for sure. She just comes out with the strangest things." Asked for the best advice she'd ever heard, Burt said, "Being random is the key to life."

Here's how key to life being random is:

On New Year's Eve 2002, Burt and several of her teammates had a party at her house. Since they had an 8:30 a.m. practice the next day—punishment for a lackadaisical practice on December 31—there wasn't a lot of carousing: they ordered pizza, ate junk food, looked at high school yearbooks, told stories, and watched the substandard kidnap thriller they'd rented, *Trapped* ("You think you live in a world where no little girls are killed; I'm the one that decides if your little girl lives or dies").

Throughout the evening, Burt had complained that she didn't feel right, but according to Payne, "she's not a complainer, and it was just something she mentioned. I went up to Kayla's room to look at the eleven o'clock news. Everyone else was downstairs. Then she came up. I was lying on her bed, and she was sitting next to me. She said, 'Loree, I feel light-headed,' and she kind of fell back, off the bed. Kayla is a clown and I told her to get up. Then I thought she was having a seizure. I yelled to everyone to get upstairs and Giuliana [Mendiola, the star of the team] called 911."

Mendiola said, "When we went up there, I got around to the other side. There wasn't very much space; there were boxes and it was a really cramped space, so we just moved the boxes and all the stuff. She wasn't unconscious at that point. She was gurgling and her eyes were kind of rolling back. So we were like, 'Kayla!' She wasn't saying hello or anything. She wasn't responding."

Burt's heart had stopped.

Mendiola: "We looked at her and it was obvious she wasn't joking around. We slapped her face to wake her up. We rolled her over: she was purple and she needed oxygen." Mendiola pumped Burt's chest; Giuliana's sister, Gioconda, gave Kayla mouth-to-mouth. "We didn't really know what we were doing. We were just doing what we remembered from TV shows." *Rescue 911* was Kayla's favorite show.

Gioconda said, "I was just blowing into her mouth. Her chest was going up and down and she gasped, so I guessed it was working."

Erica Schelly repeated CPR instructions from the Medic One operator on the phone: "Fifteen compressions to the chest, then two breaths."

"I had no idea what to do," Schelly said. "I was freaking out. The only thing that kept me sane was having this to do. I was pretty scared."

Burt didn't have a pulse. She wheezed; her body shook.

Paramedics—including Michelle Perkins, a former Washington basketball player who became an EMT after college—arrived within five minutes of the 911 call.

Schelly said, "Loree and I went outside and we looked at each other and we were just like, 'Oh my gosh, what are we going to do? What can we do? Let's just go pray, you know?' So we went outside and sat down together and prayed a little bit and went back in."

The ambulance rushed Burt to the hospital. All of the players spent the rest of that night and most of New Year's Day in the hospital. They were scheduled to travel to Los Angeles for a game against UCLA the next day, but with Burt unconscious, they didn't know whether to cancel the game.

Daugherty said, "They weren't going to leave Seattle until they had a chance to talk to Kayla and make sure she was okay, and she knew they were going to go down there and compete for her."

Late in the afternoon on New Year's Day, Burt began exhibiting consciousness.

Burt told a reporter, "I had something wrong with my heart, but I don't really remember anything. I guess I was talking and responding, but I don't remember a thing. I'm doing a lot better, though."

Her father said, "Kayla is doing well right now. We're waiting on some test results and that's about it. It's very difficult to see your daughter hooked up to machines and tubes and a ventilator."

Kristen O'Neill, who had been her rival throughout high school, said Kayla told her "she'd had a baby, named Angelica. She knew she didn't have a baby, but it was funny, like, 'You have Angelica Baby in your room.'"

Payne said, "Our team gave her a card. She got it and she read it. She'd read one side and laugh at certain people's jokes, then she'd read the back, then she'd go back and read the front again. For, seriously, like, ten minutes, she kept reading it and we were, like, 'Okay, enough.'

"She asked if we won the game. We told her we hadn't played yet. She said, 'Why not—because of me?' We said, 'No, the game isn't until tomorrow.' She told us to play and win."

Before their game against UCLA on Friday (postponed one day), Burt told Payne to tell their teammates, "I love you guys. Think about me, but don't think about me too much. Just play like you know how."

Wearing white armbands with #20 or KAYLA BURT or GET WELL, KAYLA, they shot twenty-four percent from the field and lost, 74–46, their worst loss in two years.

Payne said, "We could have told her that we won, because she doesn't remember."

On Sunday night, though, they rallied from an eleven-point deficit to beat USC in overtime.

Burt said, "I sat in my hospital room and listened on the radio. I'd never heard an actual radio broadcast before of our games, because I've always been playing. They could easily have crumpled and played horrible under the circumstances, but they played their hearts out for me. To know they did that for me—that was awesome."

In her post-game press conference, Daugherty said, "Every kid that stepped on the court just left it all out there. Most of the game, we were on the floor more than we were standing up, trying to save loose balls, helping our teammates out. In the second half, we had no energy. Every timeout, we were trying to rotate kids and remind them that they're playing for Kayla and that they have to get their energy on defense and get stops. To see them have the courage to compete and work that hard for Kayla—it's my proudest moment ever as a coach because they played a game for the right reasons. They played it for their teammate. The amount of effort and love that they put out there was amazing. They willed the win for Kayla."

Payne, who scored seventeen points, said, "It was the biggest win of my career, and we went to the Elite Eight [in 2001]. It wasn't because of basketball. It was how this team came together, fought through, and was ultimately bonded by this experience. This has truly changed everybody. We have huge goals as a team, but this makes you realize the important things in life. Everybody needs a perspective check here and there. We got a big one." Payne always seems to say the correct thing and do what she's supposed to do, as if she were perpetually running for election.

Six days after Burt's heart stopped, doctors diagnosed her with Long QT syndrome and implanted an automatic defibrillator in her chest—a device that monitors the heartbeat and applies a shock if irregularities are detected. At a press conference the next day, her cardiologist said, "Long QT is a genetic abnormality of the heart that can predispose people to sudden and unexplained and dangerous heart rhythms." *She's the most random person I've ever met.* "Kayla is a real trooper and gave the high five both going into surgery and when she came out. I told her not to do the high five on the right side because that's where we put the defibrillator." The defibrillator, inserted on her right side because she's left-handed, was supposed to allow her to live a normal life, but she still supposedly had a twenty percent chance of a repeat episode in the next year and thought her basketball career was over.

(In fact, when she wound up seeing a specialist at the Mayo Clinic, he told her that she didn't have Long QT syndrome, had no underlying heart condition, and could resume playing. After a season and a half away from the sport and after extensive discussions with UW's medical, legal, and athletic department staffs, she returned to the team as a junior—with a defibrillator implanted between her chest and right shoulder. The only Division I athlete playing with a defibrillator, she led the team in scoring and assists in the 2004–05 season, but fifteen games into her senior season, sitting on the bench during a timeout, she was jolted in a team huddle by an electric charge; the defibrillator had been activated by sensing an irregular heartbeat. Her playing career was over. She now takes a daily dose of beta-blocker drugs to regulate her heart rhythm and sees a nurse every four months for checkups and a cardiologist every eight months. Every seven years, when the doctor stops her heart in order to replace the defibrillator, she'll be briefly, clinically dead.)

At the press conference, Burt said, "I am about as lucky as anyone has ever been lucky. My heart was stopped; I was dead. I've gone through so much in just the past week. I feel so blessed by everyone and I am here and I am happy. I have amazing teammates. I can't say it enough, how much I—they're my sisters for life."

Daugherty said, "Hopefully, we will have Kayla back in school this quarter. It sounds like that is something the doctors think she can do. The sooner we can get her back with the team, the better. We haven't had the opportunity to sit down and talk about it, but she will certainly remain on scholarship and remain a huge part of this basketball family. At some point, hopefully I can recruit her to be some kind of student assistant coach. We will get to that when we get her a little bit stronger and out of the hospital."

Assistant coach Mike Daugherty, June's husband, now an assistant coach at Washington State, said about Burt, "She was such a perfect basketball player. She could have been the best one we ever had." A sophomore averaging ten points and four rebounds a game, she was leading the Pac-10 (which became the Pac-12 in 2011) in three-point field goal percentage and assists-to-turnovers ratio.

Teri Burt, Kayla's mother, said about her five teammates, "They were so courageous. They did what they needed to do and basically saved my daughter's life. For that, I will be forever grateful."

Payne said, "Under a pressure situation, what do you do? Being a student-athlete, you learn the concept of team and the concept of composure, and they definitely came into play. We can play the 'what if' game. I've done that. Believe me. I've done it a lot and made myself scared. 'What if I had gone downstairs?' 'What if I wasn't there?' But I *was* there. And there was a reason I was there." The Head Coach has a plan for all of us.

Ten days after her cardiac arrest, Burt returned to the arena. Wearing a red coat, a white turtleneck, black slacks, and high heels, she looked radiant as she stood along the baseline before the game against Arizona State, high-fiving everyone in sight. A camera crew from *Inside Edition* followed her everywhere she went.

At the beginning of the game, she walked with three teammates to center court to serve as an honorary captain. When the starting line-ups were announced, she was introduced as a special "sixth starter." She received a prolonged, passionate standing ovation from the four thousand in attendance—the largest crowd of the year. "Just to walk out there was really special. To hear that roar when I came out, it hits you real close, and it's awesome."

Placards, held mainly by teenage girls wearing their basketball uniforms, said, BURT—20, EASTLAKE GIRLS BASKETBALL WILL ALWAYS REMEMBER KAYLA BURT, HEROINES OF THE HARDWOOD, WE LOVE KAYLA.

"I want to do everything I can to be normal," she said.

Her seventeen-year-old brother said, "There's nothing normal about you."

Washington won, pushing its overall record to 11–2, 3–1 during the Pac-10 season. Giuliana Mendiola, celebrating her twenty-first birthday, scored twenty-two points, had ten rebounds and five assists, and later said, "I was just out there trying to have fun and win the game for Kayla."

Whenever her teammates made a nice play—Payne threw a showy behind-the-back pass on a two-on-one break, which sent the crowd into a frenzy—Burt stood and pumped her left fist; her right arm was still sore from the surgery. Burt said, "It seemed like every little thing was so exciting to me. Taking a charge, creating a turnover, hitting a good shot—just the little things were so awesome to me. I can't even say enough about how hard the girls played, how tough they were, and just how inspiring it was for me to be on the bench and be a part of it. I'm just so pumped to be out there. I keep a smile on my face because I'm so happy. Life is so awesome. I'm here."

After the game, Burt, surrounded by mics and cameras, addressed the crowd and wished Giuliana a happy birthday. The Mendiola sisters presented her with a drawing of themselves and Burt, who said afterward, "We're as close as we can ever be. They gave me CPR. I mean, how close can you get? We'll stay that way forever." They walked off the floor arm in arm.

These young women were used to being told what to do and where to go all day long by coaches, university officials, sponsors, professors, parents, and now they were being instructed by *Inside Edition*, Connie Chung, Lifetime, *Good Housekeeping*, and ESPN. They were the media darlings of the moment, the belles of the b-ball, objects of ceaseless attention by a (nearly exclusively) male sportswriting corps, and they never turned down a media request. They couldn't get enough of it; they were addicted to it; they knew the red light would turn off soon enough.

A couple of weeks later, Daugherty called a meeting, ostensibly to announce to the team that it was nationally ranked in the top twenty-five, but actually to surprise Burt with a visit by Seattle Super-Sonics player Desmond Mason, whom Burt, in the Washington media guide, had identified as the player whose autograph she'd most like to have. He brought her a signed jersey and tickets to the Sonics game that night. At first Burt didn't recognize him. "I'm so embarrassed," she said. "I had no idea. He came on the court, and when I figured it all out, I was like, 'Oh, gosh. This is so cool.'"

Mason said, "I heard about the situation and what happened. I'm happy to see that she's okay, still in great spirits, with great friends around her. I'm just here to tell her I appreciate her, and I'm glad she's okay."

Burt challenged Mason to a game of H-O-R-S-E. Her first shot was from beyond the three-point line. Swish. Mason's attempt clanged off the rim. He took off his baseball cap and teased her—"Is this a

women's ball?"—but she kept shooting threes and couldn't miss and
he kept missing and she won going away.

On and especially off the court, other players looked to Payne to lead.
She was the team captain and was the team spokeswoman at various press conferences following Burt's hospitalization. At these press
conferences, Payne seemed to make a particular point of holding her
head high, maintaining a tight smile. "I like being in situations where
people look to me to direct," she said. "I'm ready for that. It's a natural
role for me." (She graduated first in her class in high school and was a
member of the National Honor Society. In college, she was a psychology major with a 3.6 GPA, because she thought it would provide a
good foundation for coaching. After graduating, she was an assistant
coach at various schools, including UW; she's now head coach at University of Puget Sound, in Tacoma.)

On New Year's Eve, Payne had called downstairs to her teammates,
then waited outside to guide the ambulance toward the house, but it
was Giuliana Mendiola who called 911 and freshman Erica Schelly
who relayed instructions from the emergency operator; it was the
Mendiola sisters who performed CPR on Payne's best friend. Her
game was the same. The sixth-best scorer in UW history, she was an
excellent shooter, especially from long range, but that's all she did.
She was an average passer, couldn't penetrate to the basket, didn't
rebound, didn't defend. "I know false hustle when I see it," Boston
Celtics coach Red Auerbach once said; false hustle was her MO on
defense. She didn't work hard for or hold her position on either end
of the floor. As a senior, she possessed exactly the same strengths and
weaknesses she possessed as an incoming freshman. She wasn't very
flexible or quick, had sloppy footwork, often cherry-picked to try to
get an easy basket off the break, was monomaniacally focused on her
own shooting—didn't follow her own shot, usually clapped to herself
whenever she scored, grimaced when she missed. She rarely fought
for a loose ball, stayed away from the scrum, wasn't scrappy. (I recognize all of these weaknesses, because they were mine when I played.)
For all of her reported selflessness off the court (she frequently visited Children's Hospital and Ronald McDonald House; Daugherty
said, "She has a great spirit about her—she genuinely cares about

people—I can't even begin to talk about how much community service she does"), on the court she seemed to be quite self-centered.
This doesn't make her a hypocrite or a bad person. It just makes her
a person: full of the contradictions, confusions, internal dramas, and
mysteries that anyone else has and that she has trouble accepting
about herself.

"As I was growing up, even with success in basketball and school
and a great family, there was still something missing," Payne said,
"but I couldn't put my finger on it. Once God opened my eyes to the
fact that He was the thing missing in my life, I became complete.
There is a God place in all of us; it's the only thing that could ever
possibly give anyone true happiness. Now I find that basketball is not
my entire life; it's only something that is a part of my life, and for
that I am so thankful. I just have a different perspective now, an eternal one that really allows me to prioritize things. Not saying, by any
means, that I have it all together. That is the awesome thing about
God: He gives us grace because we *don't* have it all together. Within
this process, the more knowledge I gain, the more I realize how little
I know. It is awesome, though!"

In emails to me when she was still an undergraduate, Payne was
partial to the single, double, and even triple exclamation point. It was
important to her to be—and to be perceived to be—positive, upbeat,
Christ-fueled. To me, it's an interesting, open, and utterly unanswer-
able question: To what degree does she believe the bromidic reassurances she articulates for public consumption? Or, more precisely,
what is the relation between these reassurances and what she actually
feels in her heart of hearts? I think this would be a difficult question
even for her to answer. The bun she tucked her hair into on game
days was hard as a fist.

Shooters win games and obtain the podium, while somebody else
does the dirty work *(offense puts fannies in the seats—defense wins
championships)*. One thing Christ was teaching his disciples was to
do the dirty work, and they were having a hard time with it. Who
wouldn't, after a few miracles?

The Huskies' 2002–03 record was 22–8; they placed second in the
Pac-10, then were eliminated in the first round of the NCAA tourna-

ment. Payne was chosen All-Pac-10 for the second straight year. She averaged sixteen points and fifty-one percent from the field before New Year's Eve, thirteen points and forty percent after. She said, "I kind of went through a drought where it was hard to focus in class and on the court. I didn't feel like my natural self as a player or anything. I was trying a little too hard to get over it, because this type of thing takes time, facing the conflicting things within me. Most people don't experience something like this in their entire life, so it's not like, 'Oh, well, she's okay, so everything's okay.' I don't know how many people heard it, but Michelle [Perkins, the EMT and former Washington player] went, 'We lost her, but we brought her back.' Kayla died for a second. She was no longer with us. That was reality, right there. I was just, like, 'Whoa, hold on.' It wasn't like, 'Oh, she was never going to . . .' She was very going to." Loree Payne is half in love with easeful death.

One night in late February, a couple of days before their final game of the regular season, Burt and Payne sat in the living room of Burt's rental house, which she shared with three teammates.

Burt said about Payne, "She needs to know what's going on. She needs to know the plan, and I'm just like, 'Whatever. Let me know.' There will be times when she's freaking out and I'm like, 'Loree, relax.' I'll just say things out of the blue. That's just kind of my personality. I keep her on her toes. When we drive in her car and she's parking, she has to get it perfectly straight. And I'm like, 'It's fine!' She'll pack for trips five days in advance and I'll pack ten minutes before we go."

Payne said, "Just thinking about how close she came to being removed from our lives—I think that's the most difficult thing. You hear that ninety-five percent of people who go through this don't live. And if it would have been two minutes longer, she would have had brain damage and not been normal again. I would have been losing my best friend. It's the hardest when you're alone, reflecting on it, and you start to let the negative thoughts come in. I know I'm still dealing with it every single day, and it's hard. It takes time. If you drop her off at her house and no one's here [at the house where I was interviewing them], it's a fear that you never should have, but you do. Or you call on the cell phone and she doesn't answer and you're like, 'Aargh, why didn't she answer?' Those are feelings that normal people don't have. Things like this happen to other people. They don't happen to you."

Burt said, "It seems like every single thing that took place that night was perfect. I could have gone upstairs by myself and Loree wouldn't have been there. None of the other girls could have been here. Even where I live: The fire station is right down the road, and I think that was huge—how it only took them about four minutes to get to my house. It's all those little things which you don't really think about that are so important and which were so important in everything that happened that night."

Payne said, "I don't believe in coincidences. Things like that don't just happen, you know. It was supposed to happen that way, and there was no other way it possibly could have happened. You just have to trust in that, and that is what faith is all about, because you can't hear about everything that happened and think, *Oh, good thing it happened that way.* Or, *That was a good chance.* That is not possible.

"At our church, the pastor gave an altar call, where he asks what it means to be a Christian. Kayla gave her testimony, and eighteen people came to know the Word. It was awesome how God used Kayla to do that. Anyone who went through this situation and to be as joyous as she's been since the day she left the hospital—there's something special. If someone didn't believe in God before this, I don't see how anyone couldn't now. She's a walking witness. She's God's miracle."

Burt said, "I can honestly say I love every single person on this team and all the coaches and all the members of my family. It's so important to let the people that you love know, because those could be your last words, and that's why I don't feel ashamed or embarrassed to tell people that I love them, and if anything were to happen to any of these people, I'd want them to know how I feel about them. You gotta say things that are on your mind, because you never know.

"Yeah, it was a very serious thing that happened in my life, but the fact that it's over with and I'm basically back to normal physically, I can joke around about it and talk about it. It's not a big deal for me at all. I never even really thought about death. I mean, yeah, I heard that I actually did die and that I was brought back, but I don't think about that anymore. I've never really thought about it, just because I am alive and so it's like, Why even think about that, you know?"

Tugging down the right side of her sweatshirt a little and displaying her defibrillator, which she explained is only 1 inch by 1 inch, she said, "I don't even really notice it. It just hangs out a little. It's good. It's pretty cool."

Payne, trying to imitate Burt's jokey style, measured the defibrillator with her fingers and kept insisting it was at least 2 inches by 2 inches (in fact, it was 1 inch by 1½ inches). It wasn't funny, though: Payne didn't comprehend that Burt was a little defensive about the size of this silver device sticking out of her chest.

In a similar way, when Burt was asked what she's going to do now that her basketball career is over and she hesitated for a moment, Payne said, "Academics." (After graduating in 2006, Burt became assistant basketball coach at the University of Portland, then an EMT. She's now the outreach coordinator for an institute for cardiovascular research, in a Seattle suburb. Doctors say her condition isn't hereditary, but after nine years, they still haven't determined exactly what her condition is or why she went into cardiac arrest in the prime of her athletic career. She's thirty-four, single, and thinks "every day" about having a family, but she says the idea of becoming a mother "scares me. I wonder what my life is going to be like later.")

Burt talked about how pitifully unprepared Connie Chung was when she interviewed her, and how Daugherty had a tendency to get things wrong—which magazine was interviewing whom, where they were meeting, etc.—and at first when Payne said, "Shut up," she seemed to be teasing, but when Burt continued to undermine these authority figures, Payne—big sister, team captain, traffic advisory—repeated, with emphasis, "No. Really. Shut up."

In the Washington media guide, asked who would play themselves in a movie, Burt said Cameron Diaz; Payne said Meg Ryan.

Funny, nice; lightness, loss; life-lunging, death-trapped.

In *Trapped*, explaining his kidnapping plan to his six-year-old victim, Kevin Bacon says, "This is a machine that runs on fear."

Though occasionally, at Payne's behest, Burt gestures in the direction of religion, she seems to know she's only bones and blood; Payne thinks Burt's body is a vessel of God.

Burt thinks people saved her; Payne is certain of divine intervention.

Payne believes, anxiously, in order; Burt knows that being random is the key to life.

Pain is just weakness leaving your body.

—SLOGAN OF THE JOHNS HOPKINS UNIVERSITY CREW TEAM

BRING THE PAIN

During the 1998 and 1999 baseball seasons, while he was being sued for divorce, Atlanta Braves relief pitcher Mark Wohlers had difficulty getting the ball anywhere near the plate. In '98, his earned run average (ERA) was 10.00, which is terrible; in '99 it was 27.00, which is unheard-of awful. "I convinced myself the reason I couldn't pitch straight was because I blew out my elbow," Wohlers said, "even though deep down I don't know what it was. The mind is a powerful thing." He retired a few years later.

Karl Newell, a kinesiologist at Penn State, says, "Consciousness gets in the way. If a pianist starts worrying where his fingers go while he's playing, it will change the performance."

Atlanta Braves catcher Dale Murphy made a few bad throws to second base during a spring training game in 1977. The next day, when an opponent tried to steal second base, Murphy threw the ball to the outfield fence on one hop. Later that year, he twice hit his own pitcher in the back on throws to second base. "Your mind won't let your natural abilities flow," he said. "Instead of just throwing, your mind interferes, and you start thinking, *Where am I throwing? What am I doing?* Your mind starts working against you." Unable to even return the ball to the pitcher, he was forced to move to the outfield, where he became a perennial All-Star.

At age nineteen, Steve Gasser was one of the stars of the Minnesota Twins minor-league system. In 1988, traded to the New York Mets and pitching in Class A ball, he walked eleven batters and threw seven wild pitches in one inning, walked twenty-one batters and threw thirteen wild pitches in six innings. He never pitched again.

Allan Lans, formerly the Mets' psychiatrist, says, "Everybody brings their personality to the game. It all comes down to an anxiety response. In baseball, people talk about someone getting wild. Then everyone comes rushing to the rescue to fix it and they just make the problem worse. 'Just throw the damn ball,' I tell them. 'Stop thinking too much.'"

In *I of the Vortex: From Neurons to Self,* Rodolfo Llinás writes, "That which we call thinking is the evolutionary internalization of movement."

Science writer Brian Hayes agrees: "Only organisms that move have brains. A tree has no need of a central nervous system because it's not going anywhere, but an animal on the prowl needs to see where it's headed and needs to predict, even envision, its future place in the world. The poster child for this close connection between motricity and mentality is the sea squirt. This marine creature starts life as a motile larva, equipped with a brainlike ganglion of about three hundred neurons. But after a day or two of cavorting in the shallows, the larva finds a hospitable site on the bottom and puts down roots. As a sessile organism, it has no further use for a brain, and so it eats it."

Baseball players suffer mental blocks far more often than athletes in more frenetic, less rote sports, such as football or basketball; in baseball, there's too much time to stop and think. Shortstops and third basemen rarely suffer from the problem, since their throws are nearly always somewhat rushed. For second basemen, it's the easy throw to first base that's usually the culprit, not the difficult, rushed throw from deep behind second base; for catchers, it's the even easier throw back to the pitcher. And it happens by far the most to pitchers, who, of course, have the most time to think.

Pat Jordan's memoir *A False Spring* chronicles his experience as a minor-league pitcher whose arm went haywire: "I could not remember how I'd once delivered a baseball with a fluid and effortless motion! And even if I could remember, I somehow knew I could never transmit that knowledge to my arms and legs, my back, and shoulders. The delicate wires through which that knowledge had so often been communicated were burned out, irrevocably charred, I know now, by too much energy channeled too often along a solitary and too fragile wavelength. I lost it all that spring."

Daniel Willingham, a psychologist at the University of Virginia, makes a distinction between "implicit learning" (what the body knows) and "explicit learning" (conscious knowledge). In cases in which athletes develop mental blocks, a switch has been flipped from *implicit* to *explicit*. I played high school tennis, and I remember this happening to me once, in the district finals. I won the first set against someone who was an obviously superior player, and when I realized this fact, I suddenly couldn't get my right arm to stop moving in jagged, pixelated slow motion. I felt like a marionette operated by some unknown other. I lost the last two sets, 6–1, 6–0. David Foster Wallace called this having a bad head.

Hayes says, "None of us know—at the level of consciousness—how to walk, or breathe, or throw a baseball. If we had to take charge of these movements, issuing commands to all the hundreds of muscles in just the right sequence, who would not collapse in a quivering mass?"

"I'd never heard of throwing percentage before I came to the big leagues," then Texas Rangers catcher Mike Stanley (now a high school baseball coach) said. "I got here, and that's what catchers are judged on. We had a very slow staff, but I started thinking it was me." Although he was fixated on the percentage of base stealers he threw out, Stanley—his body in full rebellion against his mind—threw soft, high-arcing tosses to second and third base whenever anyone tried to steal. "I never realized how much of the game is mental. You can see it when guys walk up to the plate—which guys are afraid. I'm sure they could see the fear in my eyes."

Rod Dishman, director of the Exercise Psychology Lab at the University of Georgia, says, "When thinking interferes, it physiologically, neurologically leads to inappropriate tension. That causes change in velocity and delivery. It wouldn't take much tension to throw it off.

Just that split-second thought—*God, am I going to do it again?*—can affect it."

In 1997, Rick Ankiel, the High School Player of the Year, signed with the St. Louis Cardinals and received a $2.5 million bonus. In 1999, he was the Minor League Player of the Year. In 2000, his first full season with St. Louis, his won-loss record was 11–7, and in the last month of the season he was 4–0 with a 1.97 ERA. At age twenty-one, he started the first game of the National League Division Series against Atlanta. In two starts and one relief appearance in the 2000 playoffs, against the Braves and the Mets, Ankiel walked eleven batters in four innings and threw nine wild pitches, most of which sailed ten feet over the batters' heads. In a game against the Mets, he threw five of his first twenty pitches off the wire screen behind home plate.

Ankiel says, "I was always the smallest kid. I was terribly shy. Maybe it was because my dad yelled at me so much. I was afraid to mess up. If I swung at a bad pitch in Little League, he'd make me run wind sprints when I got home. It was always, *I could've done better.* He always said, 'Do what I say, not what I do.'" Rick Sr. has been arrested fifteen times and convicted seven times—burglary, carrying a concealed weapon, and, most recently, drug smuggling.

Ankiel says his father instructed him "never to show emotion on the mound, which I always thought was strange because I was never like that, anyway."

At fourteen, Ankiel told his father, "I'm never going to be in the major leagues, so I'm going to do stuff with my buddies, hang out on the beach, go surfing, go fishing" in Fort Pierce, Florida.

Ankiel's father said, "That's not gonna work. If you love the game, good things will happen."

In *The Human Motor: Energy, Fatigue, and the Origins of Modernity,* Anson Rabinbach writes, "Neurasthenia is a kind of inverted work ethic, an ethic of resistance to work in all its forms. The lack of will or energy manifested by neurasthenics is the incapacity to work productively."

When Ankiel started to have trouble throwing the ball over the plate during the 2000 playoffs, his father, Ankiel's pitching guru his entire life, had recently been sentenced to prison for six years, and his parents had just gotten divorced. With his father gone, Ankiel made sure bad things happened.

(A rare happy ending, though: He abandoned the pitcher's mound and became a relatively successful outfielder until retiring in 2014.)

Asked how he would have treated Ankiel and others like him, sports psychologist Jack Llewellyn says, "You pull out vintage throws, and then you repeat those throws eight to ten times on videotape. What you're doing is bombarding the system by showing them what they're capable of doing. They've almost forgotten over time about how good they are, since they've been bombarded lately with all the negatives. If he's strong, young, and healthy, and he's thrown well in the past, then he can get past it. But anybody who thinks he can get rid of it and not think about it again probably is kidding himself. I think it's always there. I think you can do some things mentally to push it to the back. The worst thing you can do when you start to throw better is to start to get complacent and say, 'Well, I've got that licked.'"

Another sports psychologist, Shawn Havery, says about players who have suffered this problem, "I believe that they come to, kind of first off, doubt their ability. They start to overthink something that should be really reflexive. They begin to take too much time to consider all the machinations that go with that. It destroys their ability to do what they've been practicing so long."

Onetime Mets catcher Mackey Sasser, now a college baseball coach, had to pump the ball two or three times into his glove before lobbing the ball weakly back to the pitcher, which drove Mets pitchers to distraction and allowed opposing base runners to make delayed steals. During one game between New York and Montreal, Expo players counted Sasser's tapping of the ball into his glove, then Bronx-cheered when he finally threw the ball back to the pitcher.

When Sasser struggled in spring training in 1992, Jeff Shames, cofounder of the Manhattan Stuttering Group, wrote, "The root of Sasser's problem and mine is that we think too much about performing an ordinary chore. I stutter when I think too much about the act of speaking. All of us have difficulties in daily life. Sasser's and mine are just a little more obvious. We do what we can, even if it's not as quickly as some would like."

Former Pirates manager Chuck Tanner, who died in 2011, said, "You can't be afraid to fail. If you worry about failing, you will. The biggest reason behind these throwing mysteries is players trying not to make mistakes."

The same is true of stuttering. Stuttering consists of nothing but the attempt not to stutter. One cause of my stutter: Growing up in a maniacally verbal family, I placed enormous pressure on myself to speak well and rapidly. A similar thing happened to many of these guys: they're almost all hypersensitive, hypertensive types; they wanted it too badly, and then their overstressed body rebelled.

In "On Sickness," E. M. Cioran writes, "Flesh freeing itself, rebelling, no longer willing to serve, sickness in apostasy of the organs; each insists on going its own way, each, suddenly or gradually, refusing to play the game, to collaborate with the rest, hurls itself into adventure and caprice."

A lot of these guys also had overbearing stage fathers; the moment the father was dead or in prison or non compos mentis, the son's body celebrated its freedom from tyranny by self-destructing.

I've never heard of a stutterer who couldn't talk fluently to himself; it's a psychosocial disorder, as are athletes' mental blocks. In both cases, the person is unable to exist in easy dialogue (conversation, catch) with another person—the blocked individual becoming self-conscious about a routine activity that everybody else takes for granted. That ritual of rituals, playing catch with Dad, gets problematized, so suddenly you can't make the throw to first base, because you're thinking too much. It's as if at age twenty-two or twenty-four or twenty-eight or thirty-one, these athletes newly discovered the activity (worry, contemplation, self-scrutiny) that the rest of us do all the time, or at least I do all the time. For some reason, they're thinking about something else—some failure or sadness or guilt or weakness—and now can't perform without thinking about performing.

Former Kansas City Royals catcher Fran Healy (who, like Sasser, developed a mental block about throwing the ball back to the pitcher, and who, like Wohlers, is a native of Holyoke, Mass.—that mindful town) said, "The easiest thing a catcher has to do is throw the ball to the pitcher. It's a thing that should be as easy as opening a door. It's having to think about something that simple that makes it a problem. The problem, to a degree, existed through my career. But I was able to hide it. I'd just flip it back real easy to the pitcher. I'd walk out after every pitch and say something like 'Stay low' or 'Keep on it' or 'Bad call.' As a catcher, you can disguise a problem like this. Pitchers can't.

Their careers are over." Healy has gone on to become a successful sportscaster.

The late Dick Radatz, a former Red Sox relief pitcher, once threw twenty-seven consecutive balls in a spring training game.

Playing second base for Minnesota, Chuck Knoblauch made only eight errors in 1996 and won the Gold Glove in 1997, maintaining a forty-seven-game errorless streak. In 1999, playing for the Yankees, undergoing a divorce, and watching his father (his high school baseball coach and lifelong mentor) succumb to Alzheimer's, he made twenty-six errors, including fourteen throwing errors, most of which were on routine throws to first base. On plays on which he had to hurry, Knoblauch virtually always threw the ball fine. His throwing problems inevitably occurred on routine ground balls, when he had too much time to think.

"I really think, deep down inside of me, something is going on," Knoblauch, who retired in 2002, said at the time. "Something, somewhere along the line in my life, has affected me, and I don't know what it is. It's frustrating and it's puzzling. I don't ask, 'Why me?' because I'm a firm believer that everything in life happens for a reason. But I just have this feeling that whenever this thing stops, I'll know it without even picking up a baseball and throwing it. When I get to the root of this problem, I'll know I'm better without even walking on a baseball field. A lot of people have suggested that my throwing problems are going to be fixed simply by my going to left field for a while. I don't think that's going to be the case. That says this is something I can consciously correct. I know for sure it's not."

Cioran says, "Without pain, there would not be consciousness."

"If we can just get the mental part out of this thing," then Yankees manager Joe Torre said about Knoblauch's throwing problem, "we'll be okay."

David Grand, the proponent of a system known as EMDR (Eye Movement Desensitization and Reprocessing), says, "The problem appears out of nowhere. It can happen a few times and go away or it may never go away. People think that when you add 'sport' to 'psychology,' the reasons change. People, even top athletes, bring to the plate [!] all of their life experiences. The public openness of the problem, for all professional athletes, makes it much worse. EMDR reaches deep into the nervous system and lets people work on releasing traumatic memories. Patients begin to make a connection between the memory and what they are experiencing in the present. Unless you deal with the traumas, you're pulling up the weeds without the roots. Every time Ankiel makes a bad throw, it retraumatizes him. Give me three days with Ankiel and he'll be back to where he was. Give me a week, and he'll be even better. I have no question that Knoblauch can go back to second base without the yips and return to his Gold Glove stature."

Another psychologist, preferring anonymity, asked how many athletes overcome these mental blocks, replies, "Very few. Almost none."

In 1957, at age eighteen, Von McDaniel won the first four games he pitched in the major leagues, pitched nineteen consecutive scoreless innings, including a one-hitter, a two-hitter, and a perfect game for six innings. He finished the year at 7–5, with a 3.22 ERA. In 1958 he pitched two innings, in which he walked seven batters; he never pitched again in the major leagues.

Lindy McDaniel, who pitched for many years in the major leagues, says about his brother Von, "He lost his coordination and his mechanics. There was no real explanation. Some people thought it was psychological, but who knew about those things then? They sent Von down to the minors, but he couldn't get anyone out. He kept sinking further and further until he couldn't pitch anymore. It depressed him for years after he left baseball, but he couldn't talk about it."

None of these guys can talk about what's really bothering them. That's the problem: they're all repressive depressives, strong-silent types.

A student in my class, feeling self-conscious about being much older than the other students, told me he'd been in prison. I asked him what crime he'd committed, and he said, "Shot a dude." He wrote a series of very good but very stoic stories about prison life, and when I asked him why the stories were so tight-lipped, he explained to me the jailhouse concept of "doing your own time," which means that when you're a prisoner you're not supposed to burden the other prisoners by complaining about your incarceration or regretting what you'd done or, especially, claiming you hadn't done it. *Do your own time:* It's a seductive slogan. I find that I quote it to myself occasionally, but really I don't subscribe to the sentiment. I'm not, after all, in prison. Stoicism is of no use whatsoever. What I'm a big believer in is talking about everything until you're blue in the face.

Daniel Wegner, a professor of social psychology at Harvard, says, "People will develop an obsession not because there's anything interesting about it, but because so much energy is paid in trying to suppress it. For some, the cure is to think about it on purpose. The thing to do is tell everybody you see. Talk about it, even laugh about it."

In 1980, when Philadelphia won the World Series, Phillies relief pitcher Kevin Saucier—possessor of a 7–3 record and a 3.42 ERA—was named by fans the most popular Phillie. He said, "I'm a hyper person and I've always had a funny walk on me, so when I did a good job or we needed to keep loose, I wasn't afraid to show a little emotion." Traded to Detroit, he pitched even more effectively in 1981; he had thirteen saves, a 1.65 ERA, and was the best reliever in baseball at retiring the first batter he faced. In 1982, though—while his marriage was nearly unraveling—he gave up seventeen walks in sixteen innings. Sent to the minor leagues, he gave up twenty-three walks in twenty-two innings, had an 0–4 record, and an ERA of 7.36.

In spring training in 1983, Saucier said, "That strange feeling hit me again, and it seemed like things were twice as bad as before. I wasn't just missing high or low. I was missing side to side. I was throwing pitches twenty feet behind hitters. I could have hurt somebody, but then again, I never got that close. I just didn't feel right. It was like I was under a spell. It was a feeling of being lost, like trying to type with no fingers. What do you do? You're lost. You can't help yourself. You try, you try to relax, and you can't." Saucier now works for MLB as a scout.

Renée Bright, a sports psychologist, says, "Too often, athletes with natural ability are not aware of what it is they do that makes them play well, and when they get off track, they don't know what to look for. Also, few realize how much their private lives can affect their public performance." Interesting that a female psychologist points this out, since it's not a problem women are likely to have—failing to realize that their private lives can affect their public performance. So, too, women athletes are far less likely than men to be reluctant to talk about whatever might be plaguing them. It's nearly unheard of for a woman athlete to suffer from the yips. (So, too, it's also nearly unheard of for a black athlete to suffer from the yips. Absent other pressures, other oppressions, white men apparently have a tendency to oppress themselves by overthinking. Who knew?)

In Joyce's "The Dead," which takes place at a Christmas party, Gabriel Conroy remembers a phrase from a review he wrote, "One feels that one is listening to a thought-tormented music." Later, when he gives a toast, he says, "But we are living in a sceptical and, if I may use the phrase, a thought-tormented age."

On routine plays, Texas Rangers minor leaguer Monty Fariss, a rare shortstop with this particular mind-body problem, threw timidly to first base, often allowing the batter to beat the throw, although on difficult balls into the hole, he would make strong throws across the diamond. "Everybody wants to help solve the problem," Fariss said, "or help create one." He had a very brief major-league career.

In the bullpen, Oakland A's pitcher Bill Mooneyham was so afraid of throwing a wild pitch, which could roll onto the field and delay the game, that while warming up he was able to throw only changeups. He lasted only one season.

David Mamet says, "It is in our nature to elaborate, estimate, predict—to run before the event. This is the meaning of consciousness; anything else is instinct."

In 1987, a year after throwing a no-hitter, Joe Cowley of the Chicago White Sox gave up twenty-one hits, seventeen walks, and twenty earned runs in fewer than twelve innings. He never regained his form.

In 1971 Steve Blass won fifteen games for the Pirates, with a 2.85 ERA. He won games three and seven for the Pittsburgh Pirates in the 1971 World Series. In 1972, he won nineteen games, lost eight, pitched eleven complete games, had an ERA of 2.48—sixth best in the National League—and was an All-Star. Throughout his career he had allowed fewer than three walks per nine innings.

During spring training in 1973, he walked twenty-five men in fourteen innings, throwing one pitch that was so wild it landed nearly in the third-base dugout. In the 1973 season, Blass was 3–9 with a 9.85 ERA, walking eighty-four batters in fewer than eighty-nine innings. He tried pitching from the outfield. He tried pitching while kneeling on the mound. He tried pitching with his left foot tucked up behind his right knee. He tried Transcendental Meditation. He studied slow-motion films of his delivery. Warming up or throwing on the sidelines, while working alone with a catcher, he pitched well, but the moment a batter stood in against him he struggled, especially with his fastball. Blass was permanently out of baseball the next year.

Blass recently said, "I still can't pitch, not even at my own baseball camp."

There were many theories about Blass: he was too nice; he lost his will to win; his mechanics were off; his eyesight deteriorated; he was afraid of being hit by a line drive; he was afraid of injuring a batter with a fastball; the death of his superstar teammate Roberto Clemente incapacitated him; a slump led to a loss of self-confidence, which led to a worse slump, which led to less self-confidence. . . .

Dave Giusti, Blass's close friend and fellow pitcher, said in 1975 about Blass, "He's remarkably open to all kinds of people, but I think he's closed his mind to his inner self. There are central areas you can't infringe on with him. There is no doubt that during the past two years he didn't react to a bad performance the way he used to, and you have to wonder why he couldn't apply his competitiveness to his problem. Last year I went through something like Steve's crisis. The first half of the season, I was atrocious, and I lost all my confidence, especially in my fastball. I began worrying about making big money and not performing. I worried about not contributing to the team. I worried about being traded. I thought it might be the end for me. I didn't know how to solve my problem, but I knew I had to solve it. In the end, it was talking to people that did it. I talked to everybody. Then, at some point, I turned the corner. But it was talking that did it, and my point is that Steve can't talk to people that way. Or won't."

In *Intoxicated by My Illness,* Anatole Broyard writes, "The patient has to start by treating his illness not as a disaster, an occasion for depression or panic, but as a narrative, a story. Stories are antibodies against illness and pain. When various doctors shoved scopes up my urethral canal, I found that it helped a lot when they gave me a narrative of what they were doing. Their talking translated or humanized the procedure. It prepared, strengthened, and somehow consoled me. Anything is better than an awful silent suffering."

Former Los Angeles Dodgers second baseman Steve Sax—after overcoming such a severe case of the yips (thirty errors by mid-August in '83) that it became known for a while as Steve Sax Disease—said, "It's a matter of eliminating all possibility of error as far as mechanics go. Get that down pat, make good throws, and get your confidence back."

The Dodgers tied a sock over Sax's eyes and made him throw balls to first base blindfolded.

When Philadelphia Phillies pitcher Bruce Ruffin lost his control in 1988, a fan suggested that he take the can of chewing tobacco out of his back pocket.

Everybody tells a player with a mental block not to think about it.

Sax said, "It's like a big elephant in front of you. You can't ignore it." (An even rarer case of someone who, after many years, was "cured": in 1989, Sax led the league in fielding percentage.)

Sasser said, "I've been working with people on visualization, but either the throw's going to come or it's not. What can you do? Just pray."

Mike Stanley said, "All I could visualize was making an errant throw. I couldn't even visualize making a good one."

In the Land of Pain is Alphonse Daudet's diary of the disintegration of his body (and fellow sufferers' bodies) from neurosyphilis. "No general theory about pain," he writes. "Each patient discovers his own, and the nature of pain varies, like a singer's voice, according to the acoustics of the hall."

Nobody's perfect.

Everybody's human.

A magazine editor putting together a how-to issue asked if there was any activity about which I wanted to write a how-to article. "How about a how-not-to?" I replied. There are so many basic things I can't do correctly—just for starters: snap my fingers, blow a bubble, whistle, dive, rope climb, swing higher and higher on a swing. "Winners" (Michael Jordan, Joe Montana, Wayne Gretzky, Michael Phelps, et al.) bore me silly; there's nothing compelling to me about them, because there's so little of the human predicament in their shiny glory.

Woody Allen says, "Basically, everybody is a loser, but it's only now that people are beginning to admit it."

The better story is always in the losing locker room.

Success has many fathers; failure is an orphan.

In the fairy tale, sport is supposed to be some sort of transcendence, a liftoff from life's travails.

The mind is a powerful thing.

The director John Cassavetes supported himself by acting in commercial movies. He said that he could take almost any line and make it interesting as long as he was allowed to put in pauses—in other words, to insert thinking.

Everybody's an expert.

Nobody knows anything.

HISTORY OF AMERICA, #34

The question before the court is why Charles Barkley—NBA super-star turned NBA/USA commentator—has, in the words of his TNT colleague Ernie Johnson, "diplomatic immunity." Why does Barkley get to say virtually whatever he wants (criticize anyone, any-thing), whereas, for instance, the producers of *Barbershop* were forced to apologize for having a fictional character call Martin Luther King a "ho"? Barkley says it's because he's consistent: "You know I'm going to praise you if you do good, and I'm gonna criticize you if you do bad"—which actually has very little to do with it. Johnson says, "I think it's because his softer side is well known"—which has more to do with it. NBC Sports Group chairman Mark Lazarus says, "He can straddle that line without going over it"—which has even more to do with it.

Dave Coskey, the Philadelphia 76ers' director of public relations when Barkley played there, said, "Most of these guys are jerks who want you to think they're nice guys. Charles is a genuinely nice guy who wants you to think he's a jerk." In *Look Who's Talking Now* (1993), a little girl, age three, watches over and over a tape of Barkley playing basketball. She carries around a Barkley doll and is infatuated with him. In her daydream, she plays basketball with him and he is her best friend and perfect role model; he even lets her beat him. The fantasy worked because it contradicted Barkley's bad-boy persona at the time but conformed to what we intuited about him more deeply. Why was it so funny when, on *Saturday Night Live,* Barkley played a game of one-on-one against Barney the purple dinosaur and wound up punching Barney's lights out? Because we all know Barkley is Barney. His tail bent and one eyeball dangling from its socket, Barney said, "Charles told me I'm special."

Sports Illustrated once called Charles Barkley "Alan Keyes with monster ups." The ups are over. Despite endorsing Weight Watchers, Barkley still carries two hundred and sixty pounds on his six-foot-four-inch frame; his immensity is crucial to us loving him so much. Imagine a whippet-thin Oprah. It doesn't work. In America, we need our wizards to come in warm/cuddly packages. As he likes to remind himself and us, Barkley is worth fifty million dollars (plus or minus ten million dollars; he is endlessly paying off massive gambling debts). No one ever got rich truly discomfiting the populace. Lady Gaga's meat dress—that much activism we can handle. In the same way, Barkley is the reassuring rebel, the candid huggy bear, a weird admixture of Muhammad Ali and George Foreman. Barkley's race anger is exactly the amount of race anger we can process, which is to say: not that much. He's a race man of nearly nineteenth-century vintage: He believes in everybody pulling himself up by his bootstraps. Apotheosizing Charles Barkley is the only reparation we're going to be handing out this year (or next); white America needs to know that beneath all that black rage is, finally, forgiveness, even love. Barkley is proof.

The press release for Barkley's book *I May Be Wrong But I Doubt It*—dictated to *Washington Post* sportswriter Michael Wilbon and published by Random House in 2002—compared Barkley to Bill O'Reilly and Molly Ivins. Barkley has nothing in common with such ideologues, but it's instructive that the press release would compare him to someone on the right and someone on the left, since for all his storm and noise he's resolutely middle of the road. On the book tour, when pressed, he inevitably settled for the medium-range jumper. On CNN's *Talkback,* asked for his response to Harry Belafonte calling Colin Powell, in effect, a "house nigger," Barkley said, "Well, it's unfortunate because I love Colin Powell. He's one of my heroes. He's somebody I really admire. I honestly have great respect for Mr. Belafonte also." Asked about characters in *Barbershop* making fun of Rosa Parks, Barkley said, "I had no problem with the movie. I wish they hadn't said the thing about Rosa Parks, but I'm smart enough to know that it's just comedy." Asked whether women deserve to be members at Augusta National Golf Course, Barkley said, "No, because it's a private club. It's not a public place. Most of the golf courses I play have no black members, a lot of them don't have Jewish members, and some of them don't have women. They don't want them. I mean, that is the ultimate good-ole-boy network." Not exactly *The Fire Next Time.* It's Barkley's revolution (he goes round and round), not the white liberal's dream version (of his revolution).

Fellow Arizonan John McCain blurbed Barkley's book: "Whether you think he's right or wrong, you'll never find Charles Barkley dull, evasive, or afraid. He's blunt, honest, and funny as hell, a man with strong convictions and a determination to express them without fear of offending the sensibilities of more timid souls. He's got guts, and there's as much to admire in this book as there is in the man." As many blurbs are, it's a (flattering) self-portrait in a convex mirror; it's at least as much about McCain as it is about Barkley, and it captures how what Barkley says doesn't really matter: He's mastered the televisual style of controversy sans consequence, of playing both ends against the middle, of cult of personality. He once said, "My goal in life is to be president." Asked what his agenda would be, he said, "Lock up everybody over twelve and let kids rule the world." He *is* Barney. Paul Westphal, his former coach, called him "a free spirit—John Wayne in short pants."

Westphal, a friend of Rush Limbaugh's, also said about Barkley, "He enjoys life. He believes all people are equal. He believes in reaping rewards for hard work. That ain't liberal. In fact, he's the very definition of a modern conservative." Quizzed by Robert Novak, on *Crossfire,* as to whether he was a Republican or Democrat, Barkley said, "I'm not either, to be honest with you. I made a joke with my grandmother one time. I was asking her, 'Why are we Democrats?' She said, 'Republicans are only for rich people.' And I said, 'I'm rich.' And she hasn't given me a viable answer." The person he'd most like to meet is Colin Powell. After spending four hours with Clarence Thomas, he said, "I think I'm smart, but I was learning on the go talking with him. He's achieved true greatness." Many years ago, he said, "I look at all my old friends in the hood, and they're in the same place they've always been. On welfare, mostly. All the liberals have done is give the black man an inferiority complex. They gave us a little fish, instead of teaching us how to fish." Pre-echo of Donald Trump to black voters in 2016: "What the hell do you have to lose?"

And yet, asked what the Republicans might do differently, Barkley said, "I don't know. Actually, to tell you the truth, I have no idea." Explaining why he's never voted in his life, he said, "My one vote isn't going to mean much." When he was playing for the Phoenix Suns, asked why he didn't vote in Arizona, he said, "I don't think it's fair for me to vote in Arizona because I won't be here that long. I don't have time to keep up with all the issues. I don't vote in Alabama because I don't keep up with everything there, either." Here's really why Barkley doesn't vote: "You're voting for who'll do the best for you, and I don't like that system. You should vote to help everybody." People are good; the system is fucked.

In 2006, he said, "I was a Republican until they lost their minds"—focusing on gay marriage and illegal immigration. In 2007, he made a video supporting Obama. "The Republicans are full of it," Barkley said. "The Democrats are a little less full of it." In 2008, he announced that he'd be running for governor of Alabama in 2014 as an independent. In 2010, he acknowledged that he wouldn't be a candidate. More recently, he called the Ferguson protesters "scumbags" and said he was probably going to support John Kasich for president.

And yet in 2008 he said, "Every time I hear the word 'conservative,' it makes me sick to my stomach, because they're really just fake Christians, as I call them. That's all they are. They want to be judge and jury. Like, I'm for gay marriage. It's none of my business if gay people want to get married. I'm pro-choice. And these 'Christians'—first of all, they're not supposed to judge people. They're the most hypocritical people we have in the country. And it bugs the hell out of me. They act like they're Christians. They're not forgiving at all." His largeness is largesse. He's political without being political. He's confused and confusing.

·   ·   ·

The white man's simultaneous dream date and nightmare, Barkley improvises in ways that leave most white people flat-footed and half-witted. What do you say to a racial barb that's half joke, half truth? (Most white boys don't joke back.) Asked many years ago if he would ever play again for the 76ers, he said, "I can be bought. If they paid me enough, I'd work for the Klan." In Australia, Barkley, watching someone put a million dollars' worth of rubies on a table, said, "Damn, must not be any black folks in Australia. You can't just leave a million dollars' worth of jewelry lying around the hood." When he got in trouble with the NAACP for saying this, he explained that he sometimes says to whites getting their groove on, "Man, there's nothing in the world that makes me as nervous as seeing white people dance." When a reporter-friend asked him about groupies in the NBA, he responded by saying, "That's why I hate white people." When he injured himself in his last season, cutting short his career, he said, "Just what America needs: one more unemployed black man." After the game in which he ruptured his knee that season, walking into the interview room and sitting down next to his seventy-three-year-old grandmother, he said, "Well, guys, I guess this means sex is out of the question tonight." Asked why blacks excel at basketball, he said, "It doesn't cost anything to play." Are these comments meant to reinforce stereotypes white people have of black people or to mock these stereotypes? It's impossible to tell, which is what gives them their (mild) frisson. We want to tell ourselves we're grappling with racial history and reality when we're really not, and Barkley wittily keeps the issues afloat without ever making them unduly burdensome. He gets what he wants—a raison d'être—and we get what we need: our guilt assuaged.

In *I Might Be Wrong*, his discussions of race tend to be so evenhanded as to pat everyone on the back. He says, "The hardest but most important thing is to get a dialogue going on racial issues. I think people want to do better, I really do. I just think they're afraid. Nobody wants to make the first move. We can't get past worrying about disagreement, so we don't have meaningful conversations to make a difference. Damn, to me there's a lot worse than disagreeing with each other. What's worse, people hating and acting on that hate, or disagreeing?" Regarding the South Carolina flag flap, he says, "I'm not saying I don't understand why people are upset with state flags that include the Confederate flag. It's just that those people are not going to change what they feel in their hearts because they take the flag down. I understand the power of symbols, and if I had anything on my house that seriously offended someone, I'd take it down if for no other reason than common courtesy." Barkley's likable impulse is to find common ground, then to wonder ingenuously why we can't all just get along.

Even this degree of truth-dealing is unimaginable to Michael Jordan, who, when asked why he didn't endorse the black Democratic candidate for senator from North Carolina, Harvey Gantt, against Jesse Helms, said, "Republicans buy Nikes, too." More recently, Jordan donated a million dollars each to the International Association of Chiefs of Police and to the NAACP Legal Defense and Educational Fund, but—pointedly—nothing to Black Lives Matter. Barkley seems anti-establishment primarily in contrast to the ultimate establishmentarian Jordan, Barkley's career-long rival and ex-friend. Jordan once scolded Barkley for wearing a sweater rather than a suit: "Are you trying to look like a basketball player, or do you want to appeal to corporate America?" When Jordan saw Barkley giving money to a homeless person, Jordan grabbed him and said, "Quit doing that. If they're able to ask you for some spare change, they can say, 'Welcome to McDonald's. Can I help you, please?'" Jordan says, "Charles says what's on his mind. He never holds his tongue. I like him because it's like I'm the good brother and he's the bad brother. He says a lot of things the good brother wants to say but doesn't. And I like that. I know I'm always laughing when we're together." Of course he's laughing: In *Space Jam*, a cartoon paean to Jordan, Jordan's dog is named Charles. Barkley is the voice of the dog, whose talent gets stolen. The dog is sad: He has no place in the world to go because he can't play basketball. Girls tell him he can't play with them, either. He promises a shrink that he won't swear, won't trash-talk, won't even go out with Madonna, and he winds up getting his talent back. The movie appears to be a cautionary tale of some sort.

Barkley has said that the difference between the public perception of himself and Jordan and the private reality of himself and Jordan is the difference between night and day. This is a slightly oblique way of saying Jordan is actually the bad brother and Barkley is the good brother. "I understand what Michael is doing," Barkley said when they both were playing in the NBA, "but that's not me. These are my glory days. I'm not going to spend them locked inside some room." Put simply, Barkley loves himself—his former teammate Derek Smith once said, "Charles Barkley is a bigger fan of Charles Barkley's than any other person in the world"—but (unlike, say, Jordan) he also seems to love other people, find other people interesting. He's as much a social creature as Bill Clinton, whom he called the best president America's had while he's been alive (never mind that Barkley was at the time a registered Republican). "His heart is what makes him so great," a coach once said about Barkley. In *I May Be Wrong*, he says that after 9/11 people finally understood what he's been trying to say all along: "There's no black, there's no white, there's no liberal, there's no conservative. We all want the same things in life. We're all the same, and we got to do something about it." "I've had plenty of people tell me it appears I enjoy being famous," Barkley said recently. "But I've always disagreed with that. It's that I enjoy meeting people. There are only two ways to go about life if you're famous: enjoy this damn life or be miserable. I just refuse to stop living my life and enjoying great restaurants or hanging out with friends because I'm a public person. To me, one of the great things in life is to go out and meet new people, people whose experiences are different from your own. It has nothing to do with being recognized and well known." Regarding his experience in the 1992 Olympics, he said, "I loved Barcelona. Loved it. Maybe some people don't enjoy that, but I do. I know there are times I've been walking around a city overseas, ten thousand miles from home, and I've thought, *Here I am, this little kid from Leeds, Alabama, and I'm in Barcelona or Paris or Tokyo.*" Who wouldn't find this irresistible? No one.

He once changed a stranger's tire, drove him home, then waited until the man's children arrived home from school so they'd believe that Barkley changed their father's tire. At a hotel in Atlanta where he stays for his TNT gigs, a receptionist (whom Barkley greeted with a "Hello, girl!") said, "Before I knew him, I thought he was just a big shot with a big mouth, but he's the nicest man in the world." Which is perhaps why he was a very good, even great player but probably not among the best to ever play the game. After accidentally spitting on a little girl courtside—he was aiming for a heckler next to her—he said it was the only thing he ever regretted, "but you know what? It taught me a valuable lesson. It taught me that I was getting way too intense during the game. It let me know I wanted to win way too bad. I had to calm down. I wanted to win at all costs. Instead of playing the game the right way and respecting the game, I only thought about winning."

Winning, and food. As a TNT analyst (for which he won an Emmy for sports commentary in 2012), he's an omnivore: No team, no team's player, and certainly no team's concession stand can escape his mouth. When studio host Ernie Johnson, game analyst Kenny Smith, and Barkley were discussing cooking one night, Barkley wondered, "How come y'all call white guys chefs and black guys cooks?" Another time, Johnson, Smith, and Barkley were announcing the game courtside rather than analyzing it from the studio; when the camera cut to them on the sideline, Barkley was eating a huge bag of popcorn while talking at the same time. The conversation then turned to Barkley's culinary proclivities (basically, anything) instead of the game. Smith and Barkley had a bet that Barkley couldn't get under three hundred pounds by a certain day toward the end of the 2002 season. On a half-time segment, Barkley stripped down to his shorts and weighed in at two hundred ninety-nine. He loves his body and so do Johnson and Smith. For Barkley, hate is worse than overeating. He won't let any single issue destroy his love of love, or his life.

"My momma told me long ago to let my emotions out," he said, and does. "I believe in expressing what you feel. There are people who hide everything inside, and it's guys like that who kill whole families." Praising the sportswriter Rick Reilly, Barkley said, "The more you talk about the truth—even if it's about society, racism, politics—the more his eyes kind of lock in on you. He seems like he's actually interested in what you're trying to say." This is Barkley, too, of course: When reporters ask him questions, you can see the light in his eyes rather than the gun-metal gray ninety-nine percent of athletes favor. Former Boston Celtics coach Chris Ford said, "I love Charles because he's so honest. You can see a thought form in his head and then move right out of his mouth without stopping in between." He's barkly;

he needs to bark: "I think I have an obligation to myself and to God to tell the truth. Whether people take it good or bad, that's not my worry. I think people should say to themselves, 'Is Charles telling the truth?' instead of worrying about who it offends. I don't create controversies. They're there long before I open my mouth. I just bring them to your attention."

When he was eating in a fashionable restaurant in Atlanta, a gaggle of twelve-year-old girls walked in, all wearing fancy new braids; the birthday girl's mother told Barkley that her daughter's birthday present had been a group trip to the salon. "Whatever happened to Chuck E. Cheese?" Barkley asked the girl's mother. "Ain't no Dairy Queens in Atlanta?" This is Barkley's role in the culture or at least sports culture—bringing us crashing back down to earthy reality. About current NBA players, Barkley said, "They run like deer, jump like deer, and think like deer." Informed by a British journalist during the 1992 Olympics that the other basketball teams think the United States can win just by showing up, Barkley replied, "I think those other teams got a point." "I don't want to kiss anyone's behind," he says. "I don't want to lie to the media. I don't want to lie to anybody. You ask me a question, I'll tell you the truth. You don't like it? Tough shit."

Which isn't to say Barkley isn't also full of shit himself, full of hypocrisies or at least extreme contradictions. He's both truth-teller and scam artist, purveyor of old-school values with new-school style, a social conservative who throughout his playing career was a devotee of strip clubs, an antiauthority authoritarian, a rebel reactionary. After a difficult loss, he once said he felt like going home and beating his wife—the same woman he said made him cry every time they made love. He's a relentless capitalist whose principal shtick is sticking up for the poor and downtrodden. In the notorious *Sports Illustrated* cover article for which he posed breaking out of slave's chains, he said, "Sports are a detriment to blacks, not a positive. You have a society now where every black kid in the country thinks the only way he can be successful is through athletics." Yet he is one of the very most omnipresent commercials for this idea of success through sports. Barkley—who has said repeatedly that if he ever runs for political office, his primary issue would be improving public education, especially for poor kids, especially for poor black kids—never graduated from college and didn't graduate from high school, either, refusing to complete a Spanish class he found irrelevant. He's perhaps most famous for saying, "I think the media demands that athletes be role models because there's some jealousy involved. It's as if they say, *This is a young black kid playing a game for a living and making all this money, so we're going to make it tough on him.* And what they're really doing is telling kids to look up to someone they can't become, because not many people can be like we are. Kids can't be like Michael Jordan." Still, it's difficult to think of a recent athlete who is actually more of a role model. Although he was named one of the fifty greatest players in the history of the NBA, his appeal is heavily dependent upon people understanding him to be a gallant loser who could never quite win the big game; he never won an NBA title, whereas Michael Jordan won six, and Kobe Bryant and Magic Johnson, five. He was one of the fattest players to ever play in the NBA, but his single most important asset was how quickly he could jump. He's large (or was; he's now fairly svelte). He contains multitudes. His contradictions don't mean he's dishonest; all of his contradictions are ours as well.

The biggest contradiction: In God-haunted, godless America, he's both. He's frequently said, "I think God is in my body"—according to his mother, the result of a blood transfusion to his foot when he was three months old. But he once asked the devout, poor-shooting A. C. Green, "If God's so good, how come he didn't give you a jump shot?" And, even more ambiguously, he says, toward the end of *I May Be Wrong,* "It's not like religion isn't part of my life, because it is. I grew up going to church. I believe in prayer and treating people the way you would want to be treated. Religion, to me, is your individual relationship with God, or whatever you call your Supreme Being. That's it, plain and simple." This sounds as if he's talking, or trying to talk, himself into the theological position, especially when he then quotes an agnostic friend, who asked him, "How is it that when something bad happens, you never acknowledge God?" Barkley's response: "That really made me think. I said, 'That's fair. I don't know the answer, but that's fair.'"

He's preternaturally alert to death's siren, or at least more preternaturally alert than most middle-aged, multimillionaire ex-athletes are. He wants, desperately, not to waste his life: "I think you have to live as if tomorrow isn't promised to you." A large part of Barkley's appeal is that he feels this to the bottom of his bones, and people can feel that he feels this and they want some of that. He's alive, here, on this planet, right now. He's a brilliant extemporizer, inside the moment, satyr-like, actively searching for the jugular of truth and—this is key to presenting moderation in an immoderate appetite—nearly always finding it in humor. When he misses the truth, he still recognizes the moment's need for something to be said directly about it, even if it's just Barkley, bored, saying, "This sucks." If he were ever to run for office (he won't, but he'll keep mentioning the possibility), he'd be constrained by certain ideologies, whereas now he can contradict himself every other day or every other game, can recharge any moment with meaning, whether it's a racial incident or the analysis of a back screen. "There's nobody—nobody—who knows me and doesn't like me," he once said. Apparently true. After his Phoenix Suns lost the world championship to the Chicago Bulls in 1993, he said, "I'm *still* going to Disney World." Aren't we all.

BLINDNESS

My initial reaction when I saw on the web the report that Tiger Woods was seriously injured was *What's the matter with me that I hope he's been paralyzed or killed?* Jealousy. The much vaunted Schadenfreude. The green-eyed fairway. Tiger is extremely rich, famous (now infamous), semi-handsome (losing his hair), semi-black, the best golfer ever (was going to be), married to a supermodel (no longer, of course). I wanted him to taste life's darkness. Genes and talent and hard work don't guarantee anything. Everything comes to naught. *It is not enough for me to succeed; others must fail.* Or, *I want to rise so high that when I shit everyone gets dirty.* At 2:30 a.m. on Friday, November 27, 2009, Tiger drove his 2009 Cadillac Escalade into a fire hydrant, then into a tree. A minor accident: lacerations about the face. His wife either rescued him by knocking out the back window with a golf club or caused the accident by hitting him with same (more likely the latter, given the news that emerged shortly afterward). I was disappointed that Tiger was okay (for the nonce). But, really, I think we all were.

The only reason this minor traffic accident was given so much attention at first was so that we could all pretend to cheer him on but really root for his demise (he is/was too perfect; he's now said to be, à la Mickey Mantle, a billion-dollar talent on dime-store legs). Am I uniquely horrible? Laurie and I were watching a football game on TV; the star tailback was badly injured and taken off the field in an ambulance. Laurie said, "I can never watch football for more than five minutes without falling asleep, but when someone is injured, I can't turn away. Why is that?"

Later on, what was completely absent from all the coverage of Tiger Woods's self-destruction was even the slightest recognition that for all of us the force for good can convert so easily into the force for ill, that our deepest strength is indivisible from our most embarrassing weakness, that what makes us great will inevitably get us in terrible trouble. Everyone's ambition is underwritten by a tragic flaw. We're deeply divided animals who are drawn to the creation of our own demise. Freud: "What lives wants to die again. The life drive is in them, but the death drive as well." (Note that he says "them.") Kundera: "Anyone whose goal is 'something higher' must expect someday to suffer vertigo. What is vertigo—fear of falling? No, vertigo is something other than fear of falling. It is the voice of the emptiness below us which tempts and lures us; it is the desire to fall, against which, terrified, we defend ourselves."

And the more righteous our self-presentation, the more deeply we yearn to transgress, to fall, to fail—because being bad is more interesting/exciting/erotic than being good. Even little children, especially little children, know this: When Natalie was three, she was friends with two girls, sisters age three and four. The older girl, Julia, ran away from her mother, for which she was reprimanded. The younger girl, Emily, asked why and was told that running away was bad. "I wanna do it," Emily said.

Tiger needed to demolish the perfect marble statue he'd made of himself: the image of perfect rectitude. We were shocked—shocked—that his furious will to dominate his opponents on the golf course also manifested in an insatiable desire to humiliate countless sexual partners. We all contrive different, wonderfully idiosyncratic, and revealing ways to remain blind to our own blindnesses. In the British television series *Cracker*, Eddie Fitzgerald is a brilliant forensic psychologist who can solve the riddle of every dark human heart except his own (he gambles nonstop, drinks nonstop, smokes nonstop, is fat, and is estranged from his wife). Richard Nixon had to undo himself, because—as hard as he worked to get there—he didn't believe he belonged there. Bill Clinton's fatal charm was/is his charming fatality: His magnetism is his doom; they're the same trait. Someone recently said to me about Clinton, "He could have been, should have been, one of the great presidents of the twentieth century, so it's such a shame that—" No. No. No. There's no *if only* in human nature. When W. was a young man, he said to Poppy, "Okay, then, let's go. Mano a mano. Right now." The invasion of Iraq was the not-so-indirect result. In short, what animates us inevitably ails us.

And vice versa: Because I stutter, I became a writer (in order to return to the scene of the crime and convert the bloody fingerprints into abstract expressionism). As a writer, I love language as much as any element in the universe, but I also have trouble living anywhere other than in language. If I'm not writing it down, experience doesn't really register. Language has gone from prison to refuge back to prison.

Picasso: "A great painting comes together, just barely" (I love that comma). This fine edge of excellence gets harder and harder to maintain. My favorite book by an American writer in the last forty years is Renata Adler's *Speedboat*. And I hesitate to heap any more dispraise upon her much-maligned memoir, *Gone*, which I must admit I still find utterly addictive. Surely, though, the difference between *Speedboat* and *Gone* has to do with the fact that in the earlier book the panic tone is beautifully modulated and under complete control and often even mocked, whereas in the later book it's been given, somewhat alarmingly, free rein. Success breeds self-indulgence. What was effectively bittersweet turns toxic.

When my difficult heroes (and all real heroes are difficult) self-destruct, I retreat and reassure myself that it's safer here close to shore, where I live. I distance myself from the disaster, but I gawk in glee (no less assiduously than anyone else did I study Tiger's sexts to and from Josyln James). I want the good in my heroes, the gift in them, not the nastiness, or so I pretend. Publicly, I tsk-tsk, chastising their transgressions. Secretly, I thrill to their violations, their (psychic or physical) violence, because through them I vicariously renew my acquaintance with my shadow side. By detaching, though, before free fall, I reserve my distance from death, staving off difficult knowledge about the exact ratio in myself of angel to animal.

In college, reading all those Greek tragedies and listening to the lectures about them, I would think, rather blithely, *Well, that tragic flaw thing is nicely symmetrical. Whatever makes Oedipus heroic is also . . .* What did I know then? Nothing. I didn't feel in my bones as I do now that what powers our drive assures our downfall, that our birth date is our death sentence. You're fated to kill your dad and marry your mom, so they send you away. You live with your new mom and dad, find out about the curse, run off and kill your real dad, marry your real mom. It was a setup. You had to test it. Even though you knew it would cost you your eyes, you had to do it. You had to push ahead. You had to prove who you are.

EVERYBODY'S A WINNER

The most passionate thing I did in graduate school was attend University of Iowa basketball games. Joseph Heller gave a reading the same night as the Iowa-Indiana game, and I didn't even consider going to the former. My closest friend at Iowa, Philip, liked to say his childhood was about Walt Frazier. Every night he'd hear his mother and father screaming at each other in the next room, and he'd just stare at the Knicks game on the little black-and-white TV at the edge of his bed, trying to will himself into "Clyde's" body. In the spring of 1980, when Iowa beat Georgetown to reach the Final Four, Philip and I jumped up and down and cried and hugged each other in a way we wouldn't have dreamed of doing for any other reason.

Fifteen years later—mid-nineties—both Philip and I were living in Seattle (he's now back in New York). Our team was the Seattle SuperSonics, and whenever he and I would watch their games on TV, he seemed to go out of his way to compliment good plays by the other team, and I always wanted to ask him, *Is it a conscious effort on your part not to succumb to jingoistic cheering, or are you constitutionally incapable of the monomania required?* I admired his equanimity, but

I couldn't even pretend to emulate it. Though unable to say exactly what the disease was, I wanted the Sonics to cure me.

Sports passion is deeply, infamously territorial: *Our city-state is better than your city-state because our city-state's team beat your city-state's team.* My attachment to the Sonics was approximately the reverse of this. I had lived here for less than a quarter of my life, and none of the players was originally from the Northwest, let alone Seattle. I reveled in our non-Seattleness. My particular demigod was the Sonics point guard Gary Payton, who was one of the most notorious trash-talkers in the National Basketball Association. He wasn't really bad. He was only pretend bad—I knew that—but he allowed me to fantasize about being bad, or at least talking tough.

You might have to live here to understand entirely why this was of such importance to me. The ruling ethos of Seattle is forlorn apology for our animal impulses. When I castigated a contractor for using the phrase "Jew me down," he returned later that evening to beg my forgiveness, and the next week he mailed me a mea culpa and a rebate. Seattleites use their seat belts more, return lost wallets more often, and recycle their trash more than people do in any other American city. Thirty years ago, the Republican (losing) candidate for mayor was the man who (allegedly) invented the happy face. Last month, an old crone wagged her finger at me not for jaywalking but for placing one foot off the curb while she drove past, and my first and only thought was, *This is why I loved the Sonics—this is why I miss Gary Payton.*

I used to live across the street from a fundamentalist church, and whenever the Supes played particularly well, I was filled with empathy for the churchgoers. They go to church, I sometimes thought, for the same reason fans go to games: adulthood didn't turn out to have quite as much glory as we thought it would; for an hour or two, we're in touch with something majestic.

The psychoanalyst Robert Stoller has written, "The major traumas and frustrations of early life are reproduced in the fantasies and behaviors that make up adult erotism, but the story now ends happily. This time, we win. In other words, the adult erotic behavior contains the early trauma. The two fit: the details of the adult script tell what happened to the child." This seems to me true not only of sexual imagination but also of sports passion—why we become such devoted fans of the performances of strangers. *For once,* we hope, *the breaks will go our way. We'll love our life now. This time we'll win.* (The Sonics were sold in 2006 and relocated to Oklahoma City in 2008; in 2012, as the OKC Thunder, they played for the NBA championship and lost in five games. In 2016, their star player, Kevin Durant, à la Tom Joad, left Oklahoma for Golden State. Seattle and I, still nursing our loss, cheered wildly.)

THE WHOLE OF AMERICAN LIFE IS A DRAMA
ACTED OUT UPON THE BODY OF A NEGRO GIANT

Vince Carter is now at the end of his long and illustrious but oddly disappointing NBA career. However, behold my agony more than a dozen years ago when I contemplated his attempted apotheosis. For if I joined the hallelujah chorus concerning his "work ethic" and deference to his older teammates, his absence of jewelry and tattoos and showboating, his desire to "do things the right way," his post-game ritual of calling his mom and then playing video games rather than going to bars and clubs, his apparent contentment in Toronto, I'd feel as if I'd been unwittingly enlisted in an anti–Allen Iverson, anti–Latrell Sprewell, neocon crusade in service of the old (supposed) verities—politeness, niceness, humility. Given my background and politics, I'm surprised and even a little embarrassed that, during the first and second rounds of the 1999 Eastern Conference playoffs, I rooted for Carter's Raptors against both Sprewell's Knicks and Iverson's Sixers.

In that series against New York, Carter won the final two games for Toronto only after his own teammate prodded him to assume the alpha role. In the series against Philadelphia, he was criticized by his own coach for deciding to attend graduation ceremonies in Chapel Hill the morning of the final game, which Toronto lost when he missed a shot at the buzzer. Still, it's hardly his fault that his mother was a schoolteacher and his stepfather a high school band director; that after leaving the University of North Carolina a year early for the NBA he—per the agreement he signed with his mother—took correspondence courses in order to earn his degree in African American studies; that, according to one childhood friend, "he was raised to have morals, he was raised not to act better than anyone else," and according to another friend, "whenever I need advice, I call Vince. He's the best listener I know." What's so bad about being good? Isn't our collective romance with evil getting a bit boring in its own way? Why must Iago always get the best lines? Isn't it sweet (if a bit odd) that Carter's mother is proud that he's regarded as a "mama's boy," that Carter's then teammate Dell Curry (whose son Steph is every white fan's crush) said, "Vince is definitely the man I'd like to see my sons grow up to be," and that his former coach Butch Carter once complained, "He lacks a mean streak"? This absence of a mean streak proved crucial, fatal. He lacked/lacks a killer instinct. He's known not as one of the game's greatest players ever but as one of the greatest dunkers ever. Not perhaps a designation any player would seek. Equivalent, for a writer, to being known only as a "great stylist."

Images magnify the body. Television traffics exclusively in images. The NBA traffics, almost exclusively, in African American bodies, and from the time the first slave ship pulled into harbor, African American bodies have been big sellers. "I propose," as Ralph Ellison says in *Shadow and Act,* "that we view the whole of American life as a drama acted out upon the body of a Negro giant." And now, of course, the drama is being acted out and exported around the globe. My friend, a six-foot-eight, African American businessman who worked for several months in Tokyo, said he spent a portion of nearly every lunch hour explaining to people that he wasn't a basketball player. When does history begin, in other words? When does it end? Is the NBA a sport, a business, reparation theater? To what extent are players interested in such questions? To what extent can one insist that players be interested in such questions? If you're not angry, are you just not paying attention? Are these my questions, or my parents' questions?

Who was I, in other words, to tell Vince Carter how he should feel about his own life? What's that fantasy all about—the self-congratulatory yet masochistic liberal white dream about black men and their perpetual downness? Carter didn't grow up impoverished; on the contrary, he was raised in a four-thousand-square-foot house in Daytona Beach. Nor has he publicly said he was ever the victim of any particularly overt racism. He's been treated as a deity since high school, when, beginning his junior year, scalpers gathered outside the gym two hours before his games.

Maybe the best thing to do, then, was/is to just concentrate on Vince Carter the Basketball Player, specifically Vince Carter the Dunker, since that's why he was anointed, in his own words, "the next 'man.'" A previous anointee, Grant Hill, had nothing especially spectacular about his game; there was nothing about his body begging to be fetishized. Carter, by contrast, had—at least in this one realm—what Woody Allen once called "thrill capacity": George C. Scott was a great actor, but Marlon Brando rearranged our neurons. After Carter nearly single-handedly defeated the Lakers, Kobe Bryant said, "Vince has got wings, man. I've seen him do stuff that's crazy." In a game against Dallas a decade ago, Carter took off from around the free-throw line, spun counterclockwise 360 degrees, carrying the ball in his right hand as a waiter would carry a tray; when he completed his turn, he put his left hand on the ball and jammed it through the hoop. Afterward, asked about this play, Dallas's Steve Nash said of Carter, "He's one of those guys who might do something you'll never see again."

ESPN the Magazine, naming Carter the "new millennium's athlete of the future," said, "We can't take our eyes off of him—in or out of uniform," and he "delivers the best three seconds in sports." (How long does an orgasm last, anyway?) I, too, once wanted not just to praise Carter but to hijack him for my purposes, only what exactly were those purposes? To rebel, mildly, against my parents' politics and to remind myself that even an ordinary person from the middle class might be, in his own way, amazing.

IV. PERFORMERS

Are illusions better than nothing?
Can we sustain ourselves on dream crumbs? . . . What else can we do?
What else is there but dreams, phantoms, and other people?

—HILTON ALS

THE SAME AIR

I spent pretty much the entire 1970s indoors. As the indefatigable editor of my high school newspaper, I wrote innumerable "satires" about capital punishment. In college, I took curious pride in being the last person to leave the library nearly every night for four years. In graduate school, I hammered typewriter keys so incessantly that the landlord had trouble keeping the apartment directly below mine rented.

Rita and I left Iowa City shortly after Ronald Reagan's inauguration in 1981 to move to Los Angeles, where we lived for a few months with her parents in their glass house overlooking the ocean. Rita's friend's father (who told every new inamorata that she'd "unlocked his cock") was shrink to the stars and invited us to a party in Malibu Colony at which I dined on the same back porch with, but not really in very close proximity to, Steve Martin, Dustin Hoffman, Dinah Shore, Walter Matthau, Jack Lemmon, and Beethoven's Ninth Symphony playing in the background. Walter Matthau said he'd never seen his wife without her makeup. Someone asked me what I did and I said I was a writer and she asked me what I was writing and I said a novel and she said, "Oh, you mean a pre-movie."

An odd mixture of people showed up at Rita's parents' house: Oona Chaplin, Jean Stapleton, Henry Winkler. Rita's mother and stepfather and stepsister were beautiful in a way that neither Rita nor I was. In a menagerie of priceless objects, we weren't priceless objects, which caused me to feel so self-conscious and nervous that for the first and only time in my life I developed high blood pressure. A semi-famous actress actually said to Rita that Rita reminded her of Rita's dog in that physically they weren't out of the ordinary but that once you got to know both of them you really admired their unique spirits.

Hundred-dollar haircuts newly failed to strike me as hilarious. Dermabrasion and rhinoplasty didn't seem prima facie evidence of self-hatred. I got contact lenses. Rita got such a flattering haircut that her mother made her promise on the spot that wherever she lived the rest of her life she'd fly back once a month and get her hair cut the same way by the same person.

Rita's parents somehow managed to make watching TV seem to be a glamorous and vital and also slightly outré activity. When Rita and I weren't driving into Beverly Hills to go to premieres or into Westwood to see movies on the night they opened, we were watching TV or reading the *LA Times* or reading the trades or reading screenplays or teleplays. In grad school, I almost never read anything written after World War II; I now had trouble reading anything that hadn't been written in the last few weeks.

I was born in LA, have lived there on and off as an adult, and am utterly uninterested in LA jokes. That's not what this is about. What this is about is this: other people who had been less cloistered than I may have registered the shift a little earlier, and my sudden immersion in media/celebrity culture was so extreme as to constitute something like shock therapy, but for me 1981 is the year America as we now know it became America as we now know it; 1981 is the year the world changed forever; 1981 is the year everyone suddenly started breathing the same air.

INFORMATION SICKNESS

I love all forms of taxonomy: lists, categories, compartments, containers, boundaries. When I went to the famous Amsterdam sex shops, I was struck mainly by the arrangement of movies and magazines into exceedingly minute subdivisions of pleasure and pain. I love doing errands, and what I especially love about doing errands is crossing things off my errand list. When making phone calls, running errands, or performing ablutions, I always begin with what seems to me the least personal item and conclude with what seems to me the most personal item.

(Pre-email, pre-texting) I used to be happy to play phone tag for weeks on end in order to avoid actually talking, let alone meeting, with someone. The sound of static on the car radio is, to me, reassuring, sensuous, even beautiful. At the market, I always choose self-service checkout over human interaction.

The moment I walk into a hotel room, I turn on my laptop and the TV (the latter as wallpaper), which I turn off when I go to sleep. The worst drunk I know—twelve-ounce tumblers of scotch at eight in the morning—leaves CNN on all night downstairs as a sort of lifeline in his sleep. (He's always talking about "black": black air is considered the ultimate sin; he can't tolerate black; "they went to black"; the famous six minutes of black—he's obsessed with black, afraid of it, secretly thrilled by its suggestion of depth.) I don't ordinarily drink coffee, but once, in order to stay up all night, I drank twelve cups in eight hours; the next morning, I walked into a Chec Medical Center and said, "Please, you've got to do something to turn my brain off." When I'm nervous and need to calm down, I chew blank three-by-five cards like a woodchuck.

I once ate a half-gallon carton of ice cream in a single sitting. Ditto a bag of sixty-four cookies. I know no purer joy than residence in the throes of sugar shock: the exact moment, just before you crash, when your brain turns off and you leave the planet. Before seeing friends I haven't seen for a long time, I go on a diet because I want people to think, *He doesn't seem to seek solace in overeating; he must be happy and focused.*

Once, immediately after the breakup of a relationship, I managed to lose my wallet, checkbook, and address book within the space of a week. I find that if I'm having trouble remembering something—the name of a movie, say, or a friend's phone number—I often inadvertently trigger memory by holding the item (such as a video guide or my phone) housing the information.

I prefer previews to the movie, the "about the author" notes in the back of literary magazines to the contents of the magazine, pregame hype to the game. If I'm reading a book and it seems truly interesting, I tend to start reading back to front in order not to be too deeply under the sway of forward progress.

Once, a movie marquee's misspelling of the word "nominations" irritated me so much that when the punkette in the booth outside expressed zero interest in my correction, I bought a ticket for the movie, which I'd already seen, in order to be able to go inside and urge someone to do something about the error. On the other hand, in sixth grade I "liked" a girl named Connie Cummings; classmates wrote in chalk on the playground "DS + CC = Dog Shit + Cow Crap," which, to their surprise and perhaps Connie's as well, didn't bother me in the least: it seemed, simply, clever.

I never saw my mother, whose maiden name was Hannah Bloom, giddier than when she noticed that the *New York Times* crossword puzzle clue for 5-across was "Hard-hearted girl" and the clue for 7-across was "Claire of films." And yet my parents hoped so strongly that my sister and I would never "become part of the system" that they were honestly chagrined when, at age fifteen, I received my Social Security number, whereas my main response when I recently got audited by the IRS and saw my TRW credit report was a kind of relief that my existence could be confirmed by outside sources.

When I used to jog, I would pick up my pace and really run if I thought someone was watching me, but when no longer being watched, I'd go back to jogging. In conversation I feel little compunction about asking people extremely intimate questions but tend to balk when someone asks me even the most moderately personal question. In social situations in which it would be to my disadvantage to appear heterosexual, I attempt to give the impression that it's not beyond my ken to be bisexual. At a Halloween party many years ago, costumed as a pirate, I was flirting with a woman dressed as a lioness until she told me to take off my sunglasses, then said, "Oh, you're Jewish!"; my eyes were Jewish.

If a new song grabs my heart, I'll typically play it over and over again until it's completely robbed of all significance, beauty, and power. At a museum bookstore I bought dozens of postcards, none of which had any human figures on them, and the cashier said, "You know, you might be saying something here about yourself." I was: I'm drawn to affectless people whose emptiness is a frozen pond on which I excitedly skate.

I have a persistent yearning that I don't have to live, exactly, anywhere. When I lived for several years in New York, I'd go out every night at eleven and come back with the next day's *Times* and a pint of ice cream, then eat the whole carton while reading the paper, which had the odd but, I suppose, desired effect of blotting out tomorrow before it had even happened. My nightmares—an endless network of honeycombs, a thousand cracks in a desiccated lake—are always about the multiplying of chaos. Two questions constantly occur to me: What would this look like filmed? What would the sound track be? I grew up at a very busy intersection, and to me aesthetic bliss was hearing the sound of brakes screeching, then waiting for the sound of the crash.

That is why we, snatched from sudden freedom, are able to communicate only through this celluloid vehicle that has immortalized and given a definite shape to our formless gestures; we can live as though we had caught up with time and avoid the sickness of the present, a shapeless blur as meaningless as a carelessly exposed roll of film. There is hardness and density now, and our story takes on the clear, compact shape of the plot of a novel.

—JOHN ASHBERY

WHY WE LIVE AT THE MOVIES

Whenever Laurie and I used to go to plays, they would inevitably strike us as odd and antediluvian in their absence of a mechanical framing device. The first few years of our marriage, we would spend entire afternoons and evenings in cineplexes, sneaking from movie to movie, lugging vats of popcorn and soda. We'd always stay until the absolute end of the credits: the studio logo. The appeal for her was the "sensory overload" of image, music, and speech. What I loved the most was that it was almost the only time I cried. The worse the movie, the more I cried.

Someone somewhere says that a darkened movie theater reminds us of being in the womb and that the images we see evoke the worlds we dreamed before we were born. This seems to me to be simply true: by far my favorite moment in a movie theater still comes when the final trailer is over, the last houselights dim off, and the otherwise dormant right side of my brain takes over completely.

Thirty years ago, when we were dating, Laurie and I would compete to see who could whisper first into the other person's ear the name of the movie being previewed. I would always win, because I read movie reviews the way other people eat candy. (I read movie reviews the way I eat candy.) We were members of video stores all over Seattle and video clubs all across the country. On long weekends we'd choose a film that bore rewatching and watch it on an endless loop, until it felt *physically* painful to walk around outside the environment of the movie.

She was a genius at following and predicting plot developments; I was a great one for tracing themes and analyzing motive: She would explain to me what happened, and I'd explain to her what it all meant. Together, we felt like Fellini. At first our worst arguments would occur when I'd start analyzing the movie the moment we walked out of the theater. Then our worst arguments would occur when one of us was preternaturally attracted to one of the stars of the movie. Daniel Day-Lewis, for instance. Annabella Sciorra, for instance. Daniel Day-Lewis, for instance.

Once we were married, whenever we had people over for dinner, invariably we talked about movies all during the meal, then watched movies afterward. If people came over and somehow we managed not to watch a movie and our guests left before ten, sometimes she or I would race out to the video store and return with our fix. What was this jolt we came to crave so deeply? I'd read a book, then she'd read it, and we'd talk about it. Or, out on a drive, one of us would read a story aloud to the other. Or we'd read different books together in bed. It was nice, but it wasn't the same.

The glory of watching a movie with someone else is the illusion that the same experience is being simultaneously imprinted upon both participants' brains. It's very romantic, like simultaneous orgasm or double suicide. *You (who are so different from me and who just saw what I just saw) thought and felt what I thought and felt, didn't you? The crime you saw (your understanding of the crime you saw) didn't differ from the crime I saw (my understanding of the crime I saw), did it?* She would always check to see if I had been crying.

The crucial moment in Hemingway's *The Garden of Eden* occurs when David and Catherine come to understand that everything they've been doing has been an attempt to keep alive, or perhaps to resurrect, the feelings they felt when they first fell in love with each other. Movies are the synthetic injection of these feelings: The whole world comes into focus and seems interesting and dangerous; our lives, which aren't lived on the grand scale, are lived on the grand scale. *Don't let it ever end, we very nearly pray to the screen, don't let's ever die.*

WHY WE LIVE AT THE MOVIES (ii)

Do movie stars wear sunglasses to shut us out or lock themselves in? At first my sunglasses were too dark. They also seemed to have an odd tint to them. It didn't take long, though, before I became accustomed to the discoloration and the shade. The reds and blues still looked red and blue. I found that if I wore a particular pair of shades long enough I couldn't feel them anymore. It was as if they weren't even there. Nearly everyone said these sunglasses looked good on me, but the oddest thing happened when I took them off: I felt like I suddenly couldn't see.

WHY WE LIVE AT THE MOVIES (iii)

Gore Vidal said, "There is no such thing as a famous novelist now, any more than there is such a thing as a famous poet. I use the adjective in the strict sense. According to authority, to be famous is to be much talked about, usually in a favorable way. It is as bleak and inglorious as that. Yet fifty years ago, novels were actually read and discussed by those who did not write them or, indeed, read them. A *book* could be famous then. Today the public seldom mentions a book, though people will often chatter about the screened versions of unread novels. What, after all, do we most love to talk about? Movies."

Richard Price: "There is one thing that is more powerful than dope, and that's movies. Because even people who don't like dope love movies. Everybody loves movies. All you've got to say is *Sea of Love* or *Color of Money,* and people look at you. They go weak in the knees. Like, 'Would you call him Al, or would you call him Mr. Pacino?' All of a sudden you're like this bridge standing between them and this dream factory we all grew up on. And we're all dopey about."

Cynthia Ozick, in conversation, said that William Gaddis wrote a truly great novel, but too late. By the time Gaddis wrote *The Recogni-*

tions, the time for truly great novels was already over. It simply didn't matter that Gaddis had written a truly great novel.

There's no longer any possibility, in other words, of ever reaching, as John Updike once hoped, "a vague spot a little to the east of Kansas. I think of the books on library shelves, without their jackets, years old, and a countryish teen-aged boy finding them, and having them speak to him."

In college I spent many hours in the Marxist bookstore just off campus, eating the lunch I'd bought at McDonald's; I loved slurping coffee milkshakes while reading and rereading Sartre's *The Words.* At the end of one particularly productive writing session in the library, I actually carved into the wooden wall above my carrel, I SHALL DETHRONE SHAKESPEARE.

Fueled by such ambition, I was a good bet for graduate school, where my first teacher, Vance Bourjaily, said that if he had it to do over again, he would have become a screenwriter, and my second teacher, Hilma Wolitzer, said that she wished she were as famous to the world as she was to herself. When the actor Craig T. Nelson wanted to meet me before optioning my first novel, *Heroes,* I flew to Toronto, where he was making a movie; he walked around at night and made eye contact with prostitutes until they recognized him, then he'd wink and laugh and inform them that it was cold out, better bundle up.

RADIO

When I was in sixth grade, a pseudo-joke circulated around the playground and stayed for what felt to us like an eternity— weeks, maybe months. The story was inevitably told with minor variations in background information and character development, and the setting was always shifting slightly from the North Pole to the South Pole, but the essential situation tended to remain largely intact: A male polar bear and a female polar bear live happily together on an ice floe until one day it splits apart. As Mama Polar Bear floats east and Papa Polar Bear floats west, Mama Bear calls out (and here it was vitally important to pronounce the punch line with just the right mix of interrogatory confusion and exclamatory fatigue), *"Radio!?"*

Several of us would watch as one of us told the joke to an uninitiated classmate, and when the punch line was delivered, we'd all laugh maniacally. The joke, of course, was that there was no joke, and the point was to prove how compliant all us sixth graders were. The listener always followed our lead and laughed and laughed. The instant he started to laugh, we'd all fall completely silent and ask, "What's so funny?"

"Well, you know," he'd say, still holding his stomach.

"No," we'd say, "tell us."

"Well, you know, '*Radio!*' "

Unpersuaded, we'd press him further, and he'd retreat to the position that it just sounded funny: the two polar bears, the ice floe, "*Radio!?*"

"What's funny about it?" we'd ask again.

And then he'd have to acknowledge that he laughed only because we were laughing. "Wasn't it supposed to be funny?" he'd ask.

Sooner or later we'd laugh at him and explain the situation and call him that most terrible name: "conformist." What we ignored for the most part was the process by which we, individually and collectively, had recently been introduced to the situation ourselves, and speaking strictly of myself for a moment, how comparatively late in the game I was allowed to be enlightened, occupying as I did the singular position of indisputably least popular person in the indisputably most popular group.

PROBLEMS AND SOLUTIONS TO PROBLEMS

The lobby of the NBC affiliate KING5 featured huge TV screens everywhere and couches like thrones. Everybody looked like they were going to church—dressed up, serious, whispery, slightly nervous. A plate of chocolate-chip cookies with M&M's served as a metaphor for pre- and post-Oprah; either we were, in Oprah's phrase, "ordinary folk," or we belonged on the outsize television screen on which, at three in the afternoon, preternaturally attractive soap opera figures played. Between us and Oprah was this plate of cookies. I, too, wanted to be rich and thin and famous. I abstained.

Before the show, one woman said to another, "I think your hair looks great."

"A little bit too curly. . . . Carey has coiffed her hair for the event."

Another woman said, "I saw Oprah on *The Tonight Show*. When she was talking about her weight going up and down, she spoke right to me."

Someone else said, "Hi. I'm from the sexual harassment committee."

The set of the show was made up of magazines, pink couches,

wood painted blue and pink, flowers, vases, books, plates, and paint-ings of nothing, absolutely nothing—pastels and vague landscapes. It wasn't anyone's living room.

"I have a friend who looks like Candice Bergen," said a member of the press sitting next to me. "She lives in New York and everyone always mistakes her. It's so funny."

"No one looks that similar," said her colleague.

A KING person asked if we were all big Oprah fans. Not fans of the big Oprah, but big fans, enthusiastic devotees of Oprah. Applause. A member of the audience informed us that she had sung "The Star-Spangled Banner" at the KeyArena and offered to entertain us while we waited for Oprah. The offer was noted.

"This is your opportunity to talk to Oprah, so start thinking of things, okay?" asked another KING person, in a manner remarkably similar to that of Miss Lytken, my first-grade teacher: all solicitous concern and benign neglect.

"I just wanted to make sure you guys know you won't be asking any questions during the show," the KING publicist told the press people.

"Oh, no, we're going to be harassing her," said the reporter whose friend looked like Candice Bergen. Everyone laughed; the runway had been cleared for takeoff.

"Who are we here for?" a KING person asked the audience.

"Oprah!" we shouted.

"One more time!"

"Oprah!"

"I know that with Oprah here, you won't need to be told to applaud. But when the APPLAUSE sign lights up, be able to applaud, okay?"

APPLAUSE sign.

Applause.

"Again."

APPLAUSE sign.

Applause.

The hosts of *Seattle Today,* Cliff Lenz and Susan Michaels, came out to prime the audience before Oprah actually appeared. As the audience applauded, Susan made the oddest noise, which I can equate only with the sound of a seal, as if, without meaning to, she were trying to produce for us—in parody form—the essential ingredient of our well-trained reaction. Cliff wondered why there were so many children in the audience on a school day. He was informed that it was a school holiday.

"Public schools, too?" he asked.

Cliff and Susan asked what sort of questions people would want to ask Oprah when she's on the show. People wanted to ask her what she'll do with her "fat clothes"; whether she'd ever heard of the actress Dorothy Dandridge, who was the questioner's sister; what Oprah's most significant career break was. All the questions had to do, in other words, with the gap between regular life and celebrity. Someone told Cliff that she was going to ask Oprah whether she'd pose for a picture with her. Cliff explained that Oprah was awfully busy and may not have the time.

"Well, that's the thing," the woman said. "I don't want you to answer. I want her to answer."

What Susan wanted to know was "What does she wear when she's kicking around the house? I'll bet she's my kind of lady—a sweats kind of lady." Susan looked like she hadn't seen the inside of a sweatband in her life. Reality kept getting praised, weirdly, in the middle of this discourse, whose every syllable was fantasy.

"Oprah's almost here," we were informed.

"She's in the dressing room."

"We like to tease," said a KING person, stoking the crowd, pumping his fist.

"Suck it in, folks," said Cliff. "You look fatter on the air."

"The things that bring me pleasure are the things that bring other people pleasure," Oprah told us.

"What brings you happiness?"

"A great book."

Later, asked to name her two favorite books, she named two books she was attempting to develop into movies.

"What have you learned from guests, great or not?" she was asked.

She had learned the most from "ordinary folks, just an ordinary family. I believe we're all ordinary people."

Someone from the Rape Crisis Center wanted to know whether Oprah was ever going to do a show on male victims of rape. Someone from the Northwest Women's Law Center wanted to know what she thought about abortion, then gave her a packet and a note from Gloria Steinem.

"From Gloria?" Oprah asked.

Someone from a volunteer organization asked if she was going to do a show about "volunteers, the ordinary heroes of this country."

Oprah explained that she failed as a television reporter because she'd get all choked up on the air about the people whose tragedies she was relating. As an actress, she always cried over everyone else's scenes; when it came time for her to cry, she was all dried up. In other words, she couldn't help it: she was just too empathetic.

"Has anyone on your show ever been rude, snobby, or arrogant?"

"No."

"Never?"

"No. Never."

When asked what her message was, she said she hoped that people would see the light in her and think there was maybe a little bit of that, too, in themselves.

"I hate to break," said Cliff, "but this is TV."

"Didn't she do a great job?" we were asked at the end of the show, and told to applaud one last time as she walked off the stage, leaving behind the packet the woman from the Northwest Women's Law Center had given her. *Oprah* was being broadcast on the huge screen in the lobby as we exited. The topic was stand-up comedians.

When I got home, I found a message from the KING publicist on my answering machine. I'd forgotten to wait around to find out whether a ticket for Oprah's Saturday-night performance at the Paramount would be left for me at the Four Seasons Hotel, where Oprah was staying. "I hope there wasn't a problem and that's why you left," said the publicist—member of a new race of people who love problems and solutions to problems.

RADIO (ii)

Do you know what I hate about not having a radio?" Laurie asked, pre-internet.

"What?" I said. She'd been back a day or two from Vancouver, where her antenna had been snapped off.

"You feel like you could be driving along, a nuclear disaster could occur, and you wouldn't even have contact."

"Contact?" I said. "Contact with what?"

"Everyone else."

THE SUBJECT AT THE VANISHING POINT

I attended a march against the Gulf War, and when I confessed to my father that I was constitutionally incapable of participating vivaciously in any sort of group activity, he responded by sending me a series of one-sentence postcards: "It's better to light one candle than to curse the darkness." "If you can move one grain of sand from one spot to another, the world will never be the same." "Popular culture, of which you and your generation are so enamored, is *substitute* family, *substitute* community, *substitute* love." "Never again." "It's better to die on your feet than to live on your knees." "Change the world—it needs it." I grew up with these aphorisms, these elegant dicta that were meant to explain everything.

On Friday nights, when my sister and I were in junior high school, my parents would take us to Kepler's, the bookstore of choice for Bay Area radicals; while I was supposed to be tracking down *Soul on Ice* or *Steal This Book,* I was actually scouring *The Whole Earth Catalog* and the *Evergreen Review* for pictures of naked ladies.

.　　　　.　　　　.

The summer before my first year of college, I worked as a teacher's aide in a remedial summer school in San Francisco. All the students were black, and all the teachers except me were black. Sometimes at the end of the day, the teachers screened blaxploitation films. We watched *Mandingo*, a weird Southern gothic inversion of the genre. James Mason, the white massa, acted evil; Richard Ward, his slave, plotted freedom; everybody shouted, "Right on!" Caught up in the action, I, too, shouted, "Right on!" Everyone turned around and stared icily. A line had been crossed, a taboo broken. Though I'd been completely serious, I said, "Just kidding," so we could all get back to watching the movie.

Since I was president of the eighth grade, I was directed, despite my stutter, to address, via the intercom in the principal's office, the entire junior high school on the subject of the eighth grade's appalling behavior at the recent assembly. I found the assignment so flattering, the power so intoxicating, that I didn't stutter at all. Not once. I don't think I even paused for breath.

I know nothing about planes, but a couple of DC-10s had gone down in recent weeks, so I asked the American Airlines ticket agent, "What kind of plane will we be flying?" "Were you in 'Nam?" she said. Confusion (what does asking what kind of plane we're flying have to do with Vietnam?—only now do I see the connection; she thought I might be carrying explosives) and pride (I'd been mistaken for a soldier) warred in my brain before I said, "Um . . . no."

The summer between high school and college I taped a photograph of each Watergate witness (above his most self-incriminating quotation) on the same wall that I'd once covered with pictures of the 1965 Dodgers. Heroes, villains—it hardly mattered; the subject was where I wanted him: at the vanishing point.

.　　　　.　　　　.

The former governor of California hired me to write a biography of him that would have as its subtitle "Champion of Social Justice." I quit, or he fired me, when it became increasingly apparent that no one was interested in the champion of social justice except in conjunction with his acerbic son. One day, I was walking with the champion of social justice the few blocks from a restaurant back to his law office in Beverly Hills, when he turned to me and said, "Guess how much it cost me to join the Bel-Air Country Club?" I told him I had no idea. "Fifty thousand dollars," he said.

"I don't buy Coors," I heard someone explain to his roommate in the market. "They're fascists." "They're what?" the roommate said. "They support fascist causes," the man said. "Like what?" the roommate said. "Someone told me what they were," the man said, "but I forget."

Now the only people I like are ambivalent about everything to the point of paralysis.

LIFE/ART

When I was five or six, my sister and I and the other kids on the block would run outside and play *Sea Hunt* the moment the show was over. One of us would be Mike Nelson, ex-Navy frogman turned underwater troubleshooter, and the rest of us would hide and await rescue. Whenever I was Mike Nelson, I would always be distracted by and worry endlessly about, say, a broken shoelace or an ant crawling down the back of my neck—off I'd go on a sustained crying jag. I always used to wonder how Lloyd Bridges battled sharks, octopuses, moray eels, manta rays, alligators, giant sea turtles, Aqua-Lunged badmen, and rapture of the deep but never got bogged down in minutiae from his own life, why he never appeared to feel lonely.

Toward the end of elementary school, I kept a record—dozens of yellow, legal-size pages—of Robin's "Holy" outbursts, his alliteration and assonance, his fast riffs in sharp contrast to the laconic Batman. Holy homicide, Batman. Holy hurricane, Batman. Holy whatever, Batman.

One day, oddly (characteristically, self-destructively), I sent my one and only copy of Robin's exclamations to the producers of *Batman;* I thought they might want to have it, for some reason. (I thought it would connect me in powerful, mysterious, and irrevocable ways to the show I spent all week thinking about.) I got back a letter thanking me for my interest, along with an autographed photograph of the laconic Batman. I never watched or wanted to watch the show again. I stuttered slightly worse than usual for a few days, then returned to my usual rate of disfluency.

At twelve, I couldn't not turn friends' names into nicknames based on the names of famous people. Ethan Saunders was "Satch," because of Satch Sanders, the Boston Celtics reserve forward to whom Ethan bore no resemblance whatsoever. Jim Morrow became "Agnes Moorehead," or "Aggie," for short. Gary Goodwin was "Gookus," after the Philadelphia 76ers mediocrity Matt Guokas. Everybody hated me for doing this, but the interesting thing (to me, anyway) was that the nicknames always stuck, often for years and years. We couldn't stand—I couldn't stand—our unamplified little lives.

Childhood consisted for me mainly of a set of experiments about faith and perception: believing that if I hid my face in my hands, not only could I not see anyone but no one could see me; sitting with my sister in the back of the car, pretending—as they pulled up alongside us—to recognize people in other cars, waving madly at them, getting them to pretend to recognize us and wave back; writing my name, "in cursive," over and over and over again, trying to make my signature look impressive enough to appear at the bottom of checks.

Movie titles often consist of a two-word phrase such as *Stone Cold* or *Striking Distance* or *Dead Reckoning:* a moribund metaphor literalized until it becomes a violent pun, the point of which is to persuade the viewer that life—which sometimes seems banal, predictable—has hidden reservoirs of excitement and terror.

If your picture wasn't any good, you weren't standing close enough.

—ROBERT CAPA

ROBERT CAPA, MISUNDERSTOOD

In his diminutive, hawkish handsomeness, Mike Watkiss looked not unlike my half-brother, Joseph, looked when he was in his late twenties. Watkiss's method of operation was virtually unvarying and, in its own way, brilliant. First, he asked you how many murders you'd committed recently ("Just a rough estimate—I know it's hard to keep track"), how many adulterous affairs you were currently having ("You're married, aren't you?"), whether he hadn't seen your picture somewhere recently ("In the post office perhaps?"). Then he asked you how many bodies you'd seen wash up onshore this week, how many of your friends were drug addicts, whether this wasn't the mass-murder and adultery capital of the country. Finally, he asked whether you hadn't been watching *Twin Peaks* ("Isn't everything you see on TV true?"), whether real life wasn't in fact much more exciting and corrupting than television ("Is the American public being deceived?").

Watkiss, a reporter for the television show *A Current Affair,* strolled around Snoqualmie with a cameraman, a soundman, and a production assistant, interrogating people. After hanging around with them for an hour or so, I reluctantly agreed that it seemed at least plausible that this was what they said it was: "just a light piece." My reluctance had to do with the fact that I had no idea how the footage would be edited, nor did the people being interviewed, and our uncertainty *(This guy's not serious, is he?)* was the very quality that gave the interviews their baffling imbalance. Still, as Watkiss said, he'd been told to come up here and have a look around, but it was obvious "this town is, like someone in that *Star* article said, a lot more like Mayberry than Twin Peaks." They were just having some fun with it.

Like most male movie stars (Al Pacino, Dustin Hoffman, Sylvester Stallone, Tom Cruise), Watkiss is quite short and, seemingly as a result, has extremely fine, extremely telegenic features: prominent cheekbones, dramatic eyes, a strong chin, an amazing amount of dark hair. He seemed to be an emissary not so much from New York or LA as from television itself.

Watkiss's approach was mock-melodramatic: tabloid journalism taken to parody. "You'd have to be brain dead to take this seriously," he explained. Cool presence, semi-amusing patter—at first, these seemed to be the principal techniques by which Watkiss dominated his subjects. No one could even remotely resist him. A relaxed hipster on a bicycle said how much he wanted to be interviewed, but when asked on camera how many adulterous affairs he was having, he suddenly tensed up and laboriously explained that he was single. His giddy friend, asked how many murders he'd committed that week, became oddly solemn and started talking about the Defense Department and being a survivalist. Two police officers found themselves denying, through pursed lips, that Snoqualmie was the mass-murder capital of the country. A bright, bespectacled young woman turned a little shrill and accused the show (*A Current Affair? Twin Peaks?*) of transforming the town into a joke. People who had called the crew over to come talk to them, the moment filming started, went completely deer-in-the-headlights frozen.

Upon seeing the film crew, a workman carrying a chain saw ran straight down, at a 45-degree angle, the wooden roof he was repairing, jumped onto the bed of his truck, and bounced over to the camera crew. Again, the moment filming started, he just kept grinning and could say absolutely nothing at all to what were by now to my ears all the usual questions: how many people have you mowed down with that thing this week, etc. Once the interview was over, he ran after the crew and said that he might not be a good actor—he'd been asked to say, "Until next time, America," then fire up his chain saw—but he was a really good carpenter; the chain saw felt like it was attached to his hand. He was explaining, in effect, why he'd flunked the screen test: The chain saw rather than the camera was his weapon. Still, he wanted to know when the show would be on.

Then Watkiss turned and asked whether he hadn't seen my photograph somewhere before—in the post office perhaps? Weakly I mumbled something about the FBI's Most Wanted list. He asked how many people I'd murdered that month. I tried to play along by saying, "Twenty-seven." "Does your mother know about this?" he asked, and although a few minutes later I was able to torture myself by thinking up mildly witty repartee, at the time all I was aware of were the pincer movements of the cameraman and the soundman and how I wasn't talking to Watkiss but to Watkiss in terms of the camera and the way the camera read him as a perfect and unreal absence and me as a flawed and real presence. I finally said, "I'm not going to do this anymore; turn off the camera." Ten seconds after they relented, I was instantaneously and immensely glib about the power of the camera to distort and judge and serve as a kind of actor in a triangulated drama. I even managed to launch into an exceedingly obvious diatribe against the shoddy sensationalism of *A Current Affair,* but nothing I said carried any weight the rest of the afternoon, because it was so obvious that for an endless moment I'd fallen prey to the awesome power of something toward which I pretended absolute irony: I wanted the camera to find in me, and love me for, qualities that I don't and couldn't possibly possess. The crew moved on to the next person, and I brandished my quaint pencil and notepad as earnestly as the builder had his chain saw.

DOUBT

I don't know about Adam Sandler's movies. I haven't seen any of them, with the exception of *The Wedding Singer,* whose silliness = sweetness I rather liked. I have, though, listened to "The Chanukah Song" dozens and dozens of times; it gets at Jewish ambivalence about Jewishness, at my ambivalence about Jewishness (about simultaneously wanting to be a part of the moronic goyish culture surrounding us and wanting to be apart from it), as acutely as anything I know.

Virtually every cut from Sandler's CD *What the Hell Happened to Me?*—even the title mimics Jewish angst—is a barely disguised ode to dispossessed people, animals, and things, such as a chained goat, a piece-of-shit car, a neurasthenic Southerner, a senile grandmother. Sandler begins "The Chanukah Song" by telling a live audience of college students that there are many Christmas songs but not very many Chanukah songs (Jewish apology for being Jewish in a Christian culture). So, Sandler informs us, he wrote a song for all the nice little Jewish kids who don't get to hear any Chanukah songs. This is Jew as victim, Jew as "nice." Is it important to Sandler to create a little distance between himself and nice little Jewish kids? Is it important to me to do the same? If so, why?

In the first stanza, Sandler says that Chanukah, festival of lights, is coming and is fun, so everybody should put on their yarmulkes. Repetitively strumming an electric guitar, unable to carry a tune, he sings these lines with good-Jewish-boy poignance, sweetness, yearning. (Parts 2 through 4 of "The Chanukah Song," on other CDs, don't work for me at all. The balance between feeling and mockery, which Sandler maintains so delicately in the first version, tips over completely into parody in the later version and is therefore, given my emotional geography—bound by ambivalence—off the map.) He undermines the whispery solemnity, though, when he says "eight crazy nights" with a self-conscious, Steve Martin-esque craziness. Chanukah isn't about "crazy nights"; neither is Judaism; neither am I. The song is going to make the case that Jews are capable of Dionysian craziness, and what makes the song so appealing to me is that even as Sandler makes this assertion, he also winks about it, knowing it's not especially true. I can count on one hand the number of times I've ever been drunk or high. Okay, two hands.

In the second stanza, Sandler says that Kirk Douglas, James Caan, Dinah Shore, and David Lee Roth are Jewish "just like you and me." Sandler sings these lines with ostensible self-pity, which he—again—undercuts by laying on way too much schmaltz. This list of people who are Jewish is, of course, a send-up of Jewish head-counting, of "what's good for the Jews," and yet it's also genuine boast. Sandler is a creature of popular culture, so it's natural for him to name celebrities, but to me—only to me, because I look like, or at least strive to look like, a Jewish intellectual?—it's heartbreaking that none of the four people he mentions "looks Jewish," and they all are, or were, sex symbols, based more or less on their Aryan good looks. *Here are people we're proud of,* Sandler seems to be saying, *but we're proud of them because they look like you*—the audience of college kids at the University of California at Santa Barbara to whom he's singing, blonder than whom there doesn't exist. The audience goes wild, clapping in rhythm. *We love you for being Jewish, Adam,* I seem to hear them saying, *Jewish just like us* (blonde beauties; when a girl calls out to him that she loves him, he doesn't say anything).

The third stanza does pretty much the same thing, with Paul Newman and Goldie Hawn—both half-Jewish—the new blond, blue-eyed gods. "Put them together, what a fine-lookin' Jew," Sandler says in Sammy Davis mode, reminding listeners (at least listeners my age or older) of Sammy's conversion, lampooning the sentiment at the same time that the upbeat music screams celebration. The next stanza gives us Captain Kirk and Mister Spock: "both Jewish," Sandler says in old-Jewish-man voice, mixing caricature with anti-caricature, as does the entire song. I remember how loudly my mother laughed, sitting in the bathtub and reading *Portnoy's Complaint* the summer it was published, but how she couldn't help but wish that only Jews would be allowed to read it, since it reinforced so many stereotypes.

In the fifth stanza he head-counts Rod Carew, Harrison Ford, Ann Landers, and Dear Abby, and outs former Seattle SuperSonics owner Barry Ackerley (I long wondered whether he was Jewish; is it only in Seattle that his Jewishness would have been such a closely guarded secret?). The audience cheers wildly when Sandler informs them that O.J. isn't Jewish; the performance was recorded only a few weeks after the verdict. As O.J. is the anti-Jew (unreflective to the point of being out of control; can I say that?), Rod Carew is the anti-O.J.—one of the greatest hitters in baseball history, whose success depended at least as much upon his mental agility as his physical prowess. No surprise about Ann Landers and Dear Abby—advice-giving yentas. Harrison Ford—the unJewish quarter-Jew. Sandler is riven by the same ambivalence that I am: affirm Dear Abby (Mom) or Harrison Ford (not-Dad)?

In the next stanza we learn that the Three Stooges were Jewish and some people think Ebenezer Scrooge is; "Well he's not," Sandler says with transparent and, thereby, oddly moving defensiveness. *We're tired of fighting that image of ourselves; we're about the joyful lunacy of the Stooges, not the miserliness of Scrooge.* This rather upbeat message gets rather fully contradicted, of course, as it must, since we're Jewish. Some consolation: Tom Cruise isn't Jewish, but his agent is. The stereotype—money-grubber—is true?

In the final stanza, Sandler deepens the paradox by refusing to resolve it, combining "harmonicah," "gin and tonicah," "marijua-nakah," and "Chanukah." This constitutes very modest wordplay, to be certain, but it's crucial, because through the repetition he's ridiculing his—my, our—need to Chanukahize everything, to declare that we're Jewish in a season when no one wants to be. At the same time that Sandler's pretending to affirm Jewish capacity for what I think he knows and what I know I know are unJewish Dionysian pastimes—getting drunk, getting high, getting crazy (Milton Berle, turning down a second drink at a Catholic charity event: "Jews don't drink; it interferes with our suffering")—what he's really affirming are his (my) own self-consciousness, cleverness, involution, ambivalence, pride, shame: Jewishness.

ON THE IMPORTANCE OF GETTING AND BEING STUPID

I loved Don Adams as Maxwell Smart. I loved Edward Platt as the Chief (Daddy = failure). But I really crushed out on Barbara Feldon, Agent 99 (as close as they could get to calling her agent 69 without calling her that). The purr in her voice, the way she towered over Max and yet the way he was oblivious to her worship (which was the mirror of how we were crushing out on her; she pretended to be oblivious to how much we worshipped her). Her alternate coaxing and chiding of Agent 86. Max as dumb/smart (his stupidity was his gallantry; he got that life is a joke). All the au courant Courrèges and Paco Rabanne outfits she wore, the Vidal Sasson cut. Ooh la la.

Either *Get Smart* mapped my entire sexual life over the next fifty years, or my psyche got backformed onto the show. It's very Groucho and Margaret Dumont. All the comedy is on one side—all the Jew-ishness (Don Adams was raised Catholic, his mother's faith, while his brother was raised Jewish, his father's faith, which is too perfect). Feldon as deadpan WASP, as sex goddess, ice queen as savior, as very subtle (pseudo-oblivious) sadist. The show killed me, still kills me ("missed it by *that* much").

THE ONLY SOLUTION TO THE SOUL
IS THE SENSES

Many years ago Bill Murray said in a radio interview, "I was one of the first people to really devote my entire life to the Weather Channel, which is what I do. I love the Weather Channel. The charm and the power of the fronts, you know. You get to see something really important happening. And it's dealt with in a really . . . there's even more talk about it, but nothing can be done." I'm in a swoon over Murray because he takes "my issues"—gloom, rage, self-consciousness, word-weariness—and offers ways out, solutions of sorts, all of which amount to a delicate embrace of the real, a fragile lyricism of the unfolding moment. He thus flatters me that under all my protective layers of irony I, too, might have depth of feeling as well. I admire his slouching insouciance but don't possess it, admire it precisely because I don't possess it. I realize, of course, that a certain redemptive posture is the unique property of movies and movie stars, but Murray's grace is manifest at least as often outside movies as in them. The first line of his book, *Cinderella Story: My Life in Golf,* is "The light seems to come from everywhere."

There have been many exceptions—*Groundhog Day, Broken Flow-*

ers, *Lost in Translation, Rushmore*—but Murray has been so good in so many bad movies that it's as if he makes bad movies on purpose as a way to demonstrate the truth of Denis Leary's dictum (to which I subscribe), "Life sucks—get a fuckin' helmet." Murray's movies, in general, suck; he's the fuckin' helmet. In a self-interview in which he asked himself to explain why so few of his films have succeeded, he replied, mock-solemnly, "I've had lots of good premises." *The Razor's Edge* being, again, an interesting exception, Murray seems to believe that, given the horror show of the universe, the supreme act of bad faith would be to appear in a pretentious work of art aspiring to be beautiful, whereas my impulse has always been to try to find in art my only refuge from the storm. (Over the last decade, he's appeared mainly in artier films, with distinctly uneven results—to the point of self-parody in *St. Vincent;* maybe he's simply better in bad films. . . .)

Murray's metaphor for the Sisyphean struggle: "In life, you never have to completely quit. There's some futile paddling toward some shore of relief, and that's what gets people through. Only the really lucky get a tailwind that takes them to the shore. So many get the headwind that they fight and, then, they tip over and drown." Life is futile; failure is a sign of grace; Murray is fuckup as existential fool. His loserdom is the exact opposite, though, of, say, Woody Allen's; Allen seems intolerably sniffly by comparison. I'm much, much more like Allen than I am like Murray, which is why I admire Murray (Jewish adoration of un-Jewish stoicism). Asked to name people he finds funny, Murray mentions Bob Hope, David Letterman, Eddie Izzard, Conan O'Brien—WASPy wiseguys, no whiners allowed.

In *Meatballs*, Murray is a counselor at a summer camp for losers. When they're getting demolished in a basketball game against a much tonier camp, Murray instructs his charges to run around pantsing their opponents. *Forget the score; fuck the rules; do fun things; give yourselves things to remember.* Camp Director Morty takes himself and the camp way too seriously (so many blocking figures in Murray movies are officious Jews; what's that about—Hollywood's knee-jerk self-hatred?), so Murray leads all the other kids in calling Morty "Mickey," turning him into a mouse. The great crime in any Murray movie is self-seriousness, because as Murray's fellow Irishman Oscar Wilde said, "Life is too important to take seriously." Wilde also said, "The only solution to the soul is the senses," which is a key to Murray's appeal: He's in touch with his animal self and teaches the kids to be in touch with theirs. *We're all meatballs; we're all just bodies.* (Murray's second ex-wife accused him of being a sex addict.) If I were a girl or gay, I'd have a searing crush on him in this movie, because just the way he carries his body seems to say, *Here is fun. I'm where fun happens.* When he (crucially: unsuccessfully) courts another counselor, he does so without an ounce of earnestness. Losers are winners; they get that life is an unmitigated disaster. At one point he leads the campers in a chant: "It just doesn't matter. It just doesn't matter. It just doesn't matter." My problem is that even though I know on an intellectual level that it just doesn't matter, on a daily level I treat everything as if it does. Murray is notorious for and proud of the degree to which he makes up his own lines in movies; I suppose I could look up whether "It just doesn't matter" is in the original screenplay of *Meatballs,* but I'd rather not. I want to believe it's his invention.

Murray's shtick—antistar Star, antihero Hero, idler Icon—is built in part upon the fact of his unglamorous appearance. In sketches on *Saturday Night Live,* Gilda Radner would often call him Pizza Face, and it's obvious he's never done anything to improve his deeply mottled skin. Seemingly half my adolescence was spent in a dermatologist's office. *Saturday Night Live* producer Lorne Michaels said about Murray, "He never had much vanity. There was a way he always told the truth." The qualities are of course intricately intertwined; it's his absence of vanity that allows him to get to emotional truths in a scene, as opposed to, say, Ethan Hawke, who you can tell is always concentrating only on one question: *How do I look?* I was cute enough as a little kid to appear in an advertisement for a toy store; my father took the photographs, and here I am in the family album, riding a plastic pony and brandishing a pistol with crypto-cowboy charm. Although now I'm certainly not handsome, I don't think I've ever quite outgrown that early narcissism. Murray's not fat, but he has a serious paunch; as opposed to some septuagenarian buffster like Harrison Ford, Murray's sixty-seven and looks all of it. Bless him for that: It's a gift back to us; he makes us all feel less shitty. He posed for a *New York Times Magazine* profile wearing a drooping undershirt and with uncombed thinning gray hair. This is a comparison Murray would surely loathe for its la-di-da-ness, but the photograph reminds me of Rembrandt's late self-portraits: a famous man who understands his own mortal ordinariness and is willing to show us the irredeemable sadness of his eyes in which that knowledge registers.

Murray's sadness is not other movie stars' pseudo-seriousness; he seems genuinely forlorn—always a plus in my book. Speaking to Terry Gross on *Fresh Air,* Murray said, "Movies don't usually show the failure of relationships; they want to give the audience a final, happy resolution. In *Rushmore,* I play a guy who's aware that his life is not working, but he's still holding on, hoping something will happen, and that's what's most interesting." Gross, stunned that Murray would identify so strongly with someone as bitter and remorseful as Herman Blume, tried to pull Murray up off the floor by saying, "I mean, you've found work that is meaningful for you, though, haven't you?" Murray explained that Blume is drawn to the energetic teenager Max Fischer, who is the founder and president of virtually every club at Rushmore Academy, but "sometimes it makes you sadder to see someone that's really happy, really engaged in life when you have detached." He said this as if he knew exactly what he was talking about. "Murray's glazed expression sees no cause for hope in the world," Anthony Lane once said of him. Nothing can be done. In *Quick Change,* codirected by Murray, he plays a clown named Grimm. "What kind of clown are you?" someone asks him. "The cryin'-on-the-inside kind, I guess," he says, which—maybe it's me—I take both as goof on the cliché and true confession.

The Razor's Edge, cowritten by Murray, is the film that he'd desperately been wanting to do for years and that the studio agreed to finance only after Murray first agreed to do *Ghostbusters II.* It's Murray's ur-story. The first part of the Maugham novel is set in Chicago, but Murray moved the first part of the film to Lake Forest, next door to Wilmette, the North Shore suburb in which he grew up. The bulk of the book and film are set in Paris, where Murray spent a year studying French and Gurdjieff and fleeing from post-*Ghostbusters* fame. Surrounded by cripples and sybarites, amoralists and materialists, Murray's character in *The Razor's Edge,* Larry Darrell, travels to China, Myanmar, and India, searching for meaning, and the best he can come up with is "You don't get it. It doesn't matter." It just doesn't matter. Such is the highest wisdom a Murray character can hope to achieve: Zen semi-detachment, which only deepens his dread (sounds familiar to me).

Angst translates easily to anger. Wes Anderson, explaining why he'd been somewhat anxious about directing Murray in *Rushmore,* said, "I'd heard about him throwing someone in a lake on one thing, and I'd heard that if he didn't like the situation, he's going to change it." Discussing megalomaniacal celebrities, Murray said, "Whenever I hear someone say, 'My fans,' I go right for the shotgun." In *Kingpin,* Murray plays an impossibly arrogant bowler who, in one scene, says hello to the two women sitting at the next table. The less attractive woman responds by saying, "Hi," and Murray says, "Not you [nodding to the less attractive woman]. You [nodding to the more attractive woman]." Murray explained to Terry Gross how he had ad-libbed the line: "It just came into my mind at that moment. And it was so horrible—such a horrible thing to say that there was a moment of complete disbelief and then everyone [on the set] laughed really hard because, you know, the guy should be taken out and shot. It was just the kind of thing that I think would be the most offensive thing you could do. I was trying to paint a picture of a guy who was really, really a bad guy, so that any second that Woody [Harrelson]'s character stayed with this guy was an investment in bad time." Murray can access his own cruelty but isn't defined by it. He simply doesn't radiate malevolence, as, say, James Woods once did, but neither is he cuddlesome-cute, à la Tom Hanks; this mixture keeps us productively off-balance, makes us unsure whether to embrace him or be slightly afraid of him. I strive for the same mystery in my own persona but fail miserably, since it's so evident how much neediness trumps coolness. When Murray gave his protesting-too-much explanation to Terry Gross, she responded, "I guess I've always wondered how you, so intuitively, seem to understand a certain type of really crude, ego-driven personality." With genuine hostility in his voice, Murray said, "Well, that's a loaded question, Terry." Then he quickly downshifted back to a more mild tone—again, that nervous-making mixture: "How do I understand that? I don't know. I think show business can enrich that. You can see people manifesting in a bizarre way that, you know, other people don't try to get away, wouldn't try to get away, with, but people get lost in a vanity space and just start going. You know, people that just take themselves too seriously—it's ripe for re-creation."

He seizes the regenerative power of behaving badly, being disrespectful toward condescending assholes. In his self-interview, in which he pretended to be discoursing with Santa Claus, he said, "I was at the New York Film Critics Circle Awards one year. They called me up when somebody canceled two days before the thing, and asked me to present some awards. So I went, and one of the funniest film moments I've ever had was when they introduced the New York film critics. They all stood up; *motley* isn't the word for that group. Everybody had some sort of vision problem, some sort of damage. I had to bury myself in my napkin. As they kept going, it just got funnier and funnier looking. By the time they were all up, it was like, 'You have been selected as the people who have been poisoned; you were the unfortunate people who were not in the control group that didn't receive the medication.'" IF YOU'RE NOT ANGRY, YOU'RE NOT PAYING ATTENTION—so goes my favorite bumper sticker. Murray's edginess is a product of the fact that he actually pays attention. He has what Hemingway said was the "most essential gift for a good writer: a built-in, shock-proof shit detector."

Hemingway's hometown of Oak Park is about twenty miles southwest of Murray's hometown of Wilmette; both men have or had a gimlet-eyed view of the disguises the world wears. It's more broadly midwestern, though, than only Hemingwayesque, I think. Dave Eggers, who grew up in Lake Forest, has it. So does Laurie, who grew up in the same North Shore suburb. Johnny Carson, who was raised in Nebraska, and David Letterman, who was raised in Indiana, also have it—a quality of detachment that's a way of not getting sucked in by all the shit sent your way, of holding on to some tiny piece of yourself that's immune to publicity, of wearing indifference as an inmovable mask.

Murray is, in other words, ironic. He's alert to and mortified by the distance between how things appear to be and how they are. On *Charlie Rose,* the unctuous host kept trying to get Murray to brag; in every instance, Murray deflected the praise, lightly mocking himself (his irony is bottomless but never particularly self-lacerating). In *Polyester,* Murray sings "The Best Thing," a love song; it's telling, I think, that John Waters cast Murray to sing the parody-love song in the parody-love movie. In *Michael Jordan to the Max,* a grotesquely worshipful IMAX film, Murray, as a fan in the stands, says, "It's like out of all the 50,000 top athletes since, you know, prehistoric times—brontosauruses and pterodactyls included—he [Jordan]'s right there." These are modest examples, but they betray Murray's impulse: to unhype the hype, to replace force-fed feeling with something less triumphal, more plausible and human and humble. In *Stripes,* Murray delivers a rousing speech to his fellow soldiers to encourage them to learn overnight what they haven't learned during all of boot camp—how to march. "We're Americans," he says, "we're all dogfaces, but we have within us something American that knows how to do this." Murray saves the speech from sentimentality by mocking the sentimentality. *I'm not really in this situation,* Murray's character seems to be thinking; *I'm not really in this movie,* Murray seems to be thinking. That reminds us or at least me of our own detachment and puts us in the scene, thereby making the moment credible and, ironically, moving. Here, as in so many other Murray movies, Murray somehow manages to install a level or two of Plexiglas between himself and the rest of the movie. "What's funny about Murray is not his performance," Tom Keogh writes, "but the way he hangs back from his performance." At its most dire, Murray's persona is simply antifeeling; at its most fierce it's anti–faux feeling. This is what gives his persona such an edge: It's unclear whether his self-mockery is saving grace or Nowhere Man melancholia. It's both, obviously, to which I can attest or hope to attest. Maybe detachment is a way to get to real feeling; maybe it's a dead end from which no feeling arises. That's the Murray bargain.

Murray's characteristic manner of delivering dialogue is to add invisible, ironic quotes around nearly every word he says, as if he weren't quite convinced he should go along with the program that is the script, as if he were just trying out the dialogue on himself first rather than really saying it to someone else in a movie that millions of people are going to see, as if he were still seeing how it sounds. The effect is to undermine every assertion at the moment it's asserted. As a stutterer and writer, I'm a sucker for Murray's push-pull relationship to language; it's undoubtedly one of the main sources of the deep psychic identification I've always felt toward him. Commenting upon Murray's performance as Polonius in Michael Almereyda's adaptation of *Hamlet,* Elvis Mitchell said that Murray's Polonius is "a weary, middle-aged man whose every utterance sounds like a homily he should believe in and perhaps did many years ago." Murray simultaneously embodies and empties out cliché, showing how much we don't believe it, how badly we want to. In *Tootsie*, as Dustin Hoffman's roommate who's a playwright/waiter, Murray says about his work-in-progress, "I think it's going to change theater as we know it." Murray says the line in a way that no one else could: We're aware that he's full of shit, but we're also aware that he's aware he's full of shit. For which we adore him, because he reminds us how full of shit we are every hour of every day. He's also a welcome relief from Dustin Hoffman's sincerity.

His pet technique for underlining his self-consciousness is knocking, loudly, on the fourth wall. Serving as guest broadcaster for a Chicago Cubs game, which Murray once said is the best thing he's ever done, he answered the phone in the adjoining booth, stuck out his tongue at the camera, called down to the players on the field. On the first episode of *Late Night with David Letterman*, Murray ran into the audience and led them in an insanely spirited rendition of Olivia Newton-John's "Let's Get Physical." In *Stripes*, when his girlfriend leaves him, he turns to the camera and says, "And then the depression set in." At pro-am tournaments, Murray wears goofy outfits, jokes with the crowd, hits wacky shots—in an effort to tear a hole in the sanctimonious veil surrounding the game of golf. In *Michael Jordan to the Max*, Murray shoves his tub of popcorn at the camera and asks, "Hey, can I ask you: How big does that look on IMAX? Does that look like a gigantic bucket of popcorn or not that big?" At a Carnegie Hall benefit concert with a Sinatra theme, Murray, backed by a full orchestra, sang "My Way"; Murray told an interviewer, "I basically rewrote the lyrics and changed them around to suit my own mood. I started getting laughs with it, and then I was off the click track. I mean, there's a full orchestra playing to its own charts, so they just keep playing, you know. And the fact I'm off the lyric and talking and doing things—it doesn't matter to them. They don't keep vamping; it's not like a piano bar. They just keep going to the end. So I said let's see if this big band is going to stay with me here, and they didn't. They just kept barreling right ahead. But I headed them off at the pass and turned it around and got out of it again." It's crucial to Murray's comedy that the orchestra is there, playing away, serious as society—the formal straitjacket he wriggles out of. My favorite joke, by far, goes:

Knock-knock.
Who's there?
Interrupting Cow.
Interrupt—
Moo.

I have an extraordinarily vivid memory of a very brief video clip I saw twenty-five years ago of a juggler who was riding a unicycle and pretending to have great difficulty controlling the knives he was juggling. He was in absolute control, of course, but I loved how much trouble he pretended to be having; I loved how afraid he pretended to be; I loved how it was both a parody of the form and a supreme demonstration of the form. I loved it so much (an artist pretending death was going to win, but art had it under control all along, thanks) it brought me to tears.

Murray's acute self-consciousness is paralyzing, but also curiously freeing: It frees him up to be a rebel (just barely). In *Razor's Edge,* he's the only character who is both (just) sane and (beautifully) whimsical, which is the balance he strikes in nearly every movie, his signature mixture of hip and square. He knows better than anyone else that you don't always have to do what they tell you to do, but he also tends to realize that the way out of the slough of despond is delight in other people, making him clubbable. In *Stripes,* asked by the drill sergeant what he's doing, Murray's character says, "Marching in a straight line, sir." It's not a straight line, but what he's doing is still, finally, marching. Although Murray is utterly insubordinate toward the sergeant, he winds up earning the sergeant's admiration by leading a rescue mission at the end. Murray is a goof-off and anti-establishment, but he winds up having the right stuff. He gets it together but on his own terms, if "own terms" can be defined unambitiously. Asked by an interviewer what he thought of the television show *Cheers,* Murray said, "That was like prime-time TV; I never really got it or anything." Such is the extent of Murray's rebellion—late-night versus prime-time TV. One of the many good jokes of *Tootsie* is that Murray, playing an avant-garde playwright, is nobody's idea of an avant-garde playwright: Everything about him—his competence, his responsibility—screams acceptance of things as they are. He defies without sabotaging authority. When an interviewer asked Murray whether *Rushmore* director Wes Anderson's gentle approach toward actors was effective, Murray replied, a bit huffily, "Well, that's good manners, you know? That's tact." Murray went to Loyola Academy, a prep school, in Wilmette, and all his hell-raising is in a way the unthreateningly bad behavior of a slumming preppy (he supported Romney in 2012). The ultimate effect of all his hijinks on the links is to deepen golf's hushed, moneyed silence (Murray's antics would seem redundant at a football game). There's the official way and then there's your own way; Murray does it his own way, he never gets co-opted, but—and this is his magic trick, this is the movies, this is what is so deeply reassuring about his persona—he still succeeds (rids the city of ghosts, leads the rescue mission, gets the girl). He therefore is a perfect bridge figure between, to paint in broad strokes, fifties conformity, sixties rage, seventies zaniness, eighties and nineties *capitalismo,* post-9/11 testosterone; hence his appeal: He convinces us that we're still a little rebellious inside even as we're finally doing what everyone else is doing. I'm frequently abashed by how bourgeois my yearnings have become; Murray's relatively unangry versions of *épater le bourgeois* coat my conformity in glee.

This very deep contradiction in Murray is directly related to the way corrosive irony, in him, sits atop deep sentimentality. (So, too, for myself: Walking out of the theater after *Terms of Endearment,* I subjected it to a withering critique while tears were still streaking down my face.) When he was guest commentator at the Cubs game, he mocked every player on the opposing team in a parody of fan fanaticism ("That guy shouldn't even be in the major leagues, and he knows it; he's lying to himself. He really should go back into some sort of community service in his hometown."), but he refused every opportunity the cameraman handed him to score easy points off the enormously fat African American umpire Eric Gregg, whose uniform had been lost in transit and who just couldn't get comfortable in his borrowed clothes. Before the Cubs played their first night game at Wrigley Field, Murray visited the booth again, this time for just a few minutes, mercilessly ribbing the legendary announcer Harry Caray before suddenly declaring, "This is the most beautiful park in the world." I feel so earth-bound compared to Murray, so unecstatic. In *Ghostbusters,* he pretends to be a self-absorbed asshole, but we're meant to understand that underneath the mordant pose he's a pussycat. Murray's MO is in a way classic American cowboy—Gary Cooper, John Wayne—heart of gold, encased in steel. I'm the opposite—"sensitive" surface masking homicidal maniac. Had the actors in *Mad Dog and Glory* been cast according to type—De Niro playing the mobster and Murray the neurasthenic police photographer—the movie would have made no sense. The movie wouldn't be funny, the violence wouldn't seem silly, if we didn't understand that approximately credible though Murray is as the Mafia don, he's really not a killer; he's just joking (we don't believe him for a minute). Murray has an amazing ability to deliver mean lines that somehow don't sound mean; this is because he is, I'm almost sure of this, a gentle man (who also possesses of course perfectly repressed rage—giving the gentleness its edge). With just a few exceptions (*Kingpin*, say, or *Mad Dog and Glory*), Murray is almost always the character in the movie who embodies and articulates the vision of the movie, precisely because he's so hard to dislike. Asked about his parodies of bad singers, Murray explained, "You have to see what the original center of the song was and how they destroyed it. It's the ruining of a good song that you want to recreate. You have to like the stuff and you have to, I guess, know that when you have the microphone you have the opportunity to touch somebody. And when you don't do it with the lyric of it, and your own excuse for technique comes in and steps on top of it, that's, I guess, what I object to when I'm mimicking something." Oh, that old story: rage is always only disappointed romanticism.

Disappointed romanticism, however, isn't romanticism. Murray isn't Hugh Grant (such a crush of Laurie's that her coworkers bought her a life-size cutout of the caddish Oxfordian); he never, or almost never, does romantic comedy. He likes himself too much, for as Murray says, "The romantic figure has to behave romantically even after acting like a total swine. It's 'I'm so gorgeous you're going to have to go through all kinds of hell for me,' and that isn't interesting to me. Romance is very particular. There's something about romance, that if you don't have to have someone, you're more desirable." Murray has the dignity of not having to have someone, or at least not going on and on about it.

He is, in short, male, a guy's guy, still extremely boyish though he was born in 1950, broad-shouldered (six-foot-one), upbeat about his masculinity in a way that seems quite foreign and enviable to me. My voice is high and soft, as a way to control my stutter, but also as if in apology for my Y chromosome. His father, who died when Murray was nineteen, was a lumber salesman. One of five brothers (and nine siblings), Murray now has six sons (and no daughters) from two marriages. So much of his persona, his shtick, his appeal is that he revels in and excels at the brutal but obviously affectionate teasing that is characteristic of large families, whereas more than one person has asked me, apropos of nothing in particular, whether I'm an only child. Occasionally psychotic but never neurotic, Murray plays well against nervous types, as I'm trying to make him do in this essay. He's not me. He's not Woody Allen. He's not Dustin Hoffman. In *Tootsie,* in which Dustin Hoffman plays an obnoxious actor, Michael Dorsey, who pretends to be a woman in order to get a part in a soap and, by "becoming" a woman, learns to be a better man, Murray is true north of "normal" masculinity, our ordinary-guy guide, the big galoot around whom the gender-bending bends. "I think we're getting into a weird area," he informs Hoffman when Hoffman gets preoccupied with his female alter ego's wardrobe. "Do you know what my problem is?" Hoffman asks him at one point. "Cramps?" Murray replies. When Hoffman asks Murray how he-as-she looks, Murray says, "Nice, but don't play hard to get." "Instead of trying to be Michael Dorsey the great actor or Michael Dorsey the great waiter," he advises Hoffman before ushering him into his surprise birthday party, "why don't you just try to be Michael Dorsey?" This line isn't in even fairly late drafts of the screenplay; it's pure Murray; I'd bet he came up with it. He's the king of hanging out. He already knows how to be himself and how to be kind, how to be male but not be a jerk, whereas Hoffman needs to learn how to do this. Hoffman, the high-strung Jew, must learn how to do what Murray already does instinctively—to like life, to like the opposite sex, to embrace his own anima. *Live, live, live,* as Strether, that priss, finally realizes in Henry James's *The Ambassadors,* and as Murray has always known, as Murray always conveys.

Murray's boyishness is, at its most beguiling, childlikeness: openness to surprise. In *Cinderella Story: My Life in Golf,* Murray writes, "The sum and substance of what I was hoping to express is this. In golf, just as in life—I hoped I could get that line in the book some-where [Murray's relentlessly ironic gaze, his ear for cliché]—the best wagers are laid on oneself." In *The Man Who Knew Too Little*, Murray plays Wallace Ritchie, a dim American man who, visiting his busi-nessman brother in London, thinks he's attending an avant-garde "Theater of Life" performance and unbeknownst to him is caught up in an international spy-vs.-spy scheme. Murray, as Ritchie, wins the day—defeats the bad guys, gets the girl—because he just goes with the flow, is cool and relaxed, never stops believing that he's watch-ing and participating in an unusually realistic performance. Ritchie's relaxedness is Murray's relaxedness; Ritchie's distance is Murray's: Life is theater with arbitrary rules. His bemused bafflement toward everything that happens is a handbook for Murray's acting technique and his approach to life—the absurdity of all action, but (and there-fore) grooving in the moment.

When Murray was the guest commentator at the baseball game, he somehow made everything the camera focused on—a hot-dog wrapper, an untucked shirt—seem newly resonant, of possible inter-est, because unlike every person to ever broadcast a game, Murray talked about what was actually going on in his head, was actually seeing what was going on in front of his eyes rather than viewing it through a formulaic filter, was taking in the entire ballpark rather than just the sporting event per se. His eyes haven't gone dead yet. Life, seen through such eyes, becomes existentially vivid. Broadcast-ing this game, Murray seemed as interested in the physical universe as a beagle, sniffing the ballpark for new sensory input. He's dem-onstrating the Wildean wisdom that the only solution to the soul is the senses. He's a combination of two characters from the movie *American Beauty:* the kid with the video camera who can see rib-bons of beauty in a plastic bag being blown around in the wind, and the Kevin Spacey character, who processes everything through his sulfur-spewing irony machine. I'm Spacey and want to be the kid with the video camera.

It's Murray's attempt to be authentic, and underlining of his attempt to be authentic, that I admire most. Lorne Michaels once said, "It's a cliché, but Bill is always Bill. So much of my generation's approach to comedy was a reaction against the neediness of perform-ers. When Bill was on stage, he didn't much care whether they [members of the audience] liked him. Because of that, he had enormous integrity. There was a way he always told the truth." The tape I have of Murray broadcasting the Cubs game has live audio rather than commercial breaks between innings; Murray sounds exactly the same off air as he does on. He is incapable of doing Stentorian Announcer let alone Star Turn. I adore this about him. At one point in his life he was strongly influenced by the philosophy of Gurdjieff, whose Madame Blavatsky–esque work I can't bring myself to read but one of whose titles is *Life Is Real Only Then, When "I Am."* A bad translation, to be sure, but the self-conscious quote marks around "I Am," the slight or not so slight inscrutability, the deep yearning to apprehend and embody reality—that's Murray's program.

The royal road to the authentic for Murray is through the primitive. Look at the (mock?) Stanley Kowalski way he kicks open the door to the barracks in *Stripes.* In his self-interview, he told a joke about how Ralph Lauren's dog is named Rugby, but his real name is Stickball. People who pretend that they are truly civilized Murray finds ridiculous. In *Caddyshack,* a movie about class warfare phrased as a golf comedy, he plays a groundskeeper who is obsessed with killing gophers. Chevy Chase is the embodiment of the golfing fop—moneyed, charming, handsome. Murray is riddled by doubt, self-pitying, working-class. ("I got a blue-collar chip on my shoulder," Murray has said. "That part of it was not hard.") Chase, for all his bonhomie, isn't in touch with the primitive force of the universe; Murray is (he's the only one capable of recognizing that a dark brown clump floating in the country club swimming pool isn't a turd but a Baby Ruth bar, which he eats). The movie teaches the young golfer-protagonist that Chase is wrong, Murray is right. The only way for Young Golfer to grow up is by learning how to say fuck you to the "snobatorium"—the country club's version of golf and life.

Would that rebellion were so easy. Still, when Charlie Rose advised Bill Murray to take a sabbatical, because lawyers do, Murray said, "If law firms do it, Charlie, it probably can't be right." (That "probably" is quintessential Murray—anti-establishmentarian but not utterly.) Rose also advised him about the importance of "proportionality" in one's life—balance between work and play. "I want to learn that one, too," Murray said, pretending to search for a pencil. "Let me write it down." In *Wild Things,* Murray is the lone actor among several other middle-aged actors in the movie who is granted the privilege of grasping the movie's vision: Human beings are beasts and life is a scam, so manipulate the other beasts in the jungle to your own advantage. It would be impossible to cast Murray as someone who didn't understand this.

Maybe it's not much of a revelation to anyone else, but to me it always seems to be: We're finally just physical creatures living in the physical world. If Murray didn't ad-lib the following lines in *Tootsie*, he should have: "I don't want a full house at the Winter Garden Theatre. I want ninety people who just came out of the worst rainstorm in the city's history. These are people who are alive on the planet, until they dry off. I wish I had a theater that was only open when it rained." Explaining to an interviewer that *Rushmore* director Wes Anderson isn't just knowledgeable about film and clever about alluding to film history but also able to convey strong emotion in his work, Murray said, "Let's get right down to it. It's like the French. You know, they can't play rock'n'roll to save their lives. They can't play the blues to save their lives. But if you play a song by somebody, you know, Son House, they go [French accent], 'That's Son House, the famous musician and blues player. That is from the session he did in Meridian, Mississippi. I believe that is the January twenty-fourth . . .' You know, they'll know the date, the time, and the take. They couldn't give you an ounce of the feeling of it, you know. This guy, Wes, and it's the difference, you know—mind and body, he just knows how to get these things together in one place."

Murray does the same thing; all his verbal play happens atop a foundation of understated physical grace. In *Space Jam*, Murray isn't Michael Jordan, but it's crucial that he isn't Wayne Knight, either. He's halfway between jock god and blubbery nerd—someone we can identify with. After kibitzing with Jordan at the golfing tee, wearing madras shorts and a cornball shirt and shoes, he finally whacks the hell out of the ball. So, too, at pro-am tournaments it wouldn't work if, after goofing around for twenty minutes, he couldn't finally play the game. By being both ridiculous and competent, he becomes beautifully contradictory—the unicycle-riding knife juggler who pretends to be anxiety-stricken but isn't; without the contradiction he's just pathetic (Wayne Knight) or boringly excellent (Jordan). It's that stage in between that Murray occupies so movingly.

I imagine that Murray would be a bit of a bully in the way a popular camp counselor might be—making you feel bad if you just don't want to have fun right now as Murray defines fun, not allowing you to just mope if that's what you want to do. I imagine he would be such a drill sergeant on this score—toward his sons, say—because a frenetically kept-up joie de vivre is how he's managed to paper over his fairly real despair, and if he can, he's going to bring everyone along with him out of hell. I admire this and resent it a little; why can't I mope if I want to mope? Maybe the only solution to the soul isn't the senses; maybe it's deeper soul-searching (probably not); maybe there is no soul. "To be, to be, sure beats the shit out of not to be," he writes at the end of *The Cinderella Story*. At the very end of *Where the Buffalo Roam,* in which he plays Hunter Thompson, Murray quotes Lord Buckley's epitaph: "He stomped on the terra." This is the nucleus of Murray: *We're made of clay; we better cause a little ruckus while we can.* He's the anti-Malvolio in our midst; he's Tigger vs. the suits. *Life is absurd—make it your own absurdity.* Instead of wearing basic black—my dumb uniform—Murray typically wears his own weird mix of plaids and prints of different patterns and colors: a tartan vest, for instance, with a paisley tie and a sky-blue shirt. Or black pants, a brown-striped shirt, and a tan vest. Nutty clothes—so out they're in, cool because he's wearing them.

In *What About Bob?* Murray, as Bob Wylie, the patient of a hedonic psychiatrist, Leo Marvin (the un–Lee Marvin), visits the Marvins' summer home and succeeds in making even dishwashing, for Chrissake, fun for Marvin's family, though not for Dr. Marvin, of course. Murray and Richard Dreyfuss reportedly came to despise each other in the making of the movie—Murray's unscripted silliness drove Dreyfuss crazy, in exactly the same way Bob drives Leo mad in the movie—and I know we're supposed to love Murray and hate Dreyfuss, and I do, but I'm much closer to serious, striving Dr. Marvin than I am to antic Bob, which is, I suppose, what this essay is about: my distance from Murray, my yearning to be him, the gap between us, the way he makes life seem bearable (fun, amusing) if only I could get with his giddiness. (I can't.) In Murray's golf book, Cheryl Anderson, a golf pro, says, "I was practicing at the far end of the Grand Cypress range one morning. There wasn't another soul there. Just a set of clubs in one of the stands a few yards away from me. Then a figure appeared in the distance. He was on a bicycle, at the same time carrying a boom box. It was Bill. He gave me a quick nod, then walked to the clubs, set down his box, and flipped on a tape. It was an out-there rock group called Big Head Todd and the Monsters. He hit balls to the music for a while, then picked up the box, nodded goodbye, and pedaled off."

Physical grace as a container, then, for spiritual grace, if that's not putting too fine a point on it. "A lot of *Rushmore* is about the struggle to retain civility and kindness in the face of extraordinary pain," Murray said shortly after the film was released. "And I've felt a lot of that in my life." This is what Murray knows so well and what I have been trying to learn from him: Life is a shitstorm—laugh (somehow and barely). In his self-interview, he tells Santa a story about the making of the movie *Scrooged:* "We're shooting in this Victorian set for weeks, and [Buddy] Hackett is pissed all the time, angry that he's not the center of attention, and finally we get to the scene where we've gotta shoot him at the window, saying, 'Go get my boots,' or whatever. The set is stocked with Victorian extras and little children in *Oliver* kind of outfits, and the director says, 'All right, Bud, just give it whatever you want.' And Hackett goes off on a rant. Unbelievably obscene. He's talking—this is Hackett, not me—about the Virgin Mary, a limerick sort of thing, and all these children and families . . . the look of absolute horror. He's going on and on and on, and finally he stops. The camera's still rolling; you can hear it, sort of a grinding noise. And the director says, 'Anything else, Bud?'" Murray loves the director's dignity against the shitstorm, his refusal to be cowed or fazed.

In "The Passion of Bill Murray," Greg Solman says about Murray's performance in *Mad Dog and Glory,* "What's remarkable about the performance is how well Murray can now convey the intrinsic humor of his characters and situations but differentiate them from others in his past by eliminating irony, sarcasm, and self-reflexivity." This is wrong. In the forty-plus years Murray has been acting, he's gotten better not by ever going away for a second from irony but by finding deeper and deeper levels of emotion within it (*Caddyshack, Stripes, Ghostbusters, Groundhog Day, Rushmore, Hamlet, Lost in Translation, Broken Flowers, The Life Aquatic*). That's why I value his work so much: He embodies the way—not around but through. At the end of *Groundhog Day,* after being forced to repeat February 2 over and over again until he discovers real feeling, he finally says to a sleeping Andie MacDowell, "I think you're the kindest, sweetest, prettiest person I've ever met in my life. I've never seen anyone that's nicer to people than you are. The first time I saw you, something happened to me that I never told you about. I knew that I wanted to hold you as hard as I could. I don't deserve someone like you, but if I ever could, I swear I would love you for the rest of our life." This is awfully sugary, and the only reason I believe it is because of the way Murray teases her when he's teaching her how to flip cards into a hat. At the end of *Scrooged,* Murray, the scabrous president of a television network who recovers the Christmas spirit, walks onto the set of the live Christmas special he's produced, announcing, "It's Christmas Eve. It's the one night of the year where we all act a little nicer, we smile a little easier, we cheer a little more. For a couple of hours out of the whole year we are the people that we always hoped we would be. It's a miracle, it's really a sort of a miracle, because it happens every Christmas Eve. You'll want it every day of your life, and it can happen to you. I believe in it now. I believe it's going to happen to me now. I'm ready for it." A few moments later, when he has trouble dragging his long-lost beloved, Claire, in front of the camera, Murray, clearly improvising, says, "This is like boning a marlin." It's Murray's fidelity to his own mordant consciousness and the locating of joy within that mordancy that is, to me, the miracle. I'm getting a little overadulatory, so I'll stop.

My iron grip on ironic distance—hence my adoration of Murray—hence my lifelong love of books in which a neurasthenic author contemplates his more vital second self; hence this essay. What is it about such a relationship that speaks so strongly to me? Art calling out to Life? Un-Life wanting Life? Are these just parts of myself in eternal debate, or am I really this anemic? Murray, for all his anomie, likes being in the world. Bully for him. I love standing in shadow, gazing intently at ethereal glare.

ALMOST FAMOUS

A less robust Craig Wasson; a much more neurotic John Savage; Charles Martin Smith without his likable sanity; Wallace Shawn sans self-deprecation—Bob Balaban is a character actor who looks like a balding baby wearing a beard and glasses. He is never not the quintessential schlemiel. In *Midnight Cowboy*, his debut film, he suffers five indignities in five minutes: hires Joe Buck to be the recipient of his blow job in a movie theater in Times Square; coughs and spits out Buck's cum into the bathroom sink; doesn't have the money to pay him ("I was lying"); offers him his schoolbooks as payment; and pleads with him, successfully, not to take his watch ("My mother will die").

In *Report to the Commissioner*, Balaban plays Joey Egan, a legless man scooting around Times Square on a board with wheels. Dogs attack him; he barks back and bites people's legs. After another cop, weary of "Crazy Joey's" antics, tosses Joey's board into a dumpster, Michael Moriarty, who plays undercover detective Bo Lockley, rescues Joey's board for him. Later, Balaban hitches a ride on the rear bumper of a cab, trying to help Moriarty track down an evil pimp named Stick, but for his efforts only lands headfirst in a pile of garbage. Moriarty winds up apprehending the pimp in Saks, though Moriarty—a deeply flawed hero—later kills himself. Balaban doesn't kill himself; it would seem redundant.

Nowhere Man as bureaucrat:

In *Absence of Malice* Balaban plays Elliott Rosen, the head of a Justice Department special task force investigating Mafia links to organized labor in Miami. Though in most other movies he has a beard, here he has only a trim mustache. He wears a pocket protector for his many pencils and pens, speaks rapidly in a defeated, self-canceling manner, and constantly winds and unwinds a rubber band. He tricks plucky Sally Field and attempts to arraign hunky Paul Newman, so perforce he gets fired by folksy Wilford Brimley.

In *Prince of the City* Balaban plays a patrician Justice Department official in Washington who is prosecuting corruption among mostly Italian cops in New York City. He checks people's names off a list, which means he views their lives as abstractions. Wearing a bow tie, he dresses, talks, and acts as if he's living in the wrong century: specifically, the eighteenth. As in *Absence of Malice,* he represents—in contrast to Italians, who possess joie de vivre and know how to dress—the disembodied intellect: he doesn't get what life's about; he isn't in touch with elemental forces.

In *For Love or Money,* Michael J. Fox is Doug Ireland, a concierge at a fancy New York hotel who must choose between Christian Hanover—his very wealthy backer for a renovation project involving the transformation of an abandoned castle on Roosevelt Island into a luxury hotel—and Andy Hart, Hanover's beautiful mistress, who is falling in love with Fox. Hanover bribes Ed Drinkwater (Balaban, of course, that water drinker, who doesn't get that life is a glass of champagne from which to drink lustily) to investigate Fox for tax evasion, in order for Hanover to manipulate him into signing away the rights to the property. Balaban says, "I got Leona [Helmsley]; I'll get you." Balaban says, "Nice car for a bellhop." Balaban says, "You're in deep shit, Mr. Ireland." In a movie about love being more important than money, Balaban is, first and last, money.

The yuppie swine motif:

In *Alice,* a lamentation on materialism, he concludes his marriage proposal to Mia Farrow by noting, "I have a lot of money."

Girl Friends honors, as do so many films Balaban is in, ambivalence (here, two women's choices of artistic career vs. marriage), and Balaban embodies, as he does so often, the end of ambivalence, the pejorative of the extreme position. He doesn't know how to participate in the give-and-take of the dialectic because he's the Tin Woodman: no heart. A young old fogey named Martin, he enters the movie daintily carrying finger food and correcting his wife's narration of their honeymoon slide show: Agadir, not Rabat. "When we go to Italy," he exclaims, "we're going to write down everyone's sizes!" Fastidious, workaholic, yet with a perpetually distracted air, he sniffs, sneezes, smokes European cigarettes, favors the word "exquisite." The last line of the movie is his calling out, concernedly but pitifully, the name of his wife, the woman who has made the wrong decision: given up her poetry for marriage and motherhood. The two women look at each other and laugh. Balaban is the embodiment of the idea that a husband is an early grave. (Balaban: "I think I could play a romantic leading man. I'd like to have bigger parts, and I've been offered a couple of leading roles, but I haven't liked them. When you're the star of a movie that's not very good, that can be disastrous for you.")

In *Amos & Andrew,* Andrew Sterling, a Pulitzer Prize–winning black intellectual, buys a summer house on Martha's Vineyard, but the night he moves in, his white neighbors, Phil and Judy Gillman, mistake him for a robber. When the police chief, who is running for re-election, realizes that he and his officers have been shooting at a celebrity, he arranges for Amos—a recently arrested white "career criminal"—to take Andrew hostage and whisk him out of town before the truth can emerge. Surrounded by opportunistic black protesters and racist white summer people, Amos and Andrew bond and grow: The black man teaches the bumbling white man a little self-respect, while the white man teaches the uptight black man how to be a little more down. The film is about breaking out of self-pitying definitions of oneself as a victim. Balaban, a "criminal psychologist and freelance hostage-crisis counselor" whose name is a joke from elementary school (R. A. Fink), is counterexample as always: a self-absorbed hostage negotiator who spends the entire movie on the phone, bewailing his own microscopic moments of childhood pain. "I remember my eleventh birthday," he says. "I had a party. My mom and dad hired a clown. It was a very, very funny clown and it juggled, did magic tricks. My friend Ruby peed on the floor—she was really embarrassed—but I had a good time. And then the next year my mom called his house to hire him for my twelfth birthday party and his wife answers the phone and she says, 'I'm sorry, he's not a clown anymore. He's at school, learning how to be a dental technician.' I don't think I'll ever forget that moment."

On *Seinfeld*, he plays the president of NBC, who becomes infatuated with Elaine to the point of incapacitation. Attempting to impress her (she's utterly indifferent to him), he joins Greenpeace, and on his first assignment at sea, suffers death by drowning.

In *Whose Life Is It Anyway?* he plays an incompetent attorney who stutters—occasionally and unconvincingly.

Techno geek:

Little Man Tate is about a boy genius trying to find a balance between Dede, his working-class mother who wants to give him a "normal" childhood, and Dr. Grierson, his overzealous tutor escorting him to the thirteenth annual Odyssey of the Mind, a "mental Olympics" for prodigies. Balaban is the math contest emcee at Odyssey of the Mind. His first line is "Another round of questions." *There is life-giving emotion,* the film means to say, and *death-dealing intellection;* Balaban represents the *via negativa,* the coldest star in the cosmos.

In *Catch-22,* Balaban plays bombardier Orr, a "one-man disaster area" whom Yossarian refuses to fly with, despite Orr's vow that he'll take "good care" of him. Yossarian pretends to be crazy, but Orr seems truly to be crazy: He wildly overdoes the thumbs-up sign when taking off, and in a sexual frenzy over Major Major's mistress, bites his headset. He bails out over the Mediterranean and Adriatic, crash-lands, drifts for days, gets picked up at sea. It's "good practice." What, with that goofy smile, does he know that we don't? *Catch-22* is the exception proving the rule: It's the only film in which Balaban even remotely triumphs, but, revealingly, his triumph is off screen. The primary significance of Yossarian's discovery that Orr has made it—he rowed to Sweden (his name turns out to have been a prophetic pun)—is that it inspires Yossarian to break the impasse: He sets out in his own tiny dinghy into the enormous sea. In a film constructed across the loop-the-loops of paradox, Balaban is as rigid as reinforced steel.

In *Altered States* William Hurt is Faust: Eddie Jessup, a genius psychophysiologist who immerses himself in an isolation tank and digests blood and sacred mushrooms in order to try to discover the origins of human life. Balaban (Arthur Rosenberg) is Jessup's literal-minded research assistant, who, when he helps Hurt out of the tank at the end of an immersion and says to him, "I'd like to try that sometime," transparently would not like to try that sometime. At a party at Balaban's apartment, his harridan wife tells him to go answer the door, at which stands William Hurt—in a halo of backlighting, the better to be admired by Blair Brown. Balaban's only gear is pedantic busyness: analyzing data, synthesizing drugs, fiddling with his bag lunch, "fractionating rat brains." Humble technician to Hurt's mystic seeker, he asks where the research is headed and is uncomfortable with Jessup's hip adventurousness: "We're just bootlegging." Did Faust have an errand boy? I can't remember, but I think he must have.

In *2010*, as Dr. R. Chandra, designer of the Hal 9000 computer, Balaban says, "Whether we are based on carbon or silicon makes no fundamental difference. We should each be treated with appropriate respect." The audience wonders exactly to what degree Balaban shares essential molecular structure with earthlings. As always, he's the foolish intellectual—adenoidal, aphysical, distant, unconnected to ordinary human emotion. Attempting to persuade a NASA official to allow him to bring Dr. Chandra with him on the mission, Roy Scheider says, "He designed Hal. He can reactivate him."

> NASA: I think he is Hal.
> SCHEIDER: I know.
> NASA: Yeah, but can you trust him?
> SCHEIDER: No, but I have to.

Balaban is happy only when talking to Hal, proud of Hal's ability to process information "without distortion or concealment." When, preparing to meet his doom, Hal asks, "Will I dream?" and Dr. Chandra answers, "I don't know," Chandra is crying.

In *Close Encounters of the Third Kind* he is Interpreter Laughlin, a cartographer, or, as he explains to the audience, "a mapmaker." He's not a professional interpreter, but his French is good enough to explain things to François Truffaut, who plays a UFO specialist. Balaban is pure rational intelligence. "I don't believe it," he says at one point, over and over and over. "Why is it here?" When the UFO communicates, everybody is gaga, except Balaban, who points out that the UFO is conveying its latitude and longitude. When the UFO arrives, everybody takes an involuntary step forward—to enter the mystery—except Balaban, who stands still as a slide rule.

In Balaban's book *Close Encounters of the Third Kind Diary*, one entry reads,

> At the pool today Truffaut asks me if I wouldn't mind reading a script for him. He reads English very well, but someone has sent him a SciFi script, and he is having trouble understanding some of the technical terms. I am tremendously flattered and run up to my room to read it immediately. It's not a very good script, but I read it thoroughly and take copious notes; I want to give Truffaut an accurate report. Later he asks me what I thought. I fill him in on the story. I launch into an incredibly boring scene-by-scene synopsis. Truffaut listens very politely as I ramble on for fifteen minutes, retelling every trivial incident in the complicated script. I give possible meanings and interpretations for every twist and turn of its convoluted plot. Finally he stops me. He smiles: "Could you please just tell me if you think it's good or bad?"

In Our Hands, a documentary about the anti-nuke march in Central Park in 1982, includes short interviews with dozens of singers and actors. This is so perfect it sounds as if I'm making it up, but I'm not: Balaban, alone among his colleagues, goes unidentified.

What is Bob Balaban, anyway, a professional punching bag? What indignity will the movies not subject him to? What indignity will he not accept? What depth of self-loathing allows him to be used this way? What does it mean to have a face that the camera reviles? Couldn't his life count, too, along with the beautifully real—romantic, operatic, tragic—lives whirling around him? Could he ever see himself in romantic, operatic, tragic terms? What have these roles done to him?

Like someone dead or very famous, Balaban is trapped in an absolutely unchangeable identity. In almost all his movies he's extremely

dislikable, and in almost all of these movies he's extremely dislikable in precisely the same way: humorlessly overconcerned with procedure, passive-aggressive, dogged, eunuchized, bloodless. Balaban
frequently gives his character a peculiar habit: sneezing, stuttering,
playing with his food, winding and unwinding a rubber band. It's
difficult to believe that this is only a coincidence, that various directors just happened to give him a trick for us to remember him by. On
the other hand, I find it even harder to think of Bob Balaban as Chek-
hov, knowing his character so well that he knows everything about
him: how he eats, how he talks, what he does with his hands—as
if these things somehow either excused us for despising him or
explained something or other, as if the thing we hated about him
weren't him, as if it were only this one particular flaw we couldn't
abide. The technique distances Balaban from his character, his character from us: He doesn't want to be associated with his on-screen
persona any more than we do. Balaban is there to appreciate the hero
for us. Through him we gravitate toward the mysteries, but only by
first sloughing him off as our abject substitute, the viewer's least self,
with his—with our—ordinary self-interest, self-doubt, wariness,
weakness, cowardice, incompetence, homeliness. Balaban almost
always plays Jews (all those Elliotts); he's a scapegoat Christ suffering
for our one irredeemable sin: we are not movie stars, either.

STARS

Spider-Man, which I watched maybe a hundred times with Natalie, then nine, when it came out in 2002, is about how important it is for ordinary boys to view their own bodies as instruments of power—which, incidentally, or not so incidentally, is what has allowed nation-states to go to war from Mesopotamia until now. The names of the main characters in the movie are aggressively average, parodies of *Mayberry R.F.D.* ordinariness: Aunt May, Uncle Ben, Norman Osborn (who's both normal and born of Oz), Peter Parker, who has a crush on literally the girl next door, Mary Jane Watson. The words "average," "ordinary," and "normal" recur throughout the film, whose very first lines are, "Who am I? You sure you wanna know? The story of my life is not for the faint of heart. If somebody said it was a happy little tale, if somebody told you I was just your average, ordinary guy, not a care in the world, somebody lied." While Peter says this, a yellow school bus climbs a hill in Queens, belying his assertion.

It's high school; peer pressure is the state religion. Peter has two choices: try to do what he tells his friend, Harry, spiders do—"change color to blend into their environment; it's a defense mechanism"—or he can stand out, which is terrifying: "You're taller than you look," MJ tells him. "I hunch." "Don't." Even when he punches out the bully Flash, another kid calls Peter a freak. "Don't ever be ashamed of who you are," Norman/Green Goblin tells his son, Harry. And as the Goblin more Nietzscheanly tells Peter/Spider-Man, "There are eight million people in this city, and those teeming masses exist for the sole purpose of lifting a few exceptional people onto their shoulders." Gobby crashes World Unity Day, killing dozens, whereas when he forces Spider-Man to choose between rescuing the woman he loves or a tram full of children, Spider-Man, of course, manages to rescue both MJ and the children. "You mess with one of us, you mess with all of us," a guy on a bridge informs Gobby. The movie thus figures out a way to deliver an immensely reassuring message to its predominantly male and teenage audience: the transformation of your body from a boy into a man will make you not into a monster who despises the crowd but into the kind of creature the crowd idolizes.

When Peter gets bitten by a spider and begins turning into Spider-Man, Uncle Ben tells him, "You're not the same guy lately: fights in school, shirking your chores. You barely say a word to me or your aunt—what's the story?" "There's no story." "You're changing, and that's normal," Ben responds. "This is the age when a man becomes the man he's going to be for the rest of his life. Just be careful who you change into, okay?" Peter's change from dweeb to spider is explicitly analogous to his transformation from boy to man. When MJ asks him what he imagines his future will be, he says, "I don't know. It feels like something I never felt before, whatever it is," alluding to becoming Spider-Man but also to his feeling of falling in love with her. Before he becomes Spider-Man, he wears his shirt tucked in—dork style; afterward, he wears his undershirt and shirt hanging out. He can't be contained. Neither can his chest, which is newly ripped, and his eyesight is now 20/20. The screenplay phrases male sexual maturation as the equivalent of stealing fire from the gods: "I feel all this power," Peter says, "but I don't know what it means, or how to control it, or what I'm supposed to do with it even." Asked by Mary Jane what he told Spider-Man about her, Peter says he said, "The great thing about MJ is when you look in her eyes and she's looking back in yours and smiling, well, everything feels not quite normal, because you feel stronger and weaker at the same time, and you feel excited and at the same time terrified." Teenage boys want to believe that the sex instinct trumps and transfigures the day-to-day world.

Which it does and doesn't. The first time Spider-Man rescues MJ, she says to her boyfriend, Harry, that it was "incredible." "What do you mean 'incredible'?" he keeps asking her. The second time Spider-Man rescues MJ, she asks him, "Do I get to say thank you this time?" and, pulling down his mask past his lips, passionately kisses him, sending both of them into rain-drenched ecstasy. The script makes emphatically clear that Peter's newfound Spider-Man prowess is onanistic transcendence: "He wiggles his wrist, tries to get the goop to spray out, but it doesn't come. He makes a fist. Nothing. He closes his thumb and little finger together. Nothing. He rotates his hand so the palm faces up, extends all five fingers, and brings his ring and middle fingers toward his palm, together. *Thwip.* A single strand of webbing shoots out from his wrist. The webbing flies across the alley and sticks to the side of the other building. Peter tugs on it. It's tough. He pulls harder. Can't break it. He wraps one hand around it, closes his eyes, jumps off the roof. He sails through the air." All three times Spider-Man rescues MJ, they're wrapped in a pose that looks very much like missionary sex—Spider-Man on a mission. As Peter Parker, his peter is parked; as Spider-Man, he gets to have the mythic carnival ride of sex-flight without any of the messy, emotional cleanup afterward ("No matter what I do, no matter how hard I try, the ones I love are always the ones who pay").

Spider-Man is about the concomitance of your ordinary self, which is asexual, and your Big Boy self, which is sex-driven. Virtually every male character in the film worries this division. Peter Parker/Spider-Man and Norman Osborn/Green Goblin, of course. But also, when Uncle Ben changes the lightbulb, he says, "Let there be light." When Peter fails to show up to help him paint the dining room, Ben writes a teasing note to Peter and addresses him as "Michelangelo." The testosterone-intensive announcer at the New York Wrestling Foundation has a surprisingly understated side: "'The Human Spider'?" he asks Peter. "That's it? That's the best you got? Nah, you gotta jazz it up a little." Even the "squirrelly-looking" burglar who steals the New York Wrestling Foundation's money, and who later winds up killing Ben in a carjacking, mouths, "Thanks," and flashes a sweet smile when Peter unwisely lets him pass by into the elevator.

. . .

On a Saturday afternoon several years ago, at Seattle's Green Lake Pool, in the locker room, a ten-year-old kid hummed, at first quite quietly, to himself, the *Batman* theme. In less than a minute, the tune had made its way through the locker room—about a dozen pubescent boys humming the song. Some sang seriously; others joked around. Some stood on benches; others whapped their towels at one another's asses. Some danced around buck naked; others continued getting dressed. It was surprising and mysterious and confusing and beautiful and ridiculous and thrilling.

At the end of Ann Beattie's story "The Burning House," a husband and wife (the story's narrator) confront each other. She speaks first:

> "I want to know if you're staying or going."
> He takes a deep breath, lets it out, and continues to lie very still.
> "Everything you've done is commendable," he says. "You did the right thing to go back to school. You tried to do the right thing by finding yourself a normal friend like Marilyn. But your whole life you've made one mistake—you've surrounded yourself with men. Let me tell you something. All men—if they're crazy, like Tucker, if they're gay as the Queen of May, like Reddy Fox, even if they're just six years old—I'm going to tell you something about them. Men think they're Spider-Man and Buck Rogers and Superman. You know what we all feel inside that you don't feel? That we're going to the stars."
> He takes my hand. "I'm looking down on all this from space," he whispers. "I'm already gone."

Our cat, Zoomer, is exceedingly centripetal and social. The moment I spread out my papers on the dining room table, he lies on top of them. He greets most visitors by crawling onto their laps. His favorite activity is lying in front of the fire for hours while Laurie, Natalie, and I sit near him, reading. His second-favorite activity is to lie between the three of us while we're watching a movie; he eats ice cream from our bowls while we pretend not to notice. At night, he sleeps in the crook of Laurie's neck, his paws wrapped around her forehead. And yet if we indulge him by petting him for too long, he inevitably reacts to this overdomestication by biting or scratching us. He loves to hide behind a bookcase and swat unsuspecting passersby or lie across the bookcase, one paw hanging in the air, and look out across the room—a lion surveying the savanna, scoping antelope. He wants to convince himself and us that, thoroughly pampered though he is, at heart he's still a killer.

From room to room he drags "his" teddy bear—what Natalie used to call his girlfriend—and, despite his supposedly having been fixed years ago, dry-humps it day and night, howling with a conqueror's fury. He'll spend hours scratching the window at his neighborhood nemesis, Fireball, but when presented with the opportunity to confront Fireball nose-to-nose, he always settles, pseudo-disappointedly, for the safety of imprisonment. On the rare occasions when he does go outside, he hisses, terrified, at all provocations and scoots inside on the flimsiest pretext. He needs to convince himself that he's a tough guy, but really Zoomy's a pussy.

HE WAS THERE; HE WASN'T REALLY THERE: DREAMS ABOUT KURT COBAIN

Kurt and I were in a karaoke bar. We were sitting in movie theater chairs, and the karaoke stage was kinda far away from us. It was a really surreal thing. People were just walking around. It had a really spacey feel to it. He was not sitting next to me but next to next to me. Somebody was lip-synching to "Smells Like Teen Spirit," and I was, like, "Hey, man, do you know that they are the same exact chords from Blue Oyster Cult's 'Godzilla'?" Kurt and I got into this argument about it, and then he was like, "Man, how do you know that?" I said, "I'm a musician," and he said okay. But then he just started going off: "Everybody's comin' down on me because I'm famous now." I was, like, "Well, I'm sorry." And then I said, "Well, I guess it's 'cause I'm jealous because you're not really that great a musician and you're famous and I really am a great musician and I'm still just struggling." And he said, "Okay, I can agree to that. I forgive you." It was kind of an exchange-of-angst thing. I angsted-out on him, because I didn't think he deserved it, and he angsted-out on me, saying why do you people have to angst-out on me?—Raymond, age twenty-seven

.   .   .

I dunno what the setting was, but I was kneeling, looking down the barrel of a gun, about to shoot myself in tribute to Kurt.—Ryan, seventeen

Kurt was sort of a Jim Jones figure. It wasn't a jungle setting or anything, though, just an ordinary living room. Everyone was getting in line to commit suicide. The weird part is that when you got up to the head of the line to off yourself, it wasn't Kool-Aid Kurt was handing out. It was Kaopectate.—Chris, thirty-one

I was at a Butthole Surfers show and it was like this big huge racetrack, and that's where they were playing. I got up, 'cause I couldn't hear them; they weren't loud enough. We kept trying to get closer and closer. We finally found our way backstage and Kurt was back there. We had thought he died. He was sitting in this bathtub thing. We just hung out with him and we also hung out with the Nirvana bass player dude. They couldn't hear the Buttholes, either. It's kind of weird: every time I dream about the Buttholes I can't hear them.—Dave, twenty-two

I was over at somebody's house at a party. There was a band playing a song by Hole, at which point I was reminded about Kurt's death and I started to cry and get upset about the whole thing. The weirdest thing is that I have never heard a song by Hole, but I knew that the band was doing a cover of Hole, anyway. I also remember thinking about doing covers of Nirvana songs—I'm in a band, and we've done covers of "Sliver," "Breed," and "Rape Me"—and thinking we are going to have to practice more to get them perfect.—Julian, nineteen

I was at his house with a bunch of friends and it was kind of informal. It was kind of a dream house—a feeling of anarchy and domestic tranquility. I was made to feel very welcome. He was just playing music and singing, and I just remember waking up and thinking, *Wow, that's a beautiful new song*, and looking at other friends of mine and thinking, *This guy's great, this guy's the real thing.* It was just kind of a stark and beautiful caterwauling, à la Kurt.—Darren, twenty-six

I was in Kurt's house: a big, airy room, with wood floors and big windows. It had the sense of being high up, like we were looking out over the lake maybe. Kurt was in the room along with Courtney Love and Eddie Vedder. It was a really big room, and it was like each of us was in a corner. Courtney was really kind of agitated. She was nervous and upset and excited and she kept talking about a song that was supposed to be recorded really soon. I got the sense it was a Nirvana song. She was trying to talk to Kurt. He was pretty aloof; I don't think he said anything. He was kind of at the end of the room. He just didn't say much. Eddie was on the other side of the room, kind of listening to Courtney, not really saying much either, brooding, responding a little bit to Courtney. But Kurt and Eddie weren't really into what she was saying, and she was very agitated. And there was a kind of sadness in the room, also an urgency. Courtney was really trying to get things going, and neither of them were helping her. I felt kind of bad for Courtney. I wanted to help her. These two guys were being so unresponsive. She was just so frantic, trying to get this new song recorded. She really wanted to get this song recorded soon; otherwise, it would be too late. There was a real urgent sense, and Kurt didn't care. She was dressed up, bright red lipstick, a white top—the way she looked in those pictures of her in Rome. Eddie walked in circles, rubbed his face, looked angst-ridden and brooding, like he does in concert. Kurt was doing not much at all, kinda standing there; he was there, but he wasn't really there.—Kim, thirty-four

You know those dreams where the hall lasts forever, and you finally get to the door and you're really scared to open it? This was like that. I was walking around Kurt's house and I started freaking out. I was, like, *Wait a minute, this is his house, what am I doing here?* I went to his room and opened the door, and he turned over and looked at me and said, "Life's a ball," and then pow—right in the head. I was standing there and I saw him blow his head off. One minute the house was all psychedelic colors; the next, it was black.—Melinda, fifteen

I was in the room when he was writing his suicide note. He was trying really hard to think of what to say; he couldn't really write very clearly, 'cause, you know, he was in a room with a gun. I was sorta watching from the outside of the room, looking in on him. I was just sort of observing the whole thing; I kind of came in through the window. Then he got the gun out and he put it next to the paper and just started writing with a normal pencil. Then he looked up at me and he was asking what he should say, and if this was really worth it. I was trying to give him advice, but I couldn't really think of anything to say except, "Well, what about your family—how are they going to deal with this?" And he was like, "Yes, but I don't want my daughter to turn out like me." And I said, I don't think having a father who committed suicide is going to do her much good, and he said yeah, finished his note, and looked up and said, "I'm sorry," like, to the world, sort of, and then blew himself away. He seemed really helpless. In the second before he shot himself, I saw this little boy inside, sort of crying for help, sort of a tragic hero thing.—Ariel, fifteen

I learned that Kurt had a terminal illness and that Nirvana was playing a farewell show before he died. I went to the show (which seemed to be in a high school gym; it wasn't really clear) and sat next to Courtney. We watched the show, and afterward we both sat and cried for a long time. While we were talking and crying—I remember her talking about Frances Bean, although I don't recall the context—it was announced over a loudspeaker that Kurt died. I don't remember anything after that.—Greta, twenty

I was at my old high school back in Port Townsend and I was walking through the track field late at night, and my old boyfriend told me not to walk alone, but I did it anyway, and I saw these three guys coming toward me and I'm like, "Have you guys seen Nirvana? I'm looking for Nirvana. Hasn't anybody seen Nirvana?" Like I had lost them. They're looking at me all weird. And then they started to attack me.—Morgan, twenty-three

.　　　.　　　.

The etymology of the word "Nirvana" is given in various ways. According to Colebrooke (*Transactions of the Royal Asiatic Society,* Vol. I, p. 566), it comes from *va,* "to blow" like the wind, with the prefixed negative *nir;* hence it signifies a lull or calm, but as adjective "extinguished." Obry, *Du Nirvana indien,* p. 3, says, *Nirvanam en sanscrit signifie à la lettre extinction, telle que celle d'un feu.* ("'Nirvana' in Sanskrit literally means 'extinction,' e.g., as of a fire." Tr.) According to the *Asiatic Journal,* Vol. XXIV, p. 735, it is really *Neravana,* from *nera,* "without," and *vana,* "life," and the meaning would be *annihilatio.* In Spence Hardy's *Eastern Monachism,* p. 295, *Nirvana* is derived from *vana,* "sinful desires," with the negative *nir.* I. J. Schmidt, in his translation of the *History of the Eastern Mongolians,* p. 307, says that the Sanskrit *Nirvana* is translated into Mongolian by a phrase meaning "departed from misery," "escaped from misery." According to the same scholar's lectures at the St. Petersburg Academy, *Nirvana* is the opposite of *Samsara,* which is the world of constant rebirths, of craving and desire, of the illusion of the senses, of changing and transient forms, of being born, growing old, becoming sick, and dying. In Burmese the word *Nirvana,* on the analogy of other Sanskrit words, is transformed into *Nieban,* and is translated by "complete vanishing."—Schopenhauer

I was pinning Kurt down on the bed, and I thought I heard him laughing.—Michelle, twenty

CONTEMPORARY FILM CRITICISM

Early on in our relationship, Laurie and I went to yet another movie about love overcoming numerous obstacles. She shushed the movie crowd, raucous on vacation; I admired only the dialogue I couldn't quite catch. Toward the end, the hero's friend's suicide allowed everyone in the audience to die but live. Afterward, thinking the car was stolen, I let out a yelp in the empty, misty parking lot (in the trunk were my Christmas presents for her). Laurie finally saw where we were parked. Driving with bad brakes on the slick street, I slid through a stop sign, turning 180 degrees, hopping the curb. Angry at my careless driving, she jumped out of the car and I gave her ten seconds to get back in. She refused. Gallantly, as in Italian neorealism, I left in order to return, but when I returned, the car hydroplaned again toward the sidewalk, nearly killing our appetite for more movies.

V. ALTER EGOS

The stories that we tell about ourselves are designed to sort of reveal a part of ourselves to the world. It's the part we want to show. What I learned from two years of reporting, investigation, and writing is that you can't know the whole truth. But if there is one, it lies in the space between people.

—DAVID CARR

ALMOST FAMOUS (ii)

John Melendez is now a staff writer on *The Tonight Show*, but for fifteen years, on Howard Stern's radio show on WXRK in New York (and on his cable television show), "Stuttering John"—whose favorite fictional character was Cornelius, King of the Apes, whom he resembled and imitated whenever the opportunity arose—asked, tried to ask, Barbara Eden what she sleeps in; Magic Johnson why *baseball* players are so horny; Valerie Harper whether she has breast implants and whether her husband spanks her; Gennifer Flowers whether then governor Clinton used a condom; Joey Adams when was the last time he had a solid bowel movement; Chaz Bono if he'd ever French-kissed Cher; Liz Smith why she's such a fat cow; Walter Mondale whether he ever worried that Geraldine Ferraro would have gotten cramps in office; Morton Downey Jr. if his wife would dance topless to save him from poverty; Liza Minnelli why gay guys dig her mom so much; Warren Beatty what's bigger—the Oscar or his penis.

The questions with which he discomfited celebrities were invariably sexual, which made sense: Stuttering always seems—to me, anyway—so similar to sexual tension. Melendez says that as a stuttering adolescent, "I had no problem asking other kids if they had hair down there yet. Nobody wanted to talk about it. The hardest interview was Fred Gwynne. I had to promise this girl, this beautiful publicist, that I wouldn't ask him anything about *The Munsters.* I said, 'Hey, don't worry, this is gonna be a piece about his work in the theater,' and she's right next to me, right, when I ask him if he signs his pictures 'Fred Gwynne' or 'Herman Munster.' She's there and you could see her just—that's why I stutter so much. . . . It's like picking up a girl. You've got to go up and ask her out, but it's the most uncomfortable thing. When I used to try and pick up a girl, I would have to turn my head."

Melendez's stutter got worse whenever the celebrity, stalling for time, asked him to repeat the question, but it was when he was speaking to Stern—before or after the celebrity interviews—that Melendez's voice and face lost all claim to behavioral integrity, for Stern, nicely named, is a merciless sadist:

> STERN: What happens if the show goes off the air or somethin' happens to me—what do you do? Seriously, what would you do?
>
> MELENDEZ: Well, b-b-b-by then I hope to have a record contract.
>
> STERN: Let's say a record contract is a tough thing to get, okay? You'll admit that. As much talent as you have, as much natural talent as you have, let's say that never happens. And it looks like it never is gonna happen. You're twenty-six and you're on television. I mean, I haven't seen anybody give you a record contract. What do you do if something happens to me?
>
> MELENDEZ: Cry.
>
> STERN: No, really—what do you do? What is your career path in that case?
>
> MELENDEZ: I don't know, I haven't really given it much, uh-uh-uh-uh, given it too much thought. Maybe I'll take up acting.
>
> STERN: But that's another career. In other words, you have to have, you know, you have to have something to fall back on.
>
> MELENDEZ: I want to be, I want to be in the entertainment industry, you know.

STERN: Right.

MELENDEZ: That's what I've always wanted to do, so—

STERN: All right, so you're in it. Okay, I understand your point. Well, okay.

MELENDEZ: I mean, what is anyone gonna do?

ROBIN QUIVERS [Stern's sidekick]: I like that; he doesn't even think past today.

STERN: Well, you know, they say, If you're going to be successful, don't think past today. That's what all the experts say. I took a lot of courses in this and I know. You know, he wants to be in show business and the only job he's really qualified for in show business is to sweep up elephant doody at the circus.

MELENDEZ: Could I ask you a question?

STERN: Yes, go ahead.

MELENDEZ: How come, like, you know, I go out, you know, and-and-and-and do this stuff and then, and then, and then, and then, and then you just bring me out and berate me?

STERN: I'm not berating you. I'm concerned about you, like a father to a son. It's a question.

MELENDEZ: All right. I hope that I c-c-c-c-can work with you.

STERN: But what I'm saying—what if it should happen that I am no longer in show business? What-what if I lose my voice to throat cancer?

MELENDEZ: Maybe they'll give me my own show.

STERN: Well, okay, maybe, but you're a friggin' mess.

MELENDEZ: And that's what I'll call it: *The Friggin' Mess Show.*

STERN: That's going to be some show.

Stern called him "hero of the stupid," "hero of no one," "stupid man," "king of the interns," "world's oldest intern," "stuttering baboon," "oh you poor man," "you idiot." "What's the matter with you?" "What a turd you are." "There is no show on television that would give an animal like this a job interviewing people for a living." "Look at him! What a mess!" Melendez would lock up and Stern would say, "Say it already, you dope. Come on, say something. If you got something to say, say it quick." Melendez told Stern that he auditioned for a small role in a Steve Martin movie, and Stern said, "I hope Steve Martin knows hand signals, because this is going to be some movie. This is going to be the longest film ever made. This is going to be a three-hour movie. They're going to have to release it on two separate videotapes." When Melendez's girlfriend appeared on the show and Melendez suffered a bad block, Stern repeatedly asked her whether she was embarrassed to be his girlfriend. A man with Tourette's was brought on the show to compete with Melendez for his job. Stern asked Melendez if his jaw ever gets tired, then said, "You know what I just realized? Your jaw reminds me of my mother's sewing machine. I get a headache from watching you try to talk." "Isn't it fun to wait for the stutter?" Stern asked Quivers. "Seriously, you know, we all feel guilty about it, and let's face it: We all feel terrible that we're watching a guy stutter and we're laughing at him. But you gotta admit you wait for the big stutter, don't you?"

Melendez told Stern, "You know what I think it is? I think—when you point—I think it almost kinda intimidates me."

"It intimidates you a little bit? All right, well, I won't point then," Stern said and pointed.

One wanted to ask of Melendez, as one still wants to ask of Bob Balaban, *Why do you allow yourself to be used in this way?* Pleading with Liza for the interview, he promised, "One question, and I swear I'll never talk to you again." After Melendez asked Marlo Thomas whether she and Phil Donahue still get horny for each other, if Marlo ever stuck her finger down her throat, and what the most degrading term for women is, Gloria Steinem interrupted, saying, "You're really hopeless," and Melendez responded, "Why do you say that?" As Susan Sontag said (wrongly, as always) about Michel Leiris's *Manhood: A Journey from Childhood into the Fierce Order of Virility*, "Leiris's attitude is unredeemed by the slightest tinge of self-respect. This lack of esteem or respect for himself is obscene."

Melendez insisted at the time that it was not "only funny because I stutter. It was funny 'cause I was putting these celebrities on the spot. Celebrities are used to answering the same exact questions over and over again. It was cool to have someone throw them something they're going to have to think about for a second. You saw a lot of them break down and become who they really are. People get all uptight about it. I thought it was ridiculous because, I mean, if a celebrity couldn't, you know, deal with being asked what they read on the bowl—it's a goofy question, you know, and when these guys got upset about it, you could tell—that was why it was great, it put them in a true light, out of their character, you know what I mean, out of their usual mode, like 'How'd ya get started?'—out of the mode."

If Melendez's stutter expressed the perfect mix of rage and awe we feel before celebrity, the entire operation was constructed as a geometrically exquisite paradox: Melendez didn't write the questions he asked and often was unaware of the allusions they made to the celebrity's personal problems (thus, even when Melendez was asking the questions, Stern kept him out of the loop); Melendez attempted to treat the celebrities with the same contempt with which Stern treated him, but his stutter—which was "under control, for the most part" (*New York Times*)—was so completely out of control that it immediately undermined his pretense to authoritarian cruelty; Melendez turned into the Jell-O that he was trying to turn them into; using his stutter to make them feel sorry for him and therefore let him talk to them, he exposed the shamelessness of all star-maker machinery, at the same time that he was piercing, with his disrespectful questions, the nimbus around them that they felt certain had made a nullity of us all. If they couldn't laugh at themselves the way he could—if, as most did, they went grim, got mad, or ran away; John Amos, the cookie magnate, asked him, "How did you get a job like this with a speech impediment?"—they exposed the gap between their character and their character. They couldn't stand toe-to-toe even with "Stuttering John," but when they displayed anything resembling the reservoirs of vulnerability, nerve, and wit that Melendez did, they seemed newly, touchingly, weirdly alive. When Melendez asked Reggie Jackson if he'd ever accidentally farted in the catcher's face, Reggie said, "Sure, and if you hang out long enough, I'll fart in *your* face." Valerie Harper told Melendez, "I have a dear friend who stuttered, but he communicated right through it and so do you. Isn't it great that you picked this form?"

"Well, I didn't pick it," Melendez said. "I kind of got pushed into it."

"No, I think it's great. What you did is you went into the eye of the storm. That's very courageous."

"Thanks a lot," Melendez said. "C-c-can I get a hug?"

THE SIXTIES

The sixties—which, as everybody knows, began in 1963 and ended in 1974—happened, like a sitcom, in the middle of my living room.

I was president of the sixth grade of one of the first desegregated elementary schools in California, and when the BBC came to interview me, I spoke so passionately that they had to stop the film because the cameraman was crying.

By the end of eighth grade it was a profound social embarrassment if you hadn't "gotten married," which meant lost your virginity.

The third-floor roof of our high school overlooked the pool in the middle of the courtyard. People who were tripping would jump off the top of the roof into the pool on Saturday nights. Occasionally the pool would have been drained. If someone dove into the empty pool, it was called a "header."

Yvonne, who wore miniskirts and leather jackets and was by far the school's best girl swimmer, drowned when she tried to swim all the way out to Alcatraz immediately after a huge lunch of hash brownies.

A married couple who worked for the McGovern campaign, Janice and Michael, came down from Seattle and stayed in our house from the California primary until the general election. I had such a bad crush on Janice that on the night of Nixon's landslide, I disconnected the car radio so she'd still be in a good enough mood to come with me as I took old people around to the polls until closing.

I wrote so many satires about capital punishment for the high school newspaper that students who didn't read carefully started calling me the Beheader.

I heard a rumor that Smith Corona also made munitions and immediately switched to Olivetti.

As the editor of the *Observer,* the newspaper of the California Democratic Council, my father was at times caught in the middle between opponents and defenders of the Vietnam War. He finally ran a cartoon that showed LBJ surfing off the coast of Cambodia, which made the point about American imperialism. The caption my father wrote was "Up Surf." He was fired within the month, not because of the content of the cartoon but because he didn't know the idiom.

The majority of my nieces and nephews on both sides of my family have—or at least at one point had—first names that are either colors, animals, or trees, or a combination of colors, animals, or trees.

Freshman year of high school we all had to take world geography, and the first day of class we all had to come up onstage and tell "Glen" what kind of animal we were, then portray this animal for a few seconds. The entire semester there was no mention of anything even remotely related to world geography.

The ecology club held a massive demonstration and littered the courtyard with so many placards that for once I abandoned my capital punishment theme and wrote a satire about the event; the ecology club retaliated by toilet-papering my house.

My half-brother, Joseph, had a phrase, "Tain't no big thang." No one knew where he got it, whether or when it was meant sincerely or ironically, but he said it in response to almost every possible development.

When he and his roommate were arrested for possession of those hundreds of capsules of DMT, Joseph told the cops he was going to use them to decorate a Christmas tree. "In June?" one cop asked. "Tain't no big thang," Joseph said.

For sociology class I interviewed sixteen different cliques in our high school and found that precisely three-quarters of the groups made "insider/outcast" distinctions not on the basis of money, appearance, academics, after-school job, or sports. Precisely three-quarters of the groups made "insider/outcast" distinctions on the basis of what kind of drugs you used.

Newsweek reported that our high school had the highest drug use per capita of any high school in the United States, and people threw parties for a month straight to protect our number one ranking.

My half-sister, Emily, had a life-threatening case of colitis and traveled all over India, looking for a holistic cure; she finally settled on Transcendental Meditation, which seemed to do the trick. If you asked her if she wanted to do almost anything, she'd say, "Gotta have time to smell the roses," which was, of course, just another version of "Tain't no big thang."

My sister and her best friend had a bitter fight, from which the relationship never fully recovered, over who was the cutest Monkee, Davy or Micky.

I broke up with my girlfriend when one day she decided she couldn't stand it any longer and went ahead and shaved her legs.

A friend of my father's in LA lived less than a block from where the Symbionese Liberation Army was being busted on live TV; we were visiting, so we kept one eye on the television, the other eye out the window. "It's so real I feel like I can almost smell the smoke," some-one said. "You *can* smell the smoke," my father said. The SLA was burning to death and smoke was pouring through an open window.

In the fall of 1974 I left the Bay Area to go to college in Providence, Rhode Island, which I imagined as, quite literally, Providence—a heavenly city populated by seraphic souls. I imagined Rhode Island as an actual island, the exotic edge of the eastern coast. And I saw Brown as enclosed, paradisal space in which strong boys played rugby on fields of snow, then read Ruskin by gaslight in marble libraries too old to close, and girls with thick dark hair, good bodies, and great minds talked about Goethe (which I pronounced "Go-eth") at breakfast. The first month of my first semester, black students occupied the administration building and demanded increases in black student enrollment and financial aid. These seemed to me laudable goals, so I went over to become part of the picket line outside the administration building and marched in a circle, chanting, for a few minutes, but the whole event seemed like a really weak imitation of all the demonstrations I'd been going to since I was six years old, and I wanted to get away from groups and the West Coast and my former milieu for a while. A few people from my dorm were tossing around a Frisbee on the back side of the green, and I left the picket line to go join them. That, for me, was the end of the sixties.

THE SMARTER DOG
KNOWS WHEN TO DISOBEY

In 1975, when I was a sophomore at Brown, my aunt was friends with and—the way he once pushed upon me some sort of reference book he compiled—must also have been dating a man who for years had been an editor of the *New York Times Magazine,* so I knew a bit before everyone else at school that the *Times Magazine* was planning a long article about the New Curriculum (no distribution requirements, optional pass/fail, fewer total courses required to graduate, the freedom to direct your own education, the encouragement to go deep rather than wide), which by then was quite old. When a reporter and photographer showed up one week that fall, their presence was immediately known and remarked upon. On the one hand, they were treated with almost a parody of blasé disinterest, whose purpose was to demonstrate how far we'd progressed beyond such mundane considerations as school spirit and self-promotion. On the other hand, from freshman orientation (which consisted primarily of people comparing Yale wait-list stories) through senior commencement ceremonies (which, according to those who knew, lacked the rowdy irreverence of Columbia's), never, ever in my life have I encountered a more self-conscious and insecure group of individuals than the Brown class of '78. Then again, maybe it was just me, insanely alert to rumors of my own inadequacy. There was, in any case, ambivalence toward the *Times* coverage—a certain feigned but felt indifference mixed with a childish hope that our parents back in the suburbs would read about the alarmingly bright Brown student body.

By the time the article came out, we'd forgotten all about it, and like any newspaper story whose subject you know well, it got things wrong and it was unbelievably boring. (My mother was a lifelong fan of Israel Shenker and S. J. Perelman; still, when she read Shenker's portrait of Perelman in the *Times,* she said, "Like every news story I've ever known anything about personally, it was a bummer: inept, too cute, biased, incomplete. It made me wonder about all those stories I've admired.") I don't remember much about the article except that it appeared to have been written, in general, by the Brown admissions office, dwelling as it did upon the precipitous rise in the number of applications. I do remember, however, the photographer taking picture after picture of my Latin Lit classmate Theodore "Tad" Kinney III and me as we talked about who knows what outside Wayland Arch—probably how much better Tad Kinney was at Petronius than I was. I remember opening up the magazine and seeing the picture of Tad talking to . . . no one. I still had such acute acne that every night I had to mix and then wear a complex formula my dermatologist back in the Bay Area had prescribed for me; I didn't embody Brown's "new popularity" in the way that Theodore "Tad" Kinney III, with his tortoiseshell glasses and Exeter jaw, did. The point isn't that the Elephant Man always has some slight to complain about; the photo editor probably did me a favor by cropping me out of the picture. The point is that for the purposes of the accompanying photograph, I couldn't exist.

In the work of a striking number of creative artists who are Brown grads, I see a skewed, complex, somewhat tortured stance: antipathy toward the conventions of the culture and yet a strong need to be in conversation with that culture. (You can't deconstruct something that you're not hugely interested in the construction of in the first place.) Although these impulses are obviously not unique to former or current residents of Providence, Rhode Island, I'm curious to what degree, if any, Brown can be seen as an incubator for American postmodernism. Paula Vogel, who taught playwriting at Brown for twenty years before leaving for Yale, says, "I think Brown is a strong incubator, based on (1) our actual location; (2) our history as a school (the anti-Harvard, anti-Yale); and (3) the non-integration of artists into the curriculum here: we're still on the margins and, therefore, artists who also teach a history/theory/literary curriculum are the artists who come to Brown."

Is there an analogous Harvard or Williams or Oberlin or Stanford or Amherst or Cornell or Yale or Berkeley aesthetic, and, if so, how is it different, and, if not, why does Brown have such a thing while other, "similar" institutions don't? These schools are somehow more secure in what they are and aren't (the University of Chicago probably isn't obsessed with the fact that it isn't Princeton), whereas Brown is helplessly, helpfully trapped in limbo—Brown's productively flawed, tragicomic, self-conscious relation to power/prestige/privilege. In 2004, *Women's Wear Daily* named Brown "the most fashionable Ivy"—bobo clothes made (expensively) to look like the thrifty alternative to expensive trends. Embarrassing recent poll result: Brown is the "happiest Ivy." Brown is Ivy, but it's, crucially, not Harvard, Princeton, Yale. Brown students affirm a discourse of privilege at the same time they want to undermine such a hierarchy. Brown: *We're #14* (according to a recent *U.S. News & World Report* ranking); *we try not necessarily harder but differently.*

The result, in the arts: a push-pull attitude toward the dominant narrative. Todd Haynes, pitching his 2007 film *I'm Not There* to Bob Dylan, its anti-subject: "If a film were to exist in which the breadth and flux of a creative life could be experienced, a film that could open up as opposed to consolidating what we think we already know walking in, it could never be within the tidy arc of a master narrative. The structure of such a film would have to be a fractured one, with numerous openings and a multitude of voices, with its prime strategy being one of refraction, not condensation. Imagine a film splintered between seven separate faces—old men, young men, women, children—each standing in for spaces in a single life." Documentarian Ross McElwee (whose film *Sherman's March* changed my writing life): "Any attempt at some pure form of objectivity always seemed to me impossible and, at least in my attempts, dishonest, in some ways. In all of the hue and cry about objectivity and truth being captured by a camera at twenty-four frames per second, I've missed the idea of subjectivity. Somehow melding the two—the objective data of the world with a very subjective, very interior consciousness, as expressed through voice-over and on-camera appearances—seemed to give me the clay from two different pits to work with in sculpting something that suited me better than pure cinéma vérité." Ira Glass, producer and host of *This American Life:* "I was a middle-class kid who didn't know what he believed. My religion became semiotics, which was the conspiracy theory to beat all conspiracy theories. It wasn't just that authority figures of various sorts did things that were questionable. It was that language itself was actually a system designed to keep you in your place, which, when you're nineteen or twenty, is pretty much exactly what you're ready to hear. Semiotics was how I defined myself. To a large extent, it still is. Most of what I understand about how to make radio is all filtered through what I learned in semiotics at Brown. There are certain things I learned from Robert Scholes—about, say, the way to structure a narrative to produce the most anticipation and pleasure—that I think of every day. Honestly, I wouldn't have my job now without it."

Rick Moody on exactly the kind of radio Glass was reacting against: "Humanism is a worthy goal for the literature and arts. Of course. It's indisputable. The assertion of the essential dignity and value of humankind—who can argue with it? Certainly not I. The question, however, is if the goal of humanism, the assertion thereof, can survive the problem of its representation in the medium of audio. As with contemporary literature, contemporary radio has apparently found that it has to *construct* a certain rigid notion of humanism, in order to effect this humanist epiphany in you and me. And yet as soon as the construction becomes predictable, homogenized, devoid of surprise, I for one no longer hear the humanism at all. In fact, it starts to sound manipulative, controlling, condescending, perhaps even a little sinister. It's like a piece of music that has been so compressed in the studio that the dynamic variation has been entirely squeezed out of it."

Boston Globe, 2004: "From its founding as a fledgling program in 1974 to its morphing into a full Department of Modern Culture and

Media in 1996, Brown semiotics has produced a crop of creators that, if they don't exactly dominate the cultural mainstream, certainly have grown famous sparring with it." Emphasis on "sparring": over the last thirty-five years, Brown semiotics majors and others have tended to produce work with, as Moody says, an unmistakable tendency to "infiltrate and double-cross." In the late 1960s, Scholes was invited, on the strength of his book *The Nature of Narrative,* to a semiotics conference in Italy; he'd never heard the term before. He joined the Brown faculty in 1970 and by 1974 had founded the semiotics program. Scholes says he chose the word "semiotics" because of its lack of meaning. "It didn't have a lot of baggage. It was almost a blank signifier." ("Semiotics?" I remember my mother saying. "What the hell is that?") In the immediate wake of the New Curriculum, Brown could not have been more open to "interrogate certain ideological assumptions attendant upon bourgeois notions of pleasure," according to film scholar Michael Silverman, one of Scholes's first recruits. The irony being, of course, that as novelist Samantha Gillison says, "Semiotics was an exclusive, self-contained puzzle for super-smart, super-rich kids."

"I see two distinct 'schools' of Brown writing with regard to contemporary culture," Elizabeth Searle (author of the collection *Celebrities in Disgrace,* whose title novella she adapted into an opera, *Tonya and Nancy*—about Tonya Harding and Nancy Kerrigan) wrote to me. "Some, such as Moody, engage in a full-frontal assault, perhaps influenced as I was by Robert Coover and his ahead-of-the-curve *A Night at the Movies.* Other Brown alums follow more of a lone-Hawkesian flight path regarding popular culture. Jack Hawkes [the novelist John Hawkes, who taught at Brown for thirty-five years and died in 1998] seemed to soar above the whole computerized wasteland of contemporary culture with blissful indifference. Students of his such as Joanna Scott and Mary Caponegro seem to me to have followed suit, creating their unique takes from the vantage point of distant worlds (as in Scott's *Arrogance*) or by conjuring up worlds wholly of their own making (as when Caponegro, in *The Star Café,* concocts a sexual funhouse in which a warped mirror forces lovers to view the strange, twisted postures of sex with only their own body and not the body of their partner reflected for view). What the two 'schools' seem to me to have in common is—for want of a better, fresher metaphor—an insistent, outside-the-box mentality that both Coover and Hawkes, our founding fathers, shared."

Joanna Scott, describing the subjects of her own work, adumbrates many of Hawkes's topoi as well: "Character and the motion of thought; the effects of varied narrative form; contradictory perceptions of time and place; the idiosyncrasies of voice; mystery and the impact of disclosure; beauty and ugliness; comedy, temptation, collapse, and recovery; the elusive potential of imagination."

Brown, the seventh-oldest college in America, was founded in 1764—the Baptist answer to Congregationalist Harvard and Yale, Presbyterian Princeton, and Episcopalian Columbia and Penn. At the time, Brown was the only school that welcomed students of all religious persuasions. For nearly two centuries, it was what it was: a decent-to-good regional school, though also, I gather, a bit dandyish, gentlemanly, slightly or not so slightly second tier—among the least prestigious of the universities with which it wished to associate itself. In 1954, the Ivy League athletic conference was formed; Brown was/is last or nearly last among equals (with, for instance, by far the lowest endowment, currently three billion dollars to Harvard's thirty-six). Brown still, I think, suffers from a massive superiority/inferiority complex *(We're anti-Ivy, but we're Ivy!)*, proud of the club it belongs to and anxious about its status within that club. Saith Groucho Marx, two of whose films, *Monkey Business* and *Horse Feathers,* were cowritten by S. J. Perelman (he didn't graduate), "I'd never join a club that would have me as a member." At once rebel *(We're more interesting than you are)* and wannabe *(We got 1390 on our SATs rather than 1520),* we're like Jews in upper-middle-class America: We're in the winner's circle but uncertain whether we really belong. In general, Brown is (perceived to be) not the best of the best but within shouting distance of the best of the best—which creates institutional vertigo, a huge investment in and saving irony toward prestige; ambivalence toward cultural norms; and among artists, a desire to stage that ambivalence, to blur boundaries, to confuse what's acceptable and what's not.

In 1850, Brown's fourth president, Francis Wayland, argued for greater openness in the undergraduate curriculum: Every student should be able to "study what he chose, all that he chose, and nothing but what he chose." In 1969, the New Curriculum reanimated Wayland's charge. The Brown aesthetic is a very loose translation, I would argue, of the New Curriculum: more loose limbed, more playful, more interdisciplinary, harder to define, at its worst silly (in 1974, my freshman roommate attended a lecture by Buckminster Fuller about the spiritual properties of the geodesic dome and spent all of November chanting in a teepee) and at its best mind-bending, life-altering, culture-challenging. *Harvard runs the world; Brown changes it.* The New Curriculum made, brilliantly, a virtue of necessity—took what was less traditionally pedantic and hypertensive about Brown and made it the very emblem of off-center experimentation and excitement, of off-axis cultural contributions. Brown is "branded" with a specificity that is surely the envy of other schools. Self-fulfilling prophecy: a certain kind of student now applies to Brown.

Amy Hempel, whose *Collected Stories* carries a foreword by Moody, says, "The smart dog obeys. The smarter dog knows when to disobey." Dave Eggers, the recipient of an honorary degree in 2005, said at Commencement, "Man, did I want to go here. Brown was the number one school I wanted to go to when I applied to college. I wanted to go somewhere without any rules, but I was brutally rejected."

It's important to acknowledge, of course, that such self-reflexive, genre-bending, fourth-wall-shattering gestures are hardly exclusive to Brunonians. Brown didn't invent American postmodernism. So, too, many extremely successful Brown grads in the arts are working a fairly traditional vein. As Beth Taylor, director of the Nonfiction Writing Program, says, "Certainly our Literary Arts Program has defined itself as experimental and against-the-grain since Hawkes and Coover brought it to national prominence in the 1970s. And perhaps, post-1969 New Curriculum, more Brown students have tended toward comfort with dissent than pre-1969 alums. Over the years, though, I've seen as many writers go off to mainstream publications as to alternative ones. And their stances have ranged from flip/skeptical to documentarian/fact-checked journalism." Doug Liman's Bourne trilogy does not seek to alter the face of an art form. Nathaniel Philbrick's *In the Heart of the Sea: The Tragedy of the Whaleship Essex*, which won a National Book Award, is an estimable work of traditional nonfiction. The historical novelist Thomas Mallon has positioned himself in direct opposition to pomo relativism; he credits Mary McCarthy's "premodernist" sensibility with inspiring him to become a writer, and he says about his collection of essays *In Fact* that "its prevailing moods and enthusiasms remain more retroverted and conservative than the academic and media cultures in which they were experienced." Susan Minot is a direct descendant of the literary Episcopalianism of Henry James, Edith Wharton, Shirley Hazzard, John Updike. Deborah Garrison's poetry is old-fashionedly accessible, as the irresistible title of her first book, *A Working Girl Can't Win,* would suggest. Alfred Uhry's *Driving Miss Daisy* is straight down Broadway. Kermit Champa, professor of the history of art and architecture until his death in 2004, believed in Gesamtkunstwerk—the "absolute aesthetic fullness of art." Comp Lit professor Arnold Weinstein is an ardent advocate for traditional high-modernist fiction. (I should know; I house-sat for him one summer forty years ago, and I read all the marginalia in the books on the shelves: he really, really, really doesn't like Beckett.)

The literary critic Stanley Fish, describing seventeenth-century "masterworks" such as Milton's *Paradise Lost,* coined the term "self-consuming artifact"—a perfect phrase for a lot of what is, to me, the most exciting artistic work done by Brown faculty, grads, dropouts. Eurydice Kamvisseli, the author of the novel *F/32,* "rewrote Beckett and Homer" as a very young child. "My father still has the books in his library. I erased parts of the books and added, with my childish handwriting, better versions of the plot. I didn't like anything mild." So, too, see nearly every sentence S. J. Perelman ever wrote. Pretty much everything Nathanael West wrote as well, especially *Miss Lonelyhearts* (many of the letters in which were lifted from letters West steamed open when he was working as a desk clerk in a hotel) and *A Cool Million* (a large portion of which was appropriated without attribution from a Horatio Alger novel). The exquisitely self-conscious cartoons of Edward Koren, who is now retired after teaching in the Brown art department for decades. Richard Kostelanetz's *In the Beginning* consists of the alphabet, in single- and double-letter combinations, unfolding over thirty pages. Shelley Jackson, who describes herself as a "student in the art of digression," once published a story in tattoos on the skin of 2,095 volunteers. Andrew Sean Greer, whose second novel, *The Confessions of Max Tivoli,* is told in the voice of a man who appears to age backward, says about working with Coover, "He encouraged us to write anything except conventional narrative." Even Coover's titles are self-consuming: *The Adventures of Lucky Pierre (Directors' Cut); The Public Burning; The Universal Baseball Association, Inc., J. Henry Waugh, Prop.; The Origin of the Brunists; A Night at the Movies, or, You Must Remember This.* Coover on Alison Bundy's story collection *A Bad Business:* "In these elegant tales—not so much of adventure, comedy, and romance as their residue—Bundy summons up the world's distance with bright, paradoxical immediacy that is sometimes almost magical. She is a poet to the prose line born, playing with the possibilities of plot as though it were a metrical system, rhymed with thought's assonantal drift. This is rich comic writing, delicate and sure, touched at times by a wistful longing as a kiss might be touched by irony. Or life's violence by the tenderness of dream." Paul Grellong's plays *Manuscript* and *Radio Free Emerson.* John Krasinski's (well-intentioned and abysmally bad) film adaptation of David Foster Wallace's *Brief Interviews with Hideous Men.* At the end of Michael Showalter's short film *Pizza,* in the midst of Showalter's weeping on the floor, he languidly orients himself toward the camera and poses—that nervous self-awareness that never turns off. Edwin Honig, who founded Brown's creative writing program, is the author of *Shake a Spear with Me, John Berryman.* Note again, and everywhere, that note of self-consciousness, of self-reflexivity.

Will Oldham, aka Bonnie "Prince" Billy, an actor and playwright turned country musician and founder of the Palace Records label, stayed only a semester, but he must have absorbed the ions in the air pretty damn quickly: "I didn't want to record under my own name, but also not under an implied group name. Assuming that a voice and guitar implies confession or self-expression doesn't seem like a very productive line of thinking. I suggest that a song is no guarantee of its singer's honesty, wit, sensitivity, or politics. I will always rewrite a song that seems like it's too connected to a real event, because the intention is always to create the hyperreal event, so that—ideally—more people can relate to it."

The Brown literary aesthetic: consciousness-drenched. Jaimy Gordon, author of the National Book Award–winning *Lord of Misrule* and many other difficult-to-categorize works, says, "This will sound odd, but I like having a mind. I like thinking, though I'm aware that I think eccentrically and often ridiculously, so that my thoughts threaten to isolate me, even though they take shape in the common tongue. I have confidence that what goes on in my mind, including but by no means featuring its review of personal experience, can be turned into something made of language that will be arresting to those who are susceptible to splendors of rhetoric." Which could and should serve as the epigraph to Nancy Lemann's giddily hall-of-mirrors novels, especially my favorite, *Sportsman's Paradise.* Or Maya Sonenberg's fascinatingly self-canceling story "Throwing Voices." Brian Evenson, who is former chair of the Literary Arts Program at Brown and whose first work of fiction, *Altmann's Tongue,* got him dismissed from BYU for its violation of Mormon tenets, says, "I'm fairly aware of philosophy and am especially interested in questions of epistemology, particularly theories that suggest the impossibility of knowing." Evenson's story "Prairie" ends with a character literally unsure whether he's alive or dead; his novella *The Sanza Affair* gives each detail of a story two or three times (conflictingly) and cites each version with the name of a character (in parentheses) who believes that version to be true. Jeffrey Eugenides says about his Pulitzer-winning novel, *Middlesex,* "My narrator is not entirely reliable. He's inventing the past as much as he's telling it. The bottom line is that you can't really know much about what you really don't know. There are very old-fashioned narrative techniques deployed in the book as well, but postmodernism is always recuperating old styles of narration." Hawkes, without whose encouragement I would never have become a writer (he told me that the first short story I ever wrote was about "the agony of love without communication and in the context of violence"), famously said, "I began to write fiction on the assumption that the true enemies of the novel were plot, character, setting, and theme, and having abandoned these familiar ways of thinking about fiction, I realized totality of vision or structure was really all that remained."

For quite a while I wrote in a fairly traditional manner—two linear, realistic novels and dozens of conventionally plotted stories. I'm not a big believer in major epiphanies, especially those that occur in the shower, but I had one, about twenty years ago, and it occurred in the shower: I had the sudden intuition that I could take various fragments of things—aborted stories, outtakes from novels, journal entries, lit crit—and build a story out of them. I really had no idea what the story would be about; I just knew I needed to see what it would look like to set certain shards in juxtaposition to other shards. Now I have trouble working any other way, but I can't emphasize enough how strange it felt at the time, working in this modal mode. The initial hurdle (and much the most important one) was being willing to follow this inchoate intuition, yield to the prompting, not fight it off, not retreat to SOP. I thought the story probably had something to do with obsession; I wonder where I got that idea—rummaging through boxes of old papers, riffling through drawers and computer files, crawling around on my hands and knees on the living room floor, looking for bits and pieces I thought might cohere if I could just join them together. Scissoring and taping together paragraphs from previous projects, moving them around in endless combinations, completely rewriting some sections, jettisoning others, I found a clipped, hard-bitten tone entering the pieces. My work had never been sweet, but this new voice seemed harsher, sharper, even a little hysterical. That tone is, in a sense, the plot of the story. I thought I was writing a story about obsession. I was really writing a story about the hell of obsessive ego. It was exciting to see how part of something I had originally written as an exegesis of Joyce's "The Dead" (for Scholes's course in post-structuralism) could now be turned sideways and used as the final, bruising insight into someone's psyche. All literary possibilities opened up for me with this story. The way my mind thinks—everything is connected to everything else—suddenly seemed transportable into my writing. I could play all the roles I want to play (reporter, fantasist, autobiographer, essayist, critic). I could call on my writerly strengths, bury my writerly weaknesses, be as smart on the page as I wanted to be. I'd found a way to write that seemed true to how I am in the world. My "experimentalism" isn't Hawkes's, but his influence on me is the same as Coover's on Greer.

The *Guardian*, 2006: At the opening of *Sudden Glory: Sight Gags and Slapstick in Contemporary Art,* a recent group show at the Wattis Institute in San Francisco, Ralph Rugoff suddenly found himself dangling upside down in the air. The six-foot-seven conceptual artist Martin Kersels had lumbered up behind Rugoff and swept him off his feet, suspending the curator by the ankles. "It was such an insane experience. My whole world turned inside out and I didn't know what was going on for a second," says Rugoff. "I was very thankful to Martin for doing that." . . . At the Wattis Institute, where Rugoff served as director for almost six years prior to moving to the Hayward [Gallery in London], he curated a survey of invisible art that included paintings rendered in evaporated water, a movie shot with a film-less camera, and a pedestal once occupied by Andy Warhol. "Ralph is pretty experimental; he doesn't follow the herd," says Matthew Slotover, codirector of the Frieze annual contemporary art fair.

Which brings me to the Fuck You Factor (crucial to Brown's overdog/underdog ethos): Lois Lowry's Newbery-winning and frequently banned children's book, *The Giver,* presents a dystopian view of a future society in which history is hidden, people are conditioned not to see colors, and those who do not fit within society's narrow definition of acceptability are "released" (killed). Brown's 1925 yearbook on S. J. Perelman: "He was a quiet and ingenious lower-classman, but he has since fought the good fight against Babbittism, Sham, Hypocrisy, and Mediocrity. All are supposed to quail before the vicious shakes of his pen and pencil." Moody published a burn-all-bridges essay in the *Believer* in which he defended (as if defense were needed) the unconventional, uncommercial works of fiction—rather than the usual suspects—his committee chose as the five finalists for the 2004 National Book Award. C. D. Wright, who is an NBA winner and who taught at Brown for twenty-five years until her death in 2016, said, "It's a function of poetry to locate those zones inside us that would be free, and declare them so. I've enjoyed the promise and limitations of several monikers but have never claimed them for myself. I've never been invited formally or otherwise to join an identifiable group, which doesn't mean I'm opposed to their existence. It's energizing to have an enemies list; it's useful for other reasons as well, including the sharpening business." In his senior year, James Rutherford directed a production of Sartre's *The Flies* in which he bred and released forty thousand fruit flies into the room; audience members had to sign a statement before seeing the play. Leslie Bostrom, a professor of visual art, describes her current work as "anti-landscapes with incorporation of industrial components." Vogel, whose Pulitzer-winning play,

How I Learned to Drive, was attacked by some feminists for its investigation of the connection between women and pain, says, "For me, being a feminist does not mean showing a positive image of women. Being a feminist means looking at things that disturb me, looking at things that hurt me as a woman. Wherever there is confusion or double, triple, and quadruple standards, that is the realm of theater. Drama lives in paradoxes and contradictions." Searle: "Walter Abish told our workshop, 'The single most important thing in writing is to maintain a playful attitude toward your material.' I liked the freeing, what-the-hell sound of that. I like the sense—on the page—that I'm playing with fire. I know I'm onto something when I think two things simultaneously: 'No, I could never do that' and 'Yes, that's exactly what I'm going to do.'"

Coover: "Sometimes the revolution of form seems almost accidental. Disparate elements are somehow juxtaposed, in art or life or both, creating a kind of dissonance, and an artist comes along who resolves that dissonance through the creation of a new form—a Chrétien de Troyes, for example, who secularized the monkish appetite for allegory and raised the fairy tale to an art form by enriching it with metaphor, design, fortuitous mistranslation, and exegetical tomfoolery, thereby inventing the chivalric romance, a form that dominated the world for five centuries. Something similar might be said of Cervantes as well, who brought an end to the tradition of chivalric romance by submitting its artifices to the realities of the picaroons and conquistadors of his day. Or of that eclectic 'Redactor' of Genesis, for that matter, who pressed the folk and priestly voice of his tribe into a contiguous relationship so profound that I myself am still affected by it, twenty-some centuries later. At other times—as with Ovid or Kafka or Joyce—this new form is clearly the conscious invention of a creative artist, pursuing his own peculiar, even mischievous, vision with the intransigence of a seer or an assassin. For these writers, the ossified ideologies of the world, imbedded in the communal imagination, block vision, and as artists they respond not by criticism from without but by confrontation from within. In mythopoeic dialogue, they challenge these old forms to change or die. And it is this sort of artist—whether intuitive or intellectual—that the PEN/Faulkner Award [which Coover judged in 1984] in its brief life has sought to honor. It is not surprising to me that its selections have sometimes seemed outside the 'tradition.' Its judges are prepared—obliged, even—to celebrate artistic genius wherever they find it, of course, but at its writerly heart this award belongs to the rebel, the iconoclast, the transformer. The *mainstream*." (Emphasis mine.)

Thalia Field, a professor at Brown, resisting conventional notions of and defenses of literary and artistic realism, says,

> For me it is "realistic" to be paradoxical, polyvocal, cacophonous. Stories where everything is tidy and psychologically or symbolically closed seem totally unlike lived experience. Whose universe is that? Recently at a performance in Denmark, someone asked me, "If you're a Buddhist, why is your work so difficult?" There are eighty-four thousand Buddhist tenet teachings because though truths are very simple, our neuroses are so manifestly complicated it takes eighty-four thousand teachings to begin to penetrate them. In historical terms, realism is a vast subject whose meanings have shifted drastically over the course of one hundred and fifty years. When we speak of "realism" in drama or prose, we mostly mean a proscenium naturalism in which the audience observes the "contents" as one would observe another planet. This godlike perspective, the omniscience (the unobstructed view), the ability to contain closure and entire dramatic arcs within unit "sets" (of landscapes, time frames, characters, conflicts, etc.) allow the writer and reader to believe they are invisible. We think we need consistent and immutable selves; otherwise, the world of all our opinions, careers, likes, dislikes, borders, friends, enemies will fall apart. So if we're the most traditional naturalist or the headiest philosopher, we try desperately to find coherence, whether defined through a period of a time, a theory, a series of events, even the word 'she' sitting in a few sentences. Characters are whom we love and lose, and their momentary appearance and unexplained passing are part of the ongoing drama. How rigidly we reveal or ignore this flickering ephemerality is for me a mark of "realism."

We were/are taught at Brown to question ourselves rather than naïvely and vaingloriously celebrate ourselves—to turn ourselves inside out rather than (easily) inward or outward, to mock ourselves, to simultaneously take ourselves utterly seriously and demolish ourselves. *Don't you finally want to get outside yourself? Isn't that finally what this has to be about, getting beyond the blahblahblah of your endless*—yes, yes, a thousand times yes. I mean no. Or, rather, yes and no. I want to get past myself, of course I do, but the only way I know how to do this is to ride along on my own nerve endings; the only way out is deeper in. I'm drawn to writers who appear to have Schrödinger's Cat Paradox tattooed across their forehead: The perceiver by his very presence alters the nature of what's being perceived. I admire Hilton Als's *The Women,* W. G. Sebald's *The Emigrants,* and V. S. Naipaul's *A Way in the World*—books in which the chapters, considered singly, are relatively straightforwardly biographical but, read as a whole and tilted at just the right angle, refract brilliant, harsh light back upon the author. So, too, for instance, Nicholson Baker's meditation on Updike, Geoff Dyer's on D. H. Lawrence, Beckett's on Proust, Nabokov's on Gogol: One writer attempts to write a book about another writer but, trapped in the circuitry of his own consciousness, winds up writing a book that is at least as much autobiography as biography. I'm just trying to be honest here: the only portraits I'm really interested in are self-portraits as well. I like it when a writer makes the arrow point in both directions—outward toward another person and inward toward his own head.

Several years ago I served on the nonfiction panel for the National Book Awards. One of the other panelists, disparaging a book (*Down the Nile,* by Rosemary Mahoney, who lives in Providence) I strongly believed should be a finalist, said, "The writer keeps getting in the way of the story." What could this possibly mean? The writer getting in the way of the story *is* the story, is the best story, is the only story. We semiotics concentrators (although I actually wound up changing my major to British and American literature, due to my mother's ongoing criticism of semiotics) knew that on day one.

Mary Caponegro's story collection *Five Doubts*—the perfect Brown title: There's certainty and there's doubt; I'll take doubt(s). Scholes: "My project has been to look into critical terminology and explore the confusions and contradictions lurking there, hoping, among other things, to recover the middle that they exclude." Richard Foreman, the avant-garde playwright and director, says the goal of the Ontological-Hysteric Theater, which he founded, is a "disorientation massage." He sees his work as driven by misunderstanding instead of (more Aristotelianly) conflict. A. J. Jacobs's books *The Know-It-All* and *The Year of Living Biblically* are, simultaneously and respectively, arias to and desecrations of the encyclopedia and the Bible. (White) rapper Paul Barman, dissing a rapper appearing on the same track with him: "Your talents are bite-size / It's no surprise you rhyme with white guys." Hawkes: "There is only one subject—failure."

When black students occupied the administration building my freshman year, the president of Brown was Donald Hornig, who earned his B.S. and Ph.D. from Harvard; before his presidency at Brown, he had been chair of the chemistry department at Princeton. He said, "If the private university is to continue as an important social and intellectual force, it must remain firmly in the storm center. It may mean controversy and conflict, and it may mean discomfort and dissent. Frontiers are dangerous places. The front edge of change is dangerously sharp, but it is where a great university belongs." However, when, in response to a suggestion, he said, "Well, we're not just going to drop out of the Ivy League," most of the students hooted him down—to my ear, completely unconvincingly.

A football game in Providence in 1976: At halftime, the Yale band asked, "What is Brown?" and came back with various rude rejoinders (Governor Moonbeam, the color of shit, etc.), but the only answer that really stung was the final one: "Safety school."

Anne Fadiman, in *At Large and At Small,* goes out of her way to avoid mentioning what college she attended—a very nearly unanimous gesture, I've noticed, among Harvard alumni: a pride beyond pride—the school that will not be named. Instead, she mentions the name of her *dorm,* as if Harvard is so famous that the dorm itself will suffice. Exactly the same gesture occurs in Sarah Manguso's *The Two Kinds of Decay.*

The Brown-Harvard game for the 1974 Ivy League championship: We so hoped to experience, through our boys banging shoulder pads, an image of our own excellence. Our sense of anguished consolation depended upon it. We needed to know we were stronger than the geniuses in Cambridge. We were, in point of fact, both bigger and stronger than they were, but they were faster than we were. On a fall afternoon, we lost the big game. Lopsidedly. They moved the ball better than we did; they had a superior kicking game; they deserved to win. Alternatively, they got all the breaks. We were too tight. We wanted it too badly. Our identity depended too transparently upon our performance. No late-afternoon ringing of bells on campus. My friend Alan, who was at Harvard, said, years later (when he was my friend), referring to the game, "It really did seem as if the Harvard players were simply smarter, don't you think?" He said this without hauteur or, on the other hand, irony or embarrassment. At Iowa, when each of us was asked where we'd gone to college, Alan said, "Harvard. University. In Cambridge." Here he pointed, vaguely, in a northeasterly direction. "Massachusetts." Which only had the effect, of course, of underlining the fact that Alan had attended the one school in America that exists in everyone's imagination.

My junior year an essay appeared in *Fresh Fruit,* the extremely short-lived and poorly named weekly arts supplement to the *Brown Daily Herald.* A Brown student, writing about the cultural clash at a basketball game between Brown and the University of Rhode Island, referred in passing to Brown students as "world-beaters." I remember thinking, *Really?* World-beaters? More like world-wanderers and -wonderers.

Jason Tanz, a senior editor at *Wired:* "I feel like my classmates at Brown didn't necessarily think of themselves as natural inheritors of our nation. This is a huge overgeneralization, but my sense was always that friends at, say, Princeton knew the world was theirs and they were just biding their time until they got a job at their dad's law firm; smart, snide Harvard grads had that pipeline into the TV-comedy industry. The Brown lines of influence and access weren't quite as defined, so therefore maybe we were a bit more circumspect about our place in the world."

Harvard: government; sketch comedy (same thing?). Yale: Wall Street; judiciary (same thing?). Princeton: physics; astrophysics (same thing?). Brown: art; freedom (same thing?). A myth is an attempt to reconcile an intolerable contradiction.

THE HEROIC MODE

Although the Greek Tragedy professor said that reading the play carefully, once, would probably be sufficient preparation for the test, I couldn't stop reading *Prometheus Bound* and also, for some reason, the critical commentary on it. I was a freshman and I loved how scholars felt compelled to criticize the play for not obeying certain Aristotelian dicta but were nevertheless helplessly drawn to "the almost interstellar silence of this play's remote setting," as one of them put it. I wrote to Paula that even if our father pretended to be Prometheus, he was really only Io. I blurted out quotes to Rachel, with whom I was none too secretly infatuated.

"Why are you studying so much?" she asked. "You're running yourself ragged. You know he said we could take the test after spring break, if we want. There's no reason to punish yourself."

"You must not have read the play," I said, proceeding to quote my favorite line: " 'To me, nothing that hurts shall come with a new face.' The admirable thing about Prometheus is that he accepts his fate without ever even hoping for another outcome."

"Yeah, maybe so, but at the end of the play he's still chained to a rock."

"There's a certain purity to basing your entire identity upon a single idea, don't you think? Nothing else matters except how completely I comprehend a drama written twenty-four hundred years ago. If I don't fully grasp each question, after a week of studying, I'll probably jump off the Caucasus," I said, referring to the mountains of the play and grabbing her arm. "I can sense some excitement."

"Shhh," she said, putting her finger over her lipsticked lips. "People are studying."

"You're as bad as the chorus of Oceanus's daughters, always telling Prometheus to stop pouting."

Rachel thought I was kidding and laughed, shaking her head. I told myself I was kidding and tried to believe it. I felt like a Greek New Comedy "wise fool," parading around—to everyone's astonishment—in chinos and a turtleneck. Studying until five in the morning the day of the exam, falling asleep in my room, and awaking barely in time, I stumbled into the lecture hall, where I filled four blue books in fifty minutes. My pen didn't leave paper: Whole speeches stormed from my mind. In immense handwriting (child's handwriting, out of control), I misidentified virtually every passage in the play but explicated them with such fevered devotion that the sympathetic teaching assistant gave me an A minus.

I took a train from Providence to Washington, D.C., then a cab into the suburbs, and when I appeared on her front porch in Bethesda, my aunt asked how long I'd been ill. *I groan for the present sorrow,* I thought, *I groan for the sorrow to come, I groan questioning whether there shall come a time when He shall ordain a limit to my sufferings.* When I looked at myself in the bathroom mirror, I saw black circles around my eyes. I listened to my aunt tell my mother over the phone how wonderfully I'd matured.

My uncle, at the time a stateside science advisor to the government, was in Japan on a business trip. Nearly all the books in his study, where I secluded myself for most of the Easter vacation, were technical, indecipherable, and of little interest to me—a big Aeschylus fan. Rummaging through desk drawers, I came across elaborate lists of domestic and secretarial errands for my aunt to perform and a few recent issues of *Penthouse,* which at the time I found extremely erotic because of its emphasis upon Amazonian women.

Uncle Justin's office had a small record player and a stack of classical music. He had many performances of Beethoven's Symphony no. 3, the so-called *Heroic* Symphony, and I found myself immersed, first, in all the liner notes. "Like Beethoven, Napoleon was a small man with a powerful personality," and Beethoven admired him, so when the French ambassador to Vienna suggested to Beethoven that he write a symphony about Bonaparte, Beethoven agreed. He was just about to send the finished score to Paris for Napoleon's official approval when he heard that Napoleon had proclaimed himself emperor. Beethoven tore off the title page, which had only the word "Bonaparte" on it, and changed the dedication to "Heroic Symphony—composed to celebrate the memory of a great man." Beethoven is then supposed to have said, "Is he, too, no more than a mere mortal?" Beethoven was disappointed, in other words, to discover that Napoleon was human.

What was a funeral march doing in the middle of the symphony? Why was the finale borrowed from Beethoven's ballet *The Creatures of Prometheus*? Because—one commentator surmised—Beethoven "planned his symphony as a diptych, after the manner of his favorite book, *Plutarch's Lives,* in which every modern biography is paired with an antique one like it; thus the first two movements of the *Eroica* are about Napoleon and the second two about Prometheus." *Oh, Prometheus.* I knew, as I listened over and over again to the symphony, I'd felt elated and suicidal in exactly the same way before.

And the musicologists talking about Beethoven and Napoleon sounded eerily like the classicists discussing Prometheus or like me discussing the classicists discussing Prometheus or like Peter Parker worrying about becoming Spider-Man: "What Beethoven valued in Bonaparte at the time of writing the *Eroica* was the attempt to wrest fate from the hands of the gods—the striving that, however hopeless, ennobles the man in the act." I couldn't sleep at night because I couldn't get out of my head either the two abrupt gunshots in E-flat major that began the symphony or the trip-hammer orgasm of the coda, so I outlined an essay on the parallel and contrasting uses of water imagery in Aeschylus's *Oresteia* and O'Neill's *Mourning Becomes Electra*. Rachel had urged me to abandon this topic in favor of a more "humanistic" approach. Instead, I circled every water image in both trilogies.

A high school friend was a freshman at Georgetown; I'd always wanted to get to know her better. I let the phone ring twice and hung up. I called again the next day, and the line was busy. The third time I called, she answered on the first ring, clearly expecting someone else. Her voice was newly inflected to underscore her International Relations major.

My aunt made breakfast for me every morning. We talked a lot. She asked me to define existentialism. She watched television and washed the dishes. I started agreeing with her. All this happened more than forty years ago: The documentary film *Hearts and Minds* had recently been released. I drove into Georgetown to see it, and when I returned I sat in my aunt's kitchen, excoriating the racist underpinnings of all military aggression, but I was really thinking about only one scene: the moment when two U.S. soldiers, fondling their Vietnamese prostitutes, surveyed the centerfolds taped to the mirrored walls and, for the benefit of the camera, tried to imitate heroic masculinity.

THE WOUND AND THE BOW

I know that Howard Cosell was childishly self-absorbed and petulant ("It's hard to describe the rage and frustration you feel, both personally and professionally, when you are vilified in a manner that would make Richard Nixon look like a beloved humanitarian. You can't imagine what it does to a person until you've experienced it yourself, especially when you know that the criticism is essentially unfair"); that he would obsess upon, say, the *Des Moines Register*'s critique of his performance; that too soon after he achieved prominence the beautiful balance between righteous anger and comic self-importance got lost and he was left only with anger and self-importance; that he once said that he, along with Walter Cronkite and Johnny Carson, was one of the three great men in the history of American television; that he mercilessly teased his fellow *Monday Night Football* announcers Frank Gifford and Don Meredith but pouted whenever they teased him; that he was certain he should have been a network anchor and/or a U.S. senator; that the very thing he thought needed deflating—the "importance of sports"—he was crucially responsible for inflating; that after hitching a ride on boxing and football for decades he then turned around and dismissed them when he no longer needed them ("The NFL has become a stagnant bore"; "I'm disgusted with the brutality of boxing"); that, in an attempt to assert his (nonexistent) expertise, he would frequently excoriate any rookie who had the temerity to commit an egregious error on *Monday Night Football* (dig the Cosellian diction); that he was a shameless name-dropper of people he barely knew; that he said about a black football player, "That little monkey gets loose," then, regarding the brouhaha that ensued, said, "They're conducting a literary pogrom against me"; that the *New York Times* sports columnist Red Smith once said, "I have tried hard to like Howard Cosell, and I have failed"; that the legendary sportswriter Jimmy Cannon said about him, "This is a guy who changed his name [from *Cohane* to *Cosell*], put on a toupee, and tried to convince the world he tells it like it is"; that David Halberstam said that he bullied anyone who disagreed with him; that he frequently boasted about *Monday Night Football*, "We're bigger than the game"; that he once told a Senate subcommittee, "I'm a unique personality who has had more impact upon sports broadcasting in America than any person who has yet lived"; that he once wrote, "Who the hell made *Monday Night Football* unlike any other sports program on the air? If you want the plain truth, I did"; that at the height of his fame, when fans would come up to him on the street to kibitz or get an autograph, he liked to turn to whomever he was with and say (seriously? semi-seriously?), "Witness the adulation"; that when Gene Upshaw, the head of the NFL Players Association, said about Cosell, "His footprints are in the sand," he corrected the compliment: "My footprints are cast in stone."

I know all of that and don't really care, because its first four years, when I was in high school, *Monday Night Football* mattered deeply to me and it mattered because of Cosell. I haven't watched more than a few minutes of any *MNF* game since then, and at the time I had no very coherent sense of its significance, but looking back, I would say it's not an exaggeration to claim that Howard Cosell changed my life, maybe even—at least in one sense—saved it. *MNF* was "Mother Love's traveling freak show" (Meredith's weirdly perfect description), a "happening" (Cosell's revealingly unhip attempt to be hip); it was the first sports broadcast to feature three sportscasters, nine cameras, shotgun mics in the stands and up and down and around the field. Celebrities showed up in the booth: Nixon told Gifford he wished he'd become a sportscaster instead of a politician. John Lennon told Cosell that he became a troublemaker because people didn't like his face (Cosell's comment: "I know the feeling"). Cosell stood next to Bo Derek and said with pitch-perfect, mock self-pity that here was a classic case of Beauty and the Beast. Cosell informed John Wayne that he was a terrible singer and the Duke agreed. After Cosell interviewed Spiro Agnew, Meredith said that what no one knew was that Agnew was wearing a Howard Cosell wristwatch. This was all cool and droll. It was all finally just showbiz, though. What wasn't was Cosell's relation, as an artist, to his material (I use the terms advisedly): "By standing parallel to the game and owing nothing to it, by demystifying it, by bullying it and not being bullied by it—by regarding the game as primarily an entertainment, though realizing also the social forces that impacted on it—I was able to turn *Monday Night Football* into an Event, and I do mean to use the capital E. Now it is part of American pop culture, and if it sounds like my ego is churning on overdrive for taking the lion's share of credit for it, then I'll take the mane."

My mother was the public information officer for one of the first desegregated school districts in Northern California. One day the human relations consultant informed her that the revolution wouldn't occur until white families gave up their houses in the suburbs and moved into the ghetto. My mother tried for the better part of the evening to convince us to put our house up for sale. One Easter weekend at Watts Towers, she looked smogward through some latticed wine bottles with a positively religious sparkle in her dark eyes. When my cousin Sarah married a black man from Philadelphia, Sarah's mother wasn't able to attend, so my mom substituted and brought the temple down with an a cappella finale of "Bridge over Troubled Water." My father held dozens of jobs, but perhaps the one he loved the most was director of the San Mateo poverty program during the late sixties. He sat in a one-room office without central heating and called grocery stores, wanting to know why they didn't honor food stamps; called restaurants, asking if, as the sign in the window proclaimed, they were indeed equal-opportunity employers. Sometimes, on weekends, he drove to Sacramento or flew to Washington to request more money for his program. Watts rioted; Detroit burned. My father said, "Please, I'm just doing my job." He got invited to barbecues, weddings, softball games. The salary was $7,500 a year, but I never saw him happier.

No one ever had his or her heart more firmly fixed in the right place than my father and mother, with the possible exception of Howard Cosell. Traveling in a limo through a tough part of Kansas City on the way to the airport after a game, he told the driver, Peggy, to stop the car when he saw two young black men fighting each other, surrounded by a group of guys cheering for blood. Cosell got out and instantaneously was the ringside announcer: "Now I want you to listen here. It's quite apparent to this observer that the young southpaw doesn't have a jab. And you, my friend, over here, you obviously do not have the stamina to continue. This conflict is halted posthaste." Handshakes, autographs. When Cosell got back in the limo and Peggy expressed her astonishment at what she'd just seen, Cosell leaned back, took a long drag on his cigar, and said, "Peggaroo, just remember one thing: I know who I am." Which, according to himself, was "a man of causes. My entire professional life has been predicated upon making the good fights, the fights that I believe in. And much of the time it was centered around the black athlete. My real fulfillment in broadcasting has always come from crusading journalism—fighting for the rights of people such as Jackie Robinson, Muhammad Ali, and Curt Flood. The greatest influence of my life was Jackie Roosevelt Robinson, who was [. . . the inevitable name-drop] certainly one of my closest friends." *New York Post* sportswriter Maury Allen said, "The single most significant issue in the twentieth century was race, and Howard Cosell was unafraid about race."

My father rooted for the Dodgers because they were originally from Brooklyn and then moved to Los Angeles, just as he was and had, but we as a clan stayed loyal to them because they hired the first black baseball player (Robinson) and started the highest number of nice-seeming black players (Johnny Roseboro, Jim Gilliam, Tommy Davis, et al.). The only pure moral passion I've ever felt has been for the Los Angeles Dodgers, even though I lived in LA only until age six. My proudest possession as a child was a signed copy ("To Dave with best wishes—I hope your ambitions are reached") of Robinson's biography, which my father kept for me in a safe-deposit box. I never traded a baseball card of a Dodger, even if I had seven duplicates.

Pictures of the Dodgers, obtained from Union 76 gas stations in Los Angeles, covered my bedroom walls, and I went to sleep by reciting their batting averages and ERAs; my parents weren't allowed to stop anywhere else for gas when we visited LA. I reviled Vin Scully, the Dodgers announcer, because, unlike every other team's announcer, he prided himself on appearing neutral. The Dodgers were the embodiment of good, and the San Francisco Giants were the embodiment of evil, and this was manifest in a myriad of ways: the name of the Giants' manager, Alvin Dark; the typical Giant's more threatening mien (Cepeda, Marichal, Mays, McCovey, the Alous); their very name, Giants, which evoked their monstrousness, in contrast to Dodgers (trolley dodgers, da bums, etc.), whose image of vulnerability I loved; the Giants' ghoulish black-and-orange uniforms compared with our seraphic blue-and-white; their windy Candlestick Park compared to our warm, sunny Chavez Ravine (located on Elysian Park Avenue). The first thing I did every morning of baseball season was go read the box score, and if the Dodgers had lost, I'd wail and wail, whacking my Frosted Flakes around the breakfast counter with my spoon. Whenever I hear mention, in any context, of the years 1955, 1959, 1963, 1965, 1981, or 1988, I think one thing: *victory.*

Cosell defended Ali when he refused to serve in Vietnam following his conversion to Islam. When Cosell died, Ali said, "Howard Cosell was a good man and he lived a good life. I can hear Howard now saying, 'Muhammad, you're not the man you used to be ten years ago.'" Ali was referring to Cosell standing up at a pre-fight press conference and saying to him, "Many people believe you're not the man you used to be ten years ago." Ali had replied, "I spoke to your wife, and she said you're not the man you were *two* years ago." Cosell had giggled like a schoolboy. Asked once what he stood for, Cosell replied, "I stood for the Constitution, in the case of the U.S. vs. Muhammad Ali. What the government did to this man was inhuman and illegal under the Fifth and Fourteenth amendments. Nobody says a damned word about the professional football players who dodged the draft, but Muhammad was different. He was black and he was boastful. Sportscasters today aren't concerned with causes and issues. Can you see any of those other guys putting their careers on the line for an Ali?" According to Cosell's daughter Jill, he frequently said that if people didn't stand for things, they weren't good for much else.

Music to my parents' Marxist ears. As was this: "The importance that our society attaches to sport is incredible. After all, is football a game or a religion? The people of this country have allowed sports to get completely out of hand." And this: "The sports world is an ever-spinning spiral of deceit, immorality, absence of ethics, and defiance of the public interest." And this: "There's got to be a voice such as mine somewhere, and I enjoy poking my stick at various issues and passersby." And this: "For myself, I wondered when someone other than me would tell the truth." And this: "What was it all about, Alfie? Was football that important in this country? Was it a moral crime to introduce objective commentary to the transmission of a sports event?"—after he'd been pilloried in Cleveland for saying that Browns running back Leroy Kelly hadn't been a "compelling factor" in the first half of the first *MNF* game (he hadn't). "If so, how did we as a people get this way? In the spoon-fed, Alice in Wonderland world of sports broadcasting, the public was not accustomed to hearing its heroes questioned." When, following his eulogy of Bobby Kennedy, on his *Speaking of Sports* show, and fan after fan called in to complain ("Don't tell me how to live—just give us the scores—that's what you're paid for"), Cosell said, "I began to wonder if that kind of thinking is one of the things that makes us so prone to assassination in this country. Maybe there is such an absence of intellect and sensitivity that only violence is understandable and acceptable." "The 'fan,'" Cosell pointed out, "is a telephone worker, a transit worker, a power-company worker, a steelworker, a teacher, whatever. He has never given up the right to strike and often does. When he does, the public is inconvenienced and sometimes the public health and safety are threatened. When a ballplayer strikes, the effect upon the public health and safety is nil. Nor is public convenience disturbed, for that matter. Yet the ballplayer and the owner are called upon to each give up their individual bargaining rights because the 'fan' wants baseball and 'is entitled to get it.'" "I never played the game with advertisers, with my own company, or with the sports operators," Cosell said. "And of course I never played the game as a professional athlete."

This is where it gets complicated, because I was a monomaniacal, five-foot-four-inch, one-hundred-twenty-pound freshman basketball player at Aragon High School who, somehow, was supremely confident that he was destined to become a professional athlete. From kindergarten to tenth grade all I really did was play sports, think about sports, dream about sports. I learned how to read by devouring mini-bios of jock stars. I learned math by computing players' (and my own) averages. When I was twelve I ran the fifty-yard dash in six seconds, which caused kids from all over the city to come to my school and race me. During a five-on-five weave drill at a summer basketball camp, the director of the camp, a recently retired professional basketball player, got called over to watch how accurately I could throw passes behind my back; he said he could have used a point guard like me when he was playing, and he bumped me up out of my grade level. I remember once hitting a home run in the bottom of the twelfth inning to win a Little League All-Star game and then coming home to lie down in my uniform in the hammock in our backyard, drink lemonade, eat sugar cookies, and measure my accomplishments against the fellows featured in the just arrived issue of *Sports Illustrated*. I remember thinking, *Christ, how could life possibly get any better than this?*

In junior high I would frequently take the bus crosstown, toss my backpack under my father's desk, and spend the rest of the afternoon playing basketball with black kids. I played in all seasons and instead of other sports. In seventh grade I developed a double-pump jump shot, which in seventh grade was almost unheard of. Rather than shooting on the way up, I tucked my knees, hung in the air a second, pinwheeled the ball, then shot on the way down. My white friends hated my new move. It seemed tough, mannered, teenage, vaguely Negro. The more I shot like this the more my white friends disliked me, and the more they disliked me the more I shot like this. In eighth grade, at the year-end assembly, I was named "best athlete," and my mother said that when I went up to accept the trophy, I even walked like a jock. At the time I took this as the ultimate accolade, though I realize now she meant it as gentle mockery.

My father didn't particularly mind my mindlessness, since, in addition to being director of the poverty program, he was also a lifelong athlete (runner, swimmer, trophy-winning tennis player). My mother, on the other hand, disapproved. Once, she said to me, "Sometimes when people ask me if all you ever do is play sports,

I want to tell them, 'At least he's devoted to something. At least he has an activity at which he excels,' but other times I wish you were obsessed with something a little more permanent."

"Yes, I know," I whispered; it was very late on some Sunday night.

"Sometimes I just want to tell those people, 'Leave me alone. Leave him alone. He's like a dancer on that damn playfield or ballyard or what have you.' But what I usually tell them, what I really feel, and what I guess I'm trying to tell you now is that I wish you'd dedicate yourself with the same passion to a somewhat more elevated calling."

"Yes, I know," I whispered again, turning and trotting off to sleep.

Sports and politics have always been, for me, in curiously close conversation, alliance, overlap, competition. None of the kids I played sports with were Jewish. They called me Buddha Boy (I never quite understood this moniker—Judaism was as unfathomable to them as Buddhism?) and Ignatz (my body was small and my ears were large), asked me why anyone would want to be Jewish. When Sandy Koufax refused to pitch during the World Series, I suddenly felt proud to stay home on Yom Kippur. My father derived his identity at least as much from Jewish boxers and basketball players from the 1930s and Hank Greenberg as he did from his P.S. 149 schoolmates Danny Kaye and Phil Silvers.

In high school I was athletic and thus, to a certain extent, popular. However, I worked unduly hard at it, at sports, with very little sprezzatura, which made me extremely unpopular among the really popular, really athletic people. Why? Because I made popularity or grace look like something less than a pure gift. Only the really popular, really athletic people knew I was unpopular, so I could, for instance, be elected, if I remember correctly, vice president of the sophomore class and yet be, in a sense, underappreciated.

Cosell knew the feeling, amplified. "I remember going to school in the morning," Cosell said in his *Playboy* interview. "A Jewish boy. I remember having to climb a back fence and run because the kids from St. Theresa's parish were after me. My drive, in a sense, relates to being Jewish and living in an age of Hitler. I think these things create insecurities in you that live forever." As if in proof of these insecurities, he said, "I am the most hated man on the face of the earth."

Still, he did have a point. He was voted the "most disliked sportscaster of the 1970s." One sign at a stadium said WILL ROGERS NEVER MET HOWARD COSELL. Another sign said HOWARD IS A HEMORRHOID. A contest was held: The winner got to throw a brick through a TV set when Cosell was talking. Buddy Hackett told Johnny Carson, "There are two schools of thought about Howard Cosell. Some people hate him like poison, and some people just hate him regular."

One Saturday morning, two medics carrying a stretcher stormed my family's front door, looking for someone who had supposedly fallen on the front steps. Later that afternoon, a middle-aged man, wearing a Giants windbreaker, tried to deliver a pepperoni pizza. A cop came to investigate a purported robbery. Another ambulance. A florist. An undertaker from central casting. Vehicles from most areas of the service sector were, at one point, parked virtually around the block. I was certain (though I could never prove) that my popular, athletic friends, who always gathered together to watch the proceedings with binoculars in one of their houses at the top of the hill, had orchestrated this traffic all night and into the morning. Every Halloween I cowered in my basement bedroom with the doors locked, lights out, shades down, and listened to the sound of lobbed eggs.

I had company. "Cosell, the Mouth, why don't you drop dead? There's a bomb in Rich Stadium. It will blow you up at 10 p.m., Monday." "If he comes to Green Bay on October 1, I'm going to kill him, and your sheriff's department can't stop me." "You will die now, because your government lies. I will be out in October and will be there to get you and all ABC government cheaters." The death threats always came from smaller, less cosmopolitan towns or cities—Buffalo; Green Bay; Milwaukee; Denver; Deer Lodge, Montana—to residents of which Cosell must have seemed like Sissified Civilization itself.

Every plot needs a villain, as Bill Cosby (all too prophetically) told Cosell. Cosell says that when he, Gifford, and Meredith were struggling through the first rehearsal for *MNF*, he reassured Meredith, "The Yankee lawyer and the Texas cornpone, putting each other on. You'll wear the white hat, I'll wear the black hat, and you'll have no problems from the beginning. You're going to come out of this a hero. I know this country. There's nothing this country loves more than a cowboy, especially when he's standing next to a Jew. Middle America will love you. Southern America will love you. And there are at least forty sportswriters in the country who can't wait to get at me. You'll benefit thereby. Don't worry about me, though. Because in the long run it will work for the old coach, too." Which it did, at least for a while, for longer than anyone thought possible.

Gifford was the fair-haired Hall of Famer. "People always looked for things in me they'd like to see in themselves," Gifford claimed. "I've never known what to think of it." Ah, but he did. "Look at him standing there, girls," Cosell liked to say within earshot of Gifford at meet-and-greets before *MNF* games. "A veritable Greek god. America's most famous football hero. The dream of the American working girl. The single most sexually dynamic man in the chronicle of the species." Cosell was up for this jocularity; so, in a way, was Gifford (in his memoir *The Whole Ten Yards,* he gleefully quotes his then wife Kathie Lee calling him a "love machine").

"Anyone who looked like Ichabod Crane and spoke with a nasal Brooklyn accent didn't exactly fit the sportscaster mold," Gifford said later about Cosell, in retaliation. "On top of that, Howard was Jewish."

"Of course there are critics." Cosell sighed one night on *MNF.* "There will always be critics. 'The dogs bark, but the caravan rolls on.'"

Meredith—good ole boy with a sideways wit—said, "Woof."

Another time, a receiver muffed an easy catch, and Meredith said, "Hey, he should be on *Saturday Night Live with Howard Cosell,*" which tanked after twelve shows. Cosell glowered.

Gifford, Meredith, and Cosell couldn't find anywhere to eat after a game, so the limo pulled into a McDonald's in a slum. Meredith urged Cosell to exit: "Ha'hrd, they want you. It's your constituency. You know, the poor, the downtrodden. You're always talking about them. Shit, Ha'hrd, here they are!"

When the Giants were playing the Cowboys on *MNF,* Cosell said, teasingly, that he wasn't impressed by the play of either Gifford's or Meredith's (former) respective teams, and Meredith replied, "At least we have respective teams."

Cosell should have laughed, but he didn't. I should have laughed when my faux friends made fun of me, but I didn't, I couldn't (and so they made more fun of me). Cosell was/I was . . . everything they weren't: Jewish, verbal, performative, engagé, contrarian, pretentious but insecure, despising (adoring) athletics and athletes.

Instead, Cosell would tattle to *MNF* executive producer Roone Arledge: "They're doing it again. The two jocks are out to get me. They're after me again."

Instead, he said about Gifford, "He admired my command of the language, my ability to communicate, and he was shrewd enough not to engage me in a debate. He had to know he couldn't win."

Instead, Cosell said to Meredith, "Don't start it because you don't stand a chance. Get into a duel of words with me, and I'll put you away."

Witness the adulation of words. For Cosell, language was everything, as All-American Heroism was/is for Gifford (this all blew away in a storm when Gifford's marriage and career came undone; we're in Cheever country—the perfect Connecticut home is no bulwark against the crooked timber of humanity) and Texan joie de vivre was for Meredith (this, too, was a crock; Meredith came to despise the "Dandy Don" mask that was his meal ticket). Once, on air, Meredith kissed Cosell on the cheek, pretending to gag on Cosell's toupee. Cosell immediately responded by saying, "I didn't know you—cared." The way he paused before saying "cared," and the pressure that he put on the word, thrilled me to the bottom of my fifteen-year-old toes. "You're being extremely—truculent," he once admonished Ali, and again, it was the way he paused before "truculent" and the extraordinary torque he put on the word so that he seemed to be simultaneously brandishing the word as a weapon and mocking his own sesquipedalianism. In *The Whole Ten Yards*, Gifford, surely leaning more than a little on his cowriter, *Newsweek* television writer Harry Waters, says about Cosell, "His genius lay in turning his liabilities into assets. He gave his voice"—thick New Yawk honk, full of Brooklyn bile—"a dramatic, staccato delivery that grabbed you by the ears." I, too, wanted to turn my liabilities into strengths. I knew what my liabilities were; what, though, were my strengths?

I had been aware since I was six or seven that I stuttered, but the problem would come and go; it never seemed that serious or significant. I'd successfully hid out from it, or it from me. Now, as a sophomore in high school, with my hormones trembling, my lips were, too. In class, I'd sit in back, pretending not to hear when called upon and, when pressed to respond, would produce an answer that I knew was incor-

rect but was the only word I could say. I devotedly studied the dictionary and thesaurus in the hope I could possess a vocabulary of such
immense range that for every word, I'd know half-a-dozen synonyms
and thus always be able to substitute an easy word for an unspeak-
able one. My sentences became so saturated with approximate verbal
equivalents that what I thought often bore almost no relation to what
I actually said.

One day I was asked whether the origin of the American Revolution was essentially economic or philosophical. I wanted to say, as
my mother and father had taught me, that revolution arises from an
unfair distribution of wealth, but instead I replied, "The Whigs had
a multiplicity of fomentations, ultimate or at least penultimate of
which would have to be their predilection to be utterly discrete from
colonial intervention, especially on numismatical pabulae." The
teacher looked down at his desk. The class roared. By the end of the
week I'd been scheduled to meet with the school's speech therapist.

Miss Gordon was very pretty but not especially my type: a little
too cherubic to be truly inspiring. Knowing I was a basketball player,
she brandished an impressive knowledge of the game, and for the
first half hour we talked about how it doesn't matter if a guard is
short if he knows how to protect the ball; what a shame it was the
high school had no girls' basketball team; how *A Sense of Where You
Are* was good but *The Last Loud Roar* was probably even better.

Then she had to turn on the tape recorder, hand me a mimeo-
graphed memorandum, and say, "You've been speaking really well,
Dave—only a few minor bobbles here and there. Let me hear you
read for a while."

"Oh, I read fine," I said, and wasn't being intentionally insincere. I
saw myself as a relatively articulate reader.

"That's funny," she said, and started rummaging around in her
drawer for something or other. "Almost all stutterers have at least a
little trouble when it comes to oral reading."

I, on the other hand, disliked the label. It sounded like "atheist" or
"heretic" or "cat burglar."

"I don't see myself exactly as a stutterer," I said. "It's more just a
case of getting nervous in certain situations. When I feel comfortable, I never have any trouble talking."

This wasn't true, but I felt pressed.

"Well, you feel comfortable with me, I hope. Why don't you read aloud that memo? We'll record it, play it back, and you tell me what you think."

At the time, my particular plague spot happened to be words beginning with vowels. This page, for one reason or another, was riddled with them. I kept opening my mouth and uttering air bubbles, half-human pops of empty repetition. Miss Gordon didn't have to play the tape back for me to know it had been the very embodiment of babble, but she did, and then, raising her right eyebrow, asked, "Well?"

I explained that the whirring of the tape recorder and her ostentatious tallying of my errata had made me nervous. The proof I wasn't just one more stutterer was that I could whisper.

"But, Dave," she said, "that's characteristic of stutterers."

"That's not true," I said. "You're lying. I know you are. You're just saying that. Stutterers cannot whisper. I know they can't."

"Yes, they can," she said. "Virtually all stutterers can whisper. You're a stutterer. I want you to admit that fact. It's an important step. Once you acknowledge it, we can get to work on correcting it. When you're a professional basketball player, I don't want to see you giving hesitant interviews at halftime."

The flattery tactic didn't work the second time, not least because she was wrong: As Howard Cosell well knew, the athletic aesthetic is always to assert that the ecstasies experienced by the body are beyond the reach of words. I'd regularly distinguished myself from the common run of repeaters by the fact that I could whisper; now, informed I was one among millions, I was enraged—at what or whom I didn't quite know, but enraged.

I stood and said, "I don't want your happy posters or your happy smiles or your happy basketball chitchat. I don't want to be happy. I want to be u-u-unusual." Then I did something I thought was very unusual: I tore down a poster of a seagull (A LIFE WITHOUT DREAMS IS A WINGLESS BIRD) and ran out of the room. The next day, I returned to her office and began what—forty-five years later—still feels like my life: a life limited but also defined by language.

Within a week, Miss Gordon got me switched out of Typing into Public Speaking. The Speech teacher, Mr. Phillips, much the most charismatic teacher in the school, had been the object of Paula's (and many other girls') crush for years. He was tall and lean and witty and bottomlessly, brutally ironic in a way that seemed not entirely dissimilar to Cosell's manner. Every week or so, we had to present a new speech, and with these I suffered predictably, but then I hit on the idea of doing a speech imitating Cosell. This was 1971—fall, the first month of my sophomore year, the second year of *MNF*—and so I went to school on "The Mouth" the only way I could, without the aid of a VCR, which was more than a decade away. I simply watched him and thought about him as much as I could, even more than I had before.

"The Mouth" was a good nickname for him. He was such an insatiably oral guy, talking nonstop—the way my mother and sister and Mr. Phillips did—and always pouring liquor down his throat and jamming a huge stogie in his mouth. Dick Ebersol, former president of NBC Sports, said about Cosell, "He was defined by what he said, not how he looked or spoke." As with virtually everything Dick Ebersol has ever said, this is exactly wrong. How Cosell looked and how he spoke were everything. With his rubbery skin, his stoop-shouldered walk, his ridiculous toupee, his enormous ears and schnoz, he always reminded me of nothing so much as a very verbose and Jewish elephant. The sportswriter Frank Deford's paean to him nicely conveys this quality: "He is not the one with the golden locks [Gifford] or the golden tan [Meredith], but the old one, shaking, sallow, and hunched, with a chin whose purpose is not to exist as a chin but only to fade so that his face may, as the bow of a ship, break the waves and not get in the way of that voice." The things he could do with that voice: the way, every week at halftime on *MNF*, he'd extemporize the NFL highlights in that roller-coaster rhetoric of his and, in so doing, "add guts and life to a damned football game," as he said, or as Chet Forte, executive director of *MNF* for years and years, said later, "It's not a damn football game. It's a show. That's what those guys [Gifford and Meredith] never understood. They never appreciated what Howard did. He could make two eighty-five-year-olds playing a game of marbles sound like the most exciting event in the history of sports." He'd found a way to be better than what he was reporting on, to bully reality, to make life into language.

After a week of practice, I had my Cosell imitation down. Stutterers typically don't stutter when singing, acting, or imitating someone else, and when I did my Cosell imitation, I didn't stutter. I was melodramatically grandiloquent and entertaining in the Cosellian vein. Everyone in the class loved my performance—it ended with the football purportedly landing in and thereby shutting my/Cosell's mouth—and Mr. Phillips loved it, too. For the next three years, he rarely passed me without saying softly, out of the side of his mouth, "HEL-lo, ev-uh-reBODY, this is HOW-wud Cos-SELL." It was easy to see why my sister and several of her friends had crushes on him. Still, I could imitate Howard Cosell. So what? So could and did a lot of other people. Where did that get me, exactly?

When I broke my leg on the beach that spring, my mother burst through the throng, threw up her hands, and wailed at me, "See? See what sports will do to you?" She was very sympathetic later on, but her first reaction was, approximately, *I told you so.* My left femur was badly broken, and I was in traction the entire summer, but when the doctor misread the X-ray and removed the body cast too early, I had a pin inserted in my leg and I used a leg brace and crutches my entire junior year.

I still stutter slightly, but in high school my stutter was so severe that my entire focus was upon doing one thing so well that people forgave me for, and I forgave myself for, my "disfluency" (Miss Gordon's term). With the jockocracy newly closed to me, I became, nearly overnight, an insanely overzealous chess player, carried along by the aftermath of the Fischer-Spassky World Championship. I got to the point that I dreamed in chess notation, but I was certainly never going to become a chess whiz, and I rationalized to myself that if one could be, as Bobby Fischer was, the best chess player in the world but still a monster and a moron, the game wasn't "humanly" interesting. I abandoned it after several months, joining the school paper.

By my senior year I had recovered well enough from my broken leg that I was twelfth man on the varsity basketball team and second doubles in tennis, but sports no longer meant much to me. All that physical expression had gone inside. Written language was my new channel: I suddenly loved reading; I became the editor of the paper; my parents (especially my mother) were thrilled; it was sickening. I spent no more time on my studies than I had before, but now instead of six hours a day playing sports, it was six hours a day working on the paper, writing nearly every article, taking every photograph, attending journalism conferences around the Bay Area, submitting my work to every possible high school journalism competition, submitting the paper and my work (virtually synonymous) for competitions. My bible was *The New Journalism*, an anthology edited by Tom Wolfe, which I read over and over again. I thought I'd become a new journalist, à la Joe Eszterhas or Michael Herr.

As a reporter my freshman year of college, I was trepidatious—still—about calling people on the phone (I couldn't imitate Cosell), so I crab-walked into creative writing courses. I'd become a fiction writer. I'd make stuff up, and that would be okay. The only problem, as I realized a decade or so out of graduate school, was that compared to other fiction writers, I wasn't very interested in making stuff up. I'm much more interested in contemplating the so-called real world, including, alas, the world of sports.

My first novel concerns a sportswriter's vicarious relationship with a college basketball player. *Black Planet* is my diary of an NBA season, with particular emphasis on how race is the true and taboo topic of the sport (hi, Mom and Dad!). I compiled a book of koan-like quotations uttered by the Japanese baseball player Ichiro Suzuki. And the subtitle of my book *Body Politic* is *The Great American Sports Machine*. When she was eight, Natalie said, "Daddy writes about exercise." (Perfect punchline: She's now twenty-three and her graphic memoir, *Loving Football When It Doesn't Love You Back*, is being published later this year.)

In *The Wound and the Bow*, Edmund Wilson analyzes how various writers, such as Dickens, Wharton, and Hemingway, used the central wound of their life as the major material of their art. Throughout her entire childhood, a writer I know worked fiendishly hard in the hope of becoming a professional ballet dancer, entering the Harkness Ballet trainee program at eighteen, but she left after less than a year. It's only right that her first book, published when she was in her mid-forties, is a collection of stories set in the world of ballet, and her first novel is told from the point of view of George Balanchine. In *Rocky*, asked what he sees in dowdy Adrian, Rocky says, "She fills gaps." I was a near-great child-athlete and I just assumed this play-paradise would last forever. It didn't. Writing about it filled gaps.

Although I haven't written about sports for quite some time, I do return over and over to the endlessly complex dialectic between body and mind. Whenever we talk about the body, we inevitably lie, but the body itself never lies. Our bodies always betray us—always tell us what we're really feeling (desire, fear, hatred, rapture). The body in motion is, for me, the site of the most meaning. At a deep spot in the river, Howard Cosell showed me the way across; he showed me where to look and, looking, how to stand.

THE CULTURAL CONTRADICTIONS
OF LATE CAPITALISM

I've never seen kids with so many pimples so young. You both eat too much chocolate: candy, cookies, ice cream. *Ach.* You're going to have a lot of trouble later on."

I have a very vivid memory of my father saying this to me and my sister, and although there was a definite element of truth in what he said—in fifth grade I already had to avoid red shirts because they had the effect of extending the field of my inflammation—I've often wondered what could possibly have caused him to predict such a dismal future for his children. What would have been his motivation—self-laceration taking the ritual form of infanticide? A father's laudable anger at his children's early expulsion from paradise? A discomfiting plea aimed at getting us to step up our remedial techniques? Who knows?

My sophomore year of high school my zit problem reached such catastrophic proportions that once a month I drove an hour each way to receive liquid-nitrogen treatments from an impressively serious dermatologist in South San Francisco. His office was catty-corner to a shopping center that housed a Longs drugstore, where I would always first give my prescription for that month's miracle drug to the pharmacist. Then, while I was waiting for the prescription to be filled, I'd go buy a giant bag of Switzer's red licorice. Not the cheap cherry version so much in favor now, though. The darker stuff: claret-colored. I'd tear open the bag, and even if—especially if—my face was still bleeding slightly from all the violence that had just been done to it, I'd start gobbling the licorice while standing in line for the cashier. This may sound a little gooey, but looking back, I'm hard-pressed now to see the licorice as anything other than some sort of Communion wafer—as if by swallowing the licorice, my juicy red pimples might become sweet and tasty. I'd absorb them; I'd be absolved. The purity of the contradiction I remember as a kind of ecstasy.

My senior yearbook photo was so airbrushed that people asked me, literally, who it was.

Well, time heals all wounds; so they say. This isn't even remotely true. Time passes, they say. This is true. Ten, twelve, fifteen years passed:

I craved a bag of claret-colored licorice and couldn't find one anywhere, so I wrote to Switzer's, in St. Louis: Wither the good licorice of yesteryear? "Per your inquiry," Bart Kercher, Quality Control Manager, wrote back, "our St. Louis facility produces Switzer's licorice candy, Switzer's red candy, Good & Plenty candy, and Good 'n Fruity candy. The 'claret-colored' Switzer's candy that you speak of was produced by a 'batch' cooking operation. Our plant has been modernized, and we currently have a continuous cooking system for greater candy uniformity."

A couple of weeks later, a large envelope arrived, bearing Switzer's largesse—licorice whips, strips, bits, Good & Plenty. I ripped open the bags and boxes and chewed and chewed.

NEGOTIATING AGAINST MYSELF

It's hard now to reanimate how viscerally so many people hated Bush a decade ago, but looking back on him now, I remember him as a homebody, someone who doesn't like to travel, travels with his pillow, is addicted to eight hours of sleep a night; so am I. In India, he wasn't sufficiently curious to go see the Taj Mahal. I must admit I could imagine doing the same thing. For his New Year's resolution nine months after invading Iraq, he said he wanted to eat fewer sweets; he was widely and justifiably mocked for this, but this was also my New Year's resolution the same year. He pretends to love his father, but he hates him. He pretends to admire his mother, but he reviles her. When the Dutch translator of *Dead Languages* asked if "Daddums" could be translated as "molten fool," I said, "Yep, pretty much."

He finds Nancy Pelosi sexy, but he won't admit it (cf. my imaginative relation to Sarah Palin and Michele Bachmann). He outsources every task he can. He walked into Condi Rice's office and said, "Fuck Saddam—he's going down." I could imagine saying this. He loves to watch football and eat pretzels. He did everything he could to avoid serving in the Vietnam War; in 1974, when the war and draft were long over, I registered as a conscientious objector. As do I, he prides himself on being able to assess people immediately based on their body language. When he has the tactical advantage, he presses it to the limit; when he's outflanked, he's unattractively defensive. *I don't negotiate against myself:* I'm incapable of embodying this Bush aperçu, but I quote it at least once a month.

He's not very knowledgeable about the world. He has trouble pronouncing the names of foreign leaders. He's obsessed with losing those last ten pounds. He's remarkably tongue-tied in public but supposedly relatively smart in private. He had a lower SAT score than most of his Ivy League classmates; so did I. He wildly overvalues the poetry-in-motion of athletes. He once said he couldn't imagine what it's like to be poor; I have trouble reading books by people whose sensibility is wildly divergent from my own. He wasted his youth in a fog of alcohol and drugs; I didn't do this, but sometimes I pretend I did. He reads a newspaper by glancing at the headlines—more or less what I do. He loves to get summaries of things rather than reading the thing itself. He's never happier than in the box seat of a ballpark. He takes way too much pride in throwing the ceremonial first pitch over the plate for a strike. He's slightly under six feet tall but pretends he's six feet. I'm barely six feet and claim to be six-one. He's scared to death of dying.

He was too easily seduced by Tony Blair's patter, as was I. His wife is smarter than he is, by a lot. Asked by the White House press corps what he was going to give Laura for her birthday, he tilted his head and raised his eyebrows, conveying, unmistakably, *I'm going to give* it *to her.* (My wife's name is still *Laurie.*) He's intimidated by his father's friends. He can express his affection most easily to dogs. He finds the metallics of war erotic. His knees are no damn good anymore, so he can't jog and has taken up another sport: biking (for me, swimming). He loves nicknames. He's not a good administrator. He views politics as a sporting event. He resents the *New York Times*'s (diminished but still undeniable) role in national life as pseudo-impartial arbiter; my most recent book is a critique of the same paper's front-page war photography. In a crisis he freezes up, has no idea what to do, thinks first of his own safety (note how I responded to the 2001 Nisqually earthquake).

He just wants to be secure and taken care of and left alone—pretty much my impulses. Asked what he was most proud of during his presidency, he said catching a seven-pound bass. Asked in 2011 what's on George's mind now, Laura said, "He's always worried about our small lake—whether it's stocked with bass—because he loves to fish. There's always some concern. It's too hot. It's too cold. Are the fish not getting enough feed? That's what he worries about." He's lazy (it goes without saying). He hates to admit he's wrong.

Every quality I despise in George Bush is a quality I despise in myself. He is my worst self realized. G. K. Chesterton, asked what's wrong with the world, said, "I am."

LOVE THIS

The true subject of Ben Lerner's novel *Leaving the Atocha Station*—thick with roman à clef references to his childhood in Topeka, his undergraduate and graduate education at Brown, his Fulbright year in Spain, his essay on the John Ashbery poem that gives this book its title, his poet-friends Cyrus Console, Jeff Clark, and Geoffrey G. O'Brien, his psychologist parents (his mother is the feminist writer Harriet Lerner)—is "the endemic disease of our time: the difficulty of feeling," a perfect phrase a reviewer once used in her discussion of an imperfect book of mine. Lerner never lies about how hard it is to leave the Atocha Station—to get past oneself to anything at all: "I wondered if the incommensurability of language and experience was new, if my experience of my experience issued from a damaged life of pornography and privilege, if there were happy ages when the starry sky was the map of all possible paths, or if this division of experience into what could not be named and what could not be lived just was experience, for all people for all time."

Lerner's alter ego has the aggressively unmemorable name "Adam Gordon." He incessantly wonders what it would be like to look at himself from another's perspective—for instance, imagining "I was a passenger that could see me looking up at myself looking down." He feels a rush of power to "experience the world as though under glass, and this detachment, coupled with my reduced need or capacity for sleep, gave me a kind of vampiric energy, although I was my own prey."

The book is (as what serious book is not?) born of genuine despair: Adam's notebooks are "filled with incomprehensible poems—had I tried to kill myself without my knowledge, were those so many suicide notes?" He characterizes himself as a "violent, bipolar, compulsive liar. I was a real American. I was never going to flatten space or shatter it. I hadn't seen *The Passenger,* a movie in which I starred. I was a pothead, maybe an alcoholic. When history came alive [the 2004 Madrid bombings], I was sleeping in the Ritz." When he imagines, "with a sinking feeling, a world without even the terrible excuses for poems that kept faith with the virtual possibilities of the medium, without the sort of absurd ritual [a poetry symposium] I'd participated in that evening, then I intuited an inestimable loss, a loss not of artworks but of art, and therefore infinite, the total triumph of the actual, and I realized that, in such a world, I would swallow a bottle of white pills." The issue is thereby joined: if he can't believe in poetry, he'll commit suicide.

The alienation that everybody feels when traveling is a perfect trope for Adam's knowledge that he's an impostor—"that I was a fraud had never been in question: who wasn't?" Which is precisely where, for me, the book gets interesting. *What is actual when our experiences are mediated by language, technology, medication, and the arts? Is poetry an essential art form, or merely a screen for the reader's projections?* I've lifted these last two sentences from the flap copy (surely written by Lerner). The very nature of language itself is a major part of Adam's problem. He's unable to settle on the right word in English ("reading poetry, if reading is even the word"), unable to understand Spanish ("I asked what [Adam's girlfriend Isabel's other boyfriend] Oscar was doing in Barcelona and she said either that he was a mechanic or was being retrained for something mechanical or that he sold cars or worked for a car company; I didn't care"), and revels in mistranslation as a close approximation of the incomprehensible human flux (regarding a woman Adam is smoking with at a party, he says, "Her

Spanish became a repository for whatever meaning I assigned it, and I felt I understood, although I knew I was talking to myself").

Adam pretends that his father—who patiently tries to get a spider to crawl from the carpet onto a piece of paper so he can escort it safely from house to yard—is a "fascist," that his very alive mother is dead. Like Yossarian writing from his hospital bed to his stateside correspondents that he's going on a very dangerous mission and will write again when he returns, Adam has internet access in his apartment but claims in emails to be writing from an internet café where his time is extremely limited. He pretends to be taking copious notes only when his girlfriend, Isabel, is watching him. He gives a brief speech in Spanish, written by someone else, "regarding the significance of the Spanish Civil War, about which I knew nothing, for a generation of writers, few of whom I'd read; I intended to write, I explained, a long, research-driven poem exploring the war's literary legacy. . . . Various people greeted us and Teresa [the translator of Adam's poems and the other object of his desire in addition to Isabel] detached from me to kiss them and I was acutely aware of not being attractive enough for my surroundings; luckily, I had a strategy for such situations, one I had developed over many visits to New York with the dim kids of the stars: I opened my eyes a little more widely than normal, opened them to a very specific point, raising my eyebrows and also allowing my mouth to curl up into the implication of a smile."

Adam deepens his estrangement by "remembering" imaginary experiences ("For all I knew we'd kissed and fooled around; while I doubted that, I could imagine it in a way that felt like remembering") and smoking hash; his goal, though, is to extend his alienation so far that the South Pole becomes magnetic North. Said pejoratively, "Many people, I believed, used similar drugs to remove themselves from their experience, but because, for as long as I could remember, I always already felt removed from my experience, I took the drug to intensify the vantage from said remove, and so experienced it as an intensification of presence, but only at my customary distance from myself; maybe, when I panicked, that distance was collapsing." Said more celebratorily, in reference to smoking a joint with Teresa: "To take everything personally until your personality dissolves and you can move without transition from apartment to protest or distribute yourself among a shifting configuration of bodies, saying yes to everything, affirming nothing, your own body 'giving up / Its shape in a gesture that expresses that shape.'" Adam never comes anywhere near such an apotheosis. Neither have I.

For Adam (antioriginal man seeking to name the things of the world), "none of this is real." He doesn't "like Madrid with its tourists and dust and heat and innumerable Pietàs and terrible food." He wonders if he will be the only American in history who visits Granada without seeing the Alhambra (Bush at the Taj Mahal). "Over the course of my research, I'd lost considerable weight. Other than that, I didn't think I'd undergone much change." Easy enough to judge Adam; harder to acknowledge the near-universality of such soul-sickness, circa now. "I told the waiter I was looking for a hotel whose name I didn't know on a street whose name I didn't know and could he help me; we both laughed and he said: 'Aren't we all.'" The travel cure, in general, doesn't take.

Neither does the history cure. He tries to respond to the terrorist bombings, but he's paralyzed by . . . by what exactly? "I walked to my apartment and once in my apartment read about the unfolding events of which I'd failed to form a part. . . . I considered walking back to Atocha [Station, where one of the bombings occurred], but instead I opened *El Pais* in another window and the *Guardian* in a third. . . . I said to myself that History was being made and that I needed to be with Spaniards to experience it; I should at least try to find [Teresa's brother] Arturo. I knew I was only elaborating an excuse to see Teresa. . . . While Spain was voting I was checking email."

Love is a bad bet for anyone so remote from things. Lerner is preternaturally alert to the intersection of misunderstanding, inscrutability, and Eros. Adam says, "My Spanish was getting better, despite myself, and I experienced, with the force of revelation, an obvious realization: Our relationship [his affair with Isabel] largely depended upon my never becoming fluent, on my having an excuse to speak in enigmatic fragments or koans, and while I had no fear of mastering Spanish, I wondered how long I could remain in Madrid without crossing whatever invisible threshold of proficiency would render me devoid of interest. I feared I'd be unable to be eloquent either positively or negatively and I realized with a sinking feeling that the reduction of our interactions to the literal and the transformation of our pregnant silences into dead air, a flat spectrum over a defined band, would necessarily strip my body of whatever suggestive power it had previously enjoyed, and that, when we made love, she would no longer experience her own capacity for experience, but merely my body in all its unfortunate actuality." *Love this,* he seems to be saying, *I dare you.*

Can anything rescue our fallen Adam? Can anything save us? Poetry? Yes and no. There's "nothing particularly original" about Adam's poems, composed as they are of "mistranslations intermixed with repurposed fragments from deleted emails." Adam has become a poet because "poetry, more intensely than any other practice, could not evade its anachronism and marginality and so constituted a kind of acknowledgment of my own preposterousness." "Insofar as" Adam is interested "in the arts," he's interested in the "disconnect between" his "experience of actual artworks and the claims made on their behalf; the closest" he'd "come to having a profound experience of art was probably the experience of this distance, a profound experience of the absence of profundity." He's "unworthy"; such profundity is "unavailable from within the damaged life." And yet he's willing to say, somewhat begrudgingly, that Ashbery is a great poet: "It is as though the actual Ashbery poem were concealed from you, written on the other side of a mirrored surface, and you saw only the reflection of your reading. By reflecting your reading, Ashbery's poems allow you to attend to your attention, to experience your experience, thereby enabling a strange kind of presence. It is a presence, though, that keeps the virtual possibilities of poetry intact because the true poem remains beyond you, inscribed on the far side of the mirror: 'You have it but you don't have it. / You miss it, it misses you. / You miss each other.'"

This is a lot. Still, is that the best art can now do—be a holding tank/reflecting pool for our lostness? Maybe, maybe. Lerner loves/hates life's white machine; the "great" artist's irrelevance to the indifferent museum guard; having nothing to say and saying it into a tiny phone. He asks, "Why was I born between mirrors?" An answer, of sorts: "The words are written beneath water." At the Picasso Museum, Adam approaches a canvas a child has touched—a miniature precursor of, or study for, *Les Demoiselles d'Avignon*—double-checks to make sure that no one is around, and (since the world is ending) touches the painting himself.

LOVE THIS (ii)

One of my clearest, happiest memories is of myself at fourteen, sitting up in bed, being handed a large glass of warm buttermilk by my mother because I had a sore throat, and she saying how jealous she was that I was reading *The Catcher in the Rye* for the first time. As have so many other unpopular, oversensitive American teenagers over the last sixty years, I memorized the crucial passages of the novel and carried it around with me wherever I went. The following year, my sister said that *Catcher* was good, very good in its own way, but that it was really time to move on now to *Nine Stories*, so I did. My identification with Seymour in "A Perfect Day for Bananafish" was extreme enough that my mother scheduled a few sessions for me with a psychologist friend of hers, and "For Esmé—with Love and Squalor" remains for me an example of perfection. In college, I judged every potential girlfriend according to how well she measured up to Franny in *Franny and Zooey*. In graduate school, under the influence of *Raise High the Roofbeam, Carpenters* and *Seymour: An Introduction*, I got so comma-, italics-, and parenthesis-happy one semester that my pages bore less resemblance to prose fiction than to a sort of newfangled Morse code.

When I can't sleep, I get up and pull a book off the shelves. There are no more than thirty writers whom I can reliably turn to in this situation, and Salinger is still one of them. I've read each of his books at least a dozen times. What is it in his work that offers such solace at 3:00 a.m. of the soul? For me, it's how his voice, to a different degree and in a different way in every book, talks back to itself, how it listens to itself talking, comments upon what it hears, and keeps talking. This self-awareness, this self-reflexivity is the pleasure and burden of being conscious, and the gift of his work—what makes me less lonely and makes life more livable—lies in its revelation that this isn't a deformation in how I think; this is how human beings think.

REMOTENESS

Being a writer in image-addicted America makes me feel at times somewhat marginal; being a writer in cyber-sick Seattle often makes me feel absolutely beside the point. I was born in Los Angeles (the suburbs), grew up in San Francisco (the suburbs), went to college in Providence (where I rarely left College Hill) and graduate school in Iowa City, lived on and off throughout the 1980s in New York, spent an alarming portion of my late twenties sequestered in artists' colonies, and taught at a small school in a tiny hamlet in upstate New York for two years, so when I moved to Seattle in 1989 to take a teaching job in the creative writing program at the University of Washington, I thought of Seattle not as an idyll but as a real city. A medium-sized city but a real city, nonetheless (the approximate size of Dickens's London, as Jonathan Raban—a British writer who has lived in Seattle as long as I have—likes to remind me).

Publicly, I condescended to Seattle, repeated the jokes ("When it's one p.m. in New York, it's 1972 in Seattle"), but privately I rather liked the containable snugness of Seattle. Publicly, I said it didn't matter anymore where one lived, but privately (quite unconsciously) I must have registered the remoteness of my new address, for I went from being a writer of novels and short stories to a writer of nonfiction books and personal essays. (Never mind, for the moment, that I don't of course believe in the validity of these generic distinctions.) It was as if, upon arriving here, I no longer entirely trusted the life I lived on a daily level—the material of fiction, at least the sort of autobiographical fiction I wrote—to be of sufficient interest to people living east of the Cascade Mountains and so my work became saturated with overtly public topics.

This remoteness is a crucial part of the answer to the question people so often ask, "Why Seattle?"—that is, how could such a sleepy fishing village become home to so many world-conquering companies? It's quite striking to me how many of the most successful businesses here—Boeing, Microsoft, Amazon, McCaw Cellular (which became AT&T Wireless), Paccar (Peterbilt and Kenworth trucks), UPS (which began in Seattle as a cooperative)—have created products that have the specific effect of shrinking the distance between Seattle and the rest of the country. The very remoteness of Seattle engenders the need, which creates the imagination to fill the need. (There's a proverb about this.) This doesn't happen if you're living in Montclair, New Jersey, where you think you're living near the center of the universe. "The locus of innovation has shifted westward in the United States," as the chairman of the San Francisco Museum of Modern Art likes to say. Or as my friend Joel says, "The silicon chip wasn't invented in New York; it couldn't have been."

A BBC film crew came to Seattle to document what it assumed would be a vibrant city and wound up packing up its equipment and going home without a movie because it couldn't find the vibrancy anywhere. The film crew didn't get Seattle. It didn't see that the bland face Seattle shows to the rest of the world is a workaholic's DO NOT DISTURB sign. (I feel like my self-presentation is not entirely dissimilar to Seattle's in this regard.) Less politely, LEAVE US THE FUCK ALONE. (Ditto.) It's a northern city (Scandinavian, Calvinist, Puritan) and a Pacific Rim city (Asian, self-effacing, "polite") and a Western port city (blue collar, hardworking, unshowy).

Fred Moody, the former editor of the *Seattle Weekly,* recently said to me, "Whenever I think about all this, I think about it as a native who grew up in a much more marvelous Seattle that disdained the kind of status-seeking that is endemic here now. It's hard to remember, but most of these hugely successful companies began as 'idealistic' enterprises of one kind or another. The three founders of Starbucks just wanted to make Seattle more like Italy—with these little coffee shops where people would sit around and discuss opera over espresso. Gordon Bowker, one of the Starbucks founders, is appalled by what the company has become. People forget that Microsoft was essentially a revolutionary guerrilla company intent on wresting computing power away from corporations and giving it to citizens. They also forget that it was founded by teenagers. A lot of early Microsoft people feel tremendous discomfiture over how rich they got."

I don't know—is it really all that terrible if Seattle is now a "worldwide center of ambition"? Isn't that a good, or at least a pulse-increasing, thing? Isn't the Chinese curse "May you live in interesting times" also supposed to be a blessing? As Raban once said, "I don't think you're supposed to exactly like where you live. I think you're supposed to live where you live, in a state of grumbling dissatisfaction with it."

Many years ago, *Vanity Fair* ran a long article by James Atlas making fun of the way dozens of Seattle's early retirees were spending their millions—hang gliding, opening flower shops, undertaking do-gooder projects. Atlas's rhetoric had to do with the way in which the East is supposedly about work and the West is supposedly about play. This is a fairy tale the East tells itself, as Hollywood and Silicon Valley and Seattle have remade the world. Jeff Bezos: "Reality is an interesting environment."

There is, to me, something fundamentally boring about money in the East. It maintains status quo, props up the past, feathers the nests of the patriarchs and their broods on Park Avenue and in Summit, New Jersey, and Ridgefield, Connecticut. Money in the West is about dreaming the golden dream—fantasies of the frontier, illusions of a new world to come. To people here, I'm a satirist of the city. In a couple of my books, I've made fun of Seattle's upbeat earnestness. Really, though, I love illusions of a new world to come; I don't see how anyone can live life without them. As difficult as I sometimes find this to admit, I'm a Westerner and even, now, a Seattleite. I love being a resident of a remote state, where we're forced to make everything up on our own, feverishly hoping that what we come up with will prove to be indispensable to the rest of the world, which, hemmed in by tradition, hadn't thought of that yet.

SURVIVING WITH WOLVES

The million-dollar, career-exploding, trick-tease train of misery-lit memoirs: first praised, then shamed, each taking its turn on the double-crested roller-coaster of celebrity and infamy: It's become a national tradition, each fallout more engrossing than the book itself. If you think the heart is deceitful above all things, you should meet the author. . . .

James Frey said, "I mean, I knew I'd never be the football star or the student council president and, you know, once people started saying I was the bad kid, I was like, 'All right, they think I'm the bad kid. I'll show them how bad I can be.'"

Frey's freshman-year heartsickness became a desperado run-in with the law; getting caught with a tallboy of PBR became his role as head of an Ivy League cocaine cartel; his incarceration at Hazelden, brought on by his parents' concern and perhaps their own inability to discipline effectively, became his last chance against an addiction that was certain to consume him. The process of aggrandizement: relatively ordinary problems get overblown into larger-than-life "literature." We, too, can make a myth of our own meager circumstances.

When Frey wrote his book, of course he made things up—who doesn't? He must have thought, *Sure, call it a novel, call it a memoir. Who's going to care?* I don't want to defend Frey per se—he's a terrible writer; his staccato yelling makes James Ellroy seem like Proust—but the very nearly pornographic obsession with his case a decade or so ago reveals the degree of American nervousness about the topic. The whole huge loud roar, as it returned again and again, had to do with the culture being embarrassed by how much it wants the frame of reality and, within that frame, great drama. A frankly fictional account would rob the memoirist/counterfeiter, his or her publishers, and the audience of the opportunity to attach a face to the angst.

Frey's narrative: Frat boy in free fall arose from misanthropy and was salvaged by literary industry, which is now a subset of multimedia saturation, of which Oprah (once) formed a higher denomination. Oprahcam told us that we all are abused in some way, but we need arbiters to sift through the dirt for the story that can be marketed as emblematic. We begged Frey to produce a self-flagellating myth and he complied. Frey and millions behind him line up to humiliate themselves for the sole purpose of being marketed. It's so common to expect an abuse story that we have to stifle our yawns when we hear about further deceit, recrimination, backstabbing. Frey, that Puritan, witnessed what it means to be senseless while on drugs, but he couldn't admit he had fun. He made more sense when he was wasted.

He was crucified for a handful of inaccuracies in no way essential to the character and spirit of the book. All our sins were passed onto/unto him. Violence implies redemption: our hatred of Frey was due to the fact that he didn't hurt himself badly or violently enough to justify himself as self-perpetrator.

Fragments, The Hand That Signed the Paper, The Blood Runs Like a River Through My Dreams, The Honored Society, Forbidden Love, Surviving with Wolves, Love and Consequences, Angel at the Fence, A Million Little Pieces: All were in turn used as paper tigers to define the book-length essay downward—as failed journalism. The essay, though, isn't a chronicle of experience; it's the drama of consciousness contending with experience.

You have a right, as a thinking person, to think what you think, and the closer you stick to the character of thought in your writing, the more license you have to claim that you're not making things up.

Frey, for example, wrote but didn't think, "I was in prison for three months"; instead, he probably thought something more like, *I was in prison for three months, man; I was in fucking prison for three months; give it to them; throw it down their throats; they'll take it; they don't know what I went through; I'm tough* [goes to the mirror to make sure], etc. That is, he made up the prison part: he fictionalized it (without first admitting to having done so).

Defending *A Million Little Pieces,* Oprah said, "Although some of the facts have been questioned, the underlying message of redemption in James Frey's memoir still resonates with me." A few days later, however, clearly influenced by her miffed audience, she apologized for leaving the impression "that the truth doesn't matter."

As Alice Marshall writes in "The Space Between,"

Oprah created around herself a cult of confession that offered only one prix fixe menu to those who entered her world. First, the teasing crudités of the situation, sin or sorrow hinted at. The entrée was the deep confession or revelation. Next, a palate-cleansing sorbet of regret and repentance, the delicious forgiveness served by Oprah on behalf of all humanity. Fade to commercial as the sobbing witness, who had revealed harm done to or by an uncle or a neighbor, through carelessness, neglect, evil intent, or ignorance, was applauded by the audience, comforted by Oprah. Her instincts were fine, her integrity unquestioned, and she never told us a story that wasn't true. I was disappointed not that Frey was a liar but that he wasn't a better one. He should have said, "Everyone who writes about himself is a liar. I created a person meaner, funnier, more filled with life than I could ever be." He could have talked about the parallel between a writer's persona and the public persona that Oprah herself presents to the world. Instead, he showed up for his whipping.

When Frey appeared on *Oprah* the final time, performing hara-kiri, many of the nation's newsrooms were tuned in. Even choosing what to include in a straightforward memoir involves a substantial exercise of creative license. Journalists, though, don't seem too hip to this way of thinking: bad for their business, and they have a monopoly (had a monopoly) on popular discourse.

In the aftermath of the *Million Little Pieces* outrage, Random

House reached a tentative settlement with readers who felt defrauded by James Frey. To receive a refund, hoodwinked customers had to mail in a portion of the book: For hardcover owners, it was page 163. Those with paperback copies were required to actually tear off the front cover and send it in. Also, readers had to sign a sworn statement confirming that they had bought the book with the belief it was a real memoir or, in other words, that they felt bad having accidentally read a novel.

In 2009, Oprah reversed herself again, apologizing to Frey for publicly humiliating him. In 2010, Frey, working under a pseudonym and with another writer, published a young adult novel called *I Am Number Four*, which is about a group of nine alien teenagers on a planet called Lorien. (Frey was born and raised in Cleveland, not far from Lorain, Ohio, the small, predominantly African American city in which Toni Morrison was born and raised.) Attacked by a hostile race from another planet, the nine aliens and their guardians evacuate to earth, where three are killed. The protagonist, a Lorien boy named John Smith, hides in Paradise, Ohio, disguised as a human, trying to evade his predators and knowing he is next on their list. In 2011, Frey published *The Final Testament of the Holy Bible*, a novel about a lapsed Orthodox Jew who suffers an accident and wakes up thinking he's the Messiah.

THE UNKNOWN LIFE

There was a blog, then a Twitter feed, then a phenomenally popular book, and then a TV show, which I didn't see before it was canceled. It sounds too easy—someone just collecting the one-off wisdom of his father—but Justin Halpern's *Shit My Dad Says* is, to me, a subtle meditation on Vietnam (Samuel Halpern was a medic during the war), and on the basis of a single, crucial scene, it's not inconsiderably about Sam still processing that violence, that anger. The book is also very much about being Jewish in America, about the father teaching the son how to be Jewish and male in America, which is a contradictory, complicated thing.

Each entry is 140 characters or fewer—the length of a tweet—and all the subsections and mini-chapters are extremely short; the book is essentially a tape recording of Sam's best lines, overdubbed with relatively brief monologues by Justin. It's not great or even good, probably, really, finally, but above all it's not boring. Which is everything to me. I don't want to read out of duty. I'm trying to stay awake and not bored and not rote.

What I love about *Shit My Dad Says* is the absence of space between the articulation and the embodiment of the articulation. The father is trying to teach his son that life is only blood and bones. The son is trying to express to his father his bottomless love and complex admiration. Nothing more; nothing less. There are vast reservoirs of feeling beneath the son's voice and the father's aphorisms.

Twenty years ago, David Lipsky spent a week with David Foster Wallace, then fifteen years later Lipsky went back and resurrected the notes. The resulting book, *Although Of Course You End Up Becoming Yourself*, pretends to be just a compilation of notes, and maybe that's all it is, but to me it's a debate between two sensibilities: desperate art and pure commerce. Lipsky, I hope, knows what he's doing—evoking himself as the very quintessence of everything Wallace despised.

Tara Ebrahimi, my friend and former student, emailed me, "For years I've been taking notes and collecting quotes for a book that I hope will materialize at some point, but every time I attempt to turn the notes into the book, I hate the results. Really, what I've built is a database of quotations, riffs, metaphors. I find even my notes on how the book should be structured to be full of energy, because they're an outline of my massive aspirations, most of which I have no hope of actually pulling off. It feels almost as if my book wants to be about the planning of a book: a hypothetical literature that can't exist under earth's current gravity."

Elif Batuman: "A lot of the writers I know are incredibly good email writers. I often find their emails more compelling than the things they're writing at the time. Everyone has two lives: One is open and is known to everyone, and one is unknown, running its course in secret. Email is the unknown life, and the published work is the known life."

LIFE STORY

First things first.

You're only young once, but you can be immature forever. I may grow old, but I'll never grow up. Too fast to love, too young to die. Life's a beach.

Not all men are fools—some are single. 100% Single. I'm not playing hard to get—I am hard to get. I love being exactly who I am.

Heaven doesn't want me and Hell's afraid I'll take over. I'm the person your mother warned you about. Ex-girlfriend in trunk. Don't laugh—your girlfriend might be in here.

Girls wanted, all positions, will train. Playgirl on board. Party girl on board. Sexy blonde on board. Not all dumbs are blond. Never underestimate the power of redheads. Yes, I am a movie star. 2QT4U. A4NQT. No ugly chicks. No fat chicks. I may be fat, but you're ugly and I can diet. Nobody is ugly after 2 a.m.

Party on board. Mass confusion on board. I brake for bong water. Jerk off and smoke up. Elvis died for your sins. Screw guilt. I'm Elvis—kiss me.

Ten and a half inches on board. Built to last. You can't take it with you, but I'll let you hold it for a while.

Be kind to animals—kiss a rugby player. Ballroom dancers do it with rhythm. Railroaders love to couple up. Roofers are always on top. Pilots slip it in.

Love sucks and then you die. Gravity's a lie—life sucks. Life's a bitch—you marry one, then you die. Life's a bitch and so am I. Beyond bitch.

Down on your knees, bitch. Sex is only dirty when you do it right. Liquor up front—poker in the rear. Smile—it's the second best thing you can do with your lips. I haven't had sex for so long I forget who gets tied up. I'm looking for love but will settle for sex. Bad boys have bad toys. Sticks and stones may break my bones, but whips and chains excite me. Live fast, love hard, die with your mask on.

So many men, so little time. Expensive but worth it. If you're rich, I'm single. Richer is better. Shopaholic on board. Born to shop. I'd rather be shopping at Nordstrom. Born to be pampered. A woman's place is in the mall. When the going gets tough, the tough go shopping. Consume and die. He who dies with the most toys wins. She who dies with the most jewels wins. Die, yuppie scum.

This vehicle not purchased with drug money. Hugs are better than drugs.

You are loved.

Expectant mother on board. Baby on board. Family on board. I love my kids. Precious cargo on board. Are we having fun yet? Baby on fire. No child in car. Grandchild in back.

I fight poverty—I work. I owe, I owe, it's off to work I go. It sure makes the day long when you get to work on time. Money talks—mine only knows how to say goodbye. What do you mean I can't pay off my Visa with my MasterCard?

How's my driving? Call 1-800-545-8601. If this vehicle is being driven recklessly, please call 1-800-EAT-SHIT. Don't drink and drive—you might hit a bump and spill your drink.

My other car is a horse. Thoroughbreds always get there first. Horse lovers are stable people. My other car is a boat. My other car is a Rolls-Royce. My Mercedes is in the shop today. Unemployed? Hungry? Eat your foreign car. My other car is a 747. My ex-wife's car is a broom. I think my car has PMS. My other car is a piece of shit, too. Do not wash—this car is undergoing a scientific dirt test. Don't laugh—it's paid for. If this car were a horse, I'd have to shoot it. If I go any faster, I'll burn out my hamsters. I may be slow, but I'm ahead of you. I also drive a Titleist. Pedal downhill.

Shit happens. I love your wife. Megashit happens. I'm single again. Wife and dog missing—reward for dog. The more people I meet, the more I like my cat. Nobody on board. Sober 'n' crazy. Do it sober. Drive smart—drive sober.

No more Mr. Nice Guy. Lost your cat? Try looking under my tires. I love my German shepherd. Never mind the dog—beware of owner. Don't fence me in. Don't tell me what kind of day to have. Don't tailgate or I'll flush. My kid beat up your honor student. Abort your inner child. I don't care who you are, what you're driving, who's on board, who you love, where you'd rather be, or what you'd rather be doing.

Not so close—I hardly know you. Watch my rear end, not hers. You hit it—you buy it. Hands off. No radio. No Condo/No MBA/ No BMW. You toucha my car—I breaka your face. Protected by Smith & Wesson. Warning: This car is protected by a large sheet of cardboard.

LUV2HNT. Gun control is being able to hit your target. Hunters make better lovers: They go deeper into the bush, they shoot more often, and they eat what they shoot.

Yes, as a matter of fact, I do own the whole damn road. Get in, sit down, shut up, and hold on. I don't drive fast—I just fly low. If you don't like the way I drive, stay off the sidewalk. I'm polluting the atmosphere. Can't do 55.

I may be growing old, but I refuse to grow up. Get even—live long enough to become a problem to your kids. We're outspending our children's inheritance.

Life is pretty dry without a boat. I'd rather be sailing. A man's place is on his boat. Everyone must believe in something—I believe I'll go canoeing. Who cares!

Eat dessert first—life is uncertain. Why be normal?

Don't follow me—I'm lost, too. Wherever you are, be there. No matter where you go, there you are. Bloom where you are planted.

Easy does it. Keep it simple, stupid. I'm 4 Clean Air. Go fly a kite. No matter—never mind. UFOs are real. Of all the things I've lost, I miss my mind the most. I brake for unicorns.

Choose death.

NOTES ON THE LOCAL SWIMMING HOLE

Swimming is by far the best tonic I've found yet for my bad back. I'm not a good swimmer—I do the breaststroke or elementary backstroke in the slow lane—but when I took a two-week break from swimming, I was surprised how much I missed it. When I returned to the pool, I realized it's where I get, as Evelyn Ames says in *Postcards from the Edge*, "my endolphins." I can hardly bear Sunday, when the pool is closed.

Outside the Green Lake Community Center are the healthy people—the gorgeous Rollerbladers and runners and power walkers doing laps around a large lake in the middle of the city, the buff basketball players, the junior high baseball players, the yuppie Ultimate Frisbee players, the latte drinkers checking one another out, the Euro-cool soccer players, the volleyballers, the softball players. The indoor pool is the wetland of the maimed—home to those bearing canes, knee braces, neck braces—for who else would be free or motivated to be here at, say, 1:00 p.m. on Wednesday doing laps? I'm joined by people recovering from knee surgery, spinal surgery, car accidents, obese people who weigh themselves daily but never seem to lose a pound, a man in a wheelchair with his faithful dog barking at any potential interference, another wheelchair-bound man whose assistant is an almost cruelly cheerful Nordstrom shoe salesman, the Walrus Splasher (a huge guy with a handlebar mustache whom we're all trying to build up the courage to approach about the tidal waves he sends our way as he pounds the water), and a pre-op transgender New Jerseyite who, day by day, is wearing more and more feminine attire and is sticking out his butt and chest with greater self-confidence. He's the one who one day told me the locker room was closed, owing to an outbreak of leprosy; it turned out to be just a homeless guy who had shat his pants. Nearly everyone here is trying to come back from something; you can feel it in the men's locker room, where we don't talk that much.

The good swimmers while away too much time talking; they're not desperate, as the rest of us are, to claw their way back into shape by doing their assigned thirty-six laps (one mile). The good swimmers have an uncanny ability to skid across the top of the water, while the rest of us plunge down, down, down. The falling apart of our bodies, the perfection of youthful bodies; the pool is, for me, about one thing: the tug of time.

Every swimmer seems lost in his or her own water space (accidentally touching someone's toe or shoulder always feels thrillingly, wrongly intimate). I'm never so aware of the human perplexity as when I'm at Green Lake with my fellow bodies. We're all just trying to stay alive; we have no greater purpose than glimpsing a shadow of ourselves on the surface as we glide underwater. What is the point of floating? To keep floating. I feel the weightless, gorgeous quality of existence.

LOVE IS NOT A CONSOLATION—
LOVE IS A LIGHT

Food, they say, is a substitute for love; so, they should say, is everything else. When I bumped into my ex-landlord outside the Com-
munications Building—this was quite some time ago, in the early
1990s—he told me about a lecture a friend of his from Germany
was giving later that day on campus. Karl was my ex-landlord not
because I'd moved but because he had: He moved out of the upstairs
apartment shortly after I moved in downstairs. All summer, Karl had
explained to me the nuances of the burglar alarm and meticulously
packed boxes into his car; by the time his wife returned from an NEH
seminar in anthropology at Princeton, he was gone. His ex-wife then
managed the property.

Karl taught political science, and in the short time we lived in
the same duplex, he struck me as echt-Professor: fuzzy beard, fuzzy
hair, Birkenstocks, six pens tucked into the plastic pocket protector
attached to his white shirt. He listened to National Public Repetition
day and night.

The title of the talk was "Images of Leaders in German, French,
and American Television News," which sounded interesting enough
until I walked into the room—a basement dungeon populated by

twelve professors and graduate students eating bag lunches—and was handed a flyer, which contained an abstract of the talk:

> Television news producers influence public evaluations of political leaders and issues partly by choosing how to display leaders' facial and bodily movements. Such "visual" quotations occupy almost identical amounts of time in Germany, France, and the U.S., about three minutes per newscast. Yet there are marked national differences in the *form* of this daily dosage. U.S. channels present about 40% more political leaders per newscast, zoom individual leaders about 57% nearer to the viewer's eye, and reduce exposure time on screen by about 45% compared with French and German newscasts. The leaders' complex nonverbal activity was transcribed at high resolution into a time-series protocol. First analyses suggest some specific aspects of the nonverbal pattern that account for much of the variance in person perception. Lateral head flexion has a perplexingly strong influence on the attribution of personality traits, e.g., whether a leader is viewed as "arrogant, callous, stern, rejecting" or as "affectionate, thoughtful, acquiescent, caring."

I liked that the word "form" was italicized for no particular reason, I liked the Huxleyan metaphor of "daily dosage," and I loved the confusion implicit in "perplexingly strong," but what did the rest of it mean—"time-series protocol"? "lateral head flexion"? I hadn't the faintest idea.

Karl introduced his friend and colleague Siegfried Frey, a psychologist, engineer, political scientist, instructor in the psychology department at the University of Duisburg, and "student of the impact of pharmaceuticals on human behavior." Karl said he was "looking forward with bated breath to finding out the significance of lateral head flexion." So were we all.

Siegfried Frey had a perplexingly strong resemblance to Mikhail Gorbachev, only younger and without the birthmark. He began his presentation by flashing onto an overhead projector three quotations that seemed uncontroversial to the point of being self-evident:

> There is no meaning in a message except what people put into it. When we study communication, therefore, we study people.
>
> —WILBUR SCHRAMM

In everyday life, we respond to gestures with an extreme alertness, and one might almost say, in accordance with an elaborate and secret code that is written nowhere, known by none, and understood by all.

—EDWARD SAPIR

We look at a person and immediately a certain impression of his character forms itself in us. A glance, a few spoken words are sufficient to tell us a story about a highly complex matter.

—SOLOMON ASCH

Dr. Frey explained that a linguist in Paris, a government professor in New Hampshire, and he had each monitored two television stations in France, the United States, and Germany for a full month: March 1987. They had gathered more than four thousand individual clips; they had a database of eleven and a half hours. There were amusing little statistical revelations: French television news had the longest delay until the first leader was presented, as well as the longest intervals between sequences of political leaders; U.S. news programs rarely displayed any film clips longer than twenty seconds, while Germany and France often had lengthier samples; U.S. news rarely displayed more than one political leader simultaneously, which contradicted, to my mind, anyway, Dr. Frey's flattering assertion that "the more democratic approach of the U.S." was responsible for the fact that nearly twice as many political leaders appear on U.S. television news than on French or German programs; there was no systematic difference in the nonverbal communication of Mu'ammar Gaddhafi and Ronald Reagan.

But the two-headed lady that had enticed us into the circus tent, what we were looking forward to with bated breath, was, of course, lateral head flexion. What in the world was it and how did it ramify? It was really interesting and it ramified across the board. On the overhead projector, Dr. Frey showed us a transparency he had made of the October 20, 1986, cover of *Time*. The large cover lines were,

NO DEAL—
STAR WARS
SINKS SUMMIT

Reagan's head was tilted slightly to the right in his characteristic *Mr. Smith Goes to Washington* posture—that is, it displayed lateral flexion. Gorbachev's head was straight up, chin out.

A few weeks later, *Time* had printed a letter from a reader who thought that the pictures on the cover "said it all": Gorbachev was "arrogant, hard, uncompromising," while Reagan "showed concern, frustration, and disappointment." Dr. Frey's research indicated that for men and for women, for blacks and whites, for children and adults, for Japanese and Westerners, "lateral head flexion" had a "noticeable impact" upon a viewer's evaluation of the person being depicted. Not just Gorbachev but anyone whose head was straight up was identified with such adjectives as "proud, aloof, self-confident, arrogant, self-assured, callous, stern, stiff, conceited"; not just Reagan but anyone whose head was tilted ever so slightly was perceived as being "humble, kind, sad, thoughtful, alert, friendly, sympathetic, tense, tender, vulnerable." According to Dr. Frey, artists for centuries have used lateral head flexion in a "manneristic way" to control the viewer's response to figures. He flashed photographs and drawings at us, and it was simply uncanny the degree to which the slight tilt of a person's head determined one's reading of that person's character.

Dr. Frey refused to speculate on the "possible psychological semantics of lateral head flexion." It was simply a "curious coincidence of nonverbal communication." I, on the other hand, have always been a fan of the wildly sweeping generalization, and I asked my fellow colloquium attendees whether one couldn't at least speculate that this difference in how viewers respond was related in some sense to yielding a stance of authority—for instance, to an adult acting childlike: Reagan always seemed to be trying to look so boyish whenever he dropped his head sideways like that. Dr. Frey said this was interesting but unverifiable. A woman to my immediate left caught the spirit and suggested that a viewer looked favorably on someone whose head was tilted because such a posture suggested a mother nursing an infant. Unverifiable, said Dr. Frey, but interesting.

Then Karl, who until now seemed to have been busy eating the lunch he had brought to the colloquium, brought his right hand—slowly, and with great care and patience—from a vertical position into a horizontal position until it was lying snugly on top of his left hand, and proceeded to offer two tentative theses concerning the symbolic power of lateral head flexion: first, that tilting your head suggested that you were trying to see the world from another perspective; and, second, that it was a physically intimate gesture, implying, as it does, a movement from the vertically isolated to the horizontally intertwined. It was by far the most astonishing thing I'd heard in an already fairly eye-opening afternoon. It seemed not only interesting and verifiable but the language itself by which to describe what anyone would miss about marriage.

A man's life of any worth is a continual allegory.

—KEATS

ALL OUR SECRETS ARE THE SAME

Many writers pretend that they don't read reviews of their books and that, in particular, life is too short to subject themselves to reading bad reviews. Kingsley Amis said that a bad review may spoil breakfast, but you shouldn't allow it to spoil lunch. Jean Cocteau suggested, "Listen carefully to first criticisms of your work. Note carefully just what it is about your work that the critics don't like, then cultivate it. That's the part of your work that's individual and worth keeping."

Sane advice; I don't follow it. I read my reviews, though by no means every word of every one of them. The really positive ones are boring after a while—your own most generous self-appraisal quoted back to yourself—but I must admit I find bad reviews fascinating. They're the much-ballyhooed train wreck, only you're in the train; will all those mangled bodies at the bottom of the ravine tell you something unexpected about yourself?

More than fifteen years ago—as an experiment, I suppose, in psychic survival—I reread every horrific review of my first five books. It was a genuinely odd and, in a way, riveting experience; I felt as if I were locked in a room, getting worked over by a dozen supposedly well-meaning guidance counselors. Suddenly my body felt like it had gotten filled with liquid cement.

One otherwise fairly positive review of *Dead Languages* concluded, "The novel as a whole doesn't quite uncurl from its fetal position, doesn't open out from self-consciousness toward reconciliation." A reviewer of my novel-in-stories, *Handbook for Drowning,* said about the book's protagonist, "The smudged eye turns into the eye that smudges what it sees. Clinging to the child role of bearing witness to itself, it doesn't undertake the adult role of bearing witness to everything else. Cramped, Walter tells a cramped story. The glimpses we see, varied and subtle as they may be, are all gray. It is the grayness of life seen through a caul that has never been shed."

My first reaction, when I reread these reviews, was to think, *You know, they're right: I really must figure out how to open out from self-consciousness toward reconciliation; I really must bear witness to everything else,* but then I realized that I don't do reconciliation. I don't do unself-conscious witness to everything else. Nabokov writes, "I do not know if it has ever been noted before that one of the main characteristics of life is discreteness. Unless a film of flesh envelops us, we die. Man exists only insofar as he is separated from his surroundings. The cranium is a space-traveler's helmet. Stay inside or you perish. Death is divestment, death is communion. It may be wonderful to mix with the landscape, but to do so is the end of the tender ego." I think of my work as an attempt to explore the conundrum, whereas one reviewer of my book *Black Planet* called it the "wretched musings of one white guy with a panicky ego, a pitiable heart, and too much time on his hands."

"Pitiable heart" interests me, as does this judgment about the same book: "At least it should make some white readers feel good about themselves. They may be screwed up about race, but they're not as annoyingly screwed up as David Shields." The impulse on reviewers' part to use me to get well—to brandish their own more evolved morality, psyche, humanity—flies in the face of what is to me an essential assumption of the compact between reader and writer: *Doesn't everybody have a pitiable heart? Aren't we all Bozos on this bus?*

Robert Dana says, "Was Keats a confessional poet? When he talks about youth that grows 'pale and spectre-thin, and dies,' he's talking about his kid brother, Tom, who died of tuberculosis, but he's talking about more than that. The word 'confessional' implies the need to purge oneself and go receive forgiveness for one's life. I don't think that's what confessional poetry is about at all. I think it's a poetry that comes out of the stuff of the poet's personal life, but he's trying to render this experience in more general and inclusive, or what used to be called 'universal,' terms. He's presenting himself as a representative human being. He's saying, 'This is what happens to us because we're human beings in this flawed and difficult world, where joy is rare.'" My shtick, exactly. When I present myself as a "tube boob" (one review) in *Remote* or as a "pathetically guilty white liberal" (another review) in *Black Planet*, I mean for "David Shields" to be a highly stylized figure through whom cultural energies and all manner of mad human needs flow.

One reviewer said about *Remote*, "The futuristically formless nature of the collection gets irritating; it's an ambivalent comment on bookmaking, and before long it's got us feeling ambivalent, too." Another reviewer said about the same book, "The danger, of course, in writing about fluff and modern life is that you spend too much time thinking about fluff and modern life, until you resemble not a little the prostitutes in *You'll Never Make Love in This Town Again*, trapped, mired, in it." I understand these comments are meant as dispraise, but if you're feeling ambivalent about it, that's a good thing. If I seem to you to be trapped, mired in it, that's the point or at least part of the point. Theodor Adorno said that a "successful work is not one that resolves objective contradictions in a spurious harmony, but one that expresses the idea of harmony negatively by embodying the contradictions, pure and uncompromised, in its innermost structure." I don't know about "pure and uncompromised," but all I'm ever seeking to do is embody the contradictions.

A reviewer of *Remote* said, "Shields wouldn't thank anyone who suggested, on the basis of the material presented in this book, that as the child of 'Jewish liberal activists,' he might have chosen passivism as the subtlest form of rebellion." Why would the reviewer think I included this information, unless I wanted readers to make precisely this kind of connection? If via my pitiable heart the reader intuits something about his own, that, to me, is a worthwhile trade-off. This *Remote* reviewer concluded by mentioning a relatively minor misdeed I acknowledged committing, and then said, "Presumably, by now we're past the stage of being expected to say, 'Hell, we've all done that.'" Not done that—*thought* that. Goethe said, "I've never heard of a crime that I couldn't imagine committing myself." To me, it's almost unfathomable that a reviewer would say, as one did about *Black Planet,* "The author escapes the morass of self-doubt as so many others do—by vicarious identification with a professional athlete; Shields idolizes Sonics player Gary Payton to the point of unnerving fixation," and then not figure that I'm up to something other than chronicling my own fandom. Another reviewer of *Black Planet* asked, "Do we really need to know what David Shields is fantasizing about when he's having sex? Does he imagine his foibles are our own?" I'm certain my foibles are your own, if only you're willing to acknowledge them.

"I," Rimbaud informed us, "is another."

A NOTE ABOUT THE AUTHOR

David Shields is the internationally best-selling author of twenty books, including *Reality Hunger* (named one of the best books of 2010 by more than thirty publications), *The Thing About Life Is That One Day You'll Be Dead* (*New York Times* best seller), and *Black Planet* (finalist for the National Book Critics Circle Award). James Franco's film adaptation of *I Think You're Totally Wrong: A Quarrel* will be released in February 2017. The recipient of Guggenheim and NEA fellowships, Shields has published essays and stories in the *New York Times Magazine, Harper's, Esquire, Yale Review, Village Voice, Salon, Slate, McSweeney's,* and *Believer.* His work has been translated into twenty languages.

A NOTE ON THE TYPE

This book was set in Minion, a typeface produced by the Adobe Corporation specifically for the Macintosh personal computer and released in 1990. Designed by Robert Slimbach, Minion combines the classic characteristics of old-style faces with the full complement of weights required for modern typesetting.

Composed by North Market Street Graphics, Lancaster, Pennsylvania

Printed and bound by Berryville Graphics, Berryville, Virginia

Designed by Maggie Hinders